A Dream of

An Introduction to Romantic Opera as Literature

❦

An Interdisciplinary Exploration of
La Bohème, Carmen, La Traviata
and *The Rake's Progress*

To Aiko —

*With all my very best wishes
and gratitude!*

WILLIAM WALLIS

Bill

L.A., 12.6.07

Stone & Scott, *Publishers*
Sherman Oaks, California

ALSO BY WILLIAM WALLIS

Poetry
Poems
Biographer's Notes
Four Valley Poets (with others)
Ruth
Asher
Eros
Dutton's Books
Joshua
Twins
Simple Gifts
Selected Poems

Prose
A Meeting of Cultures
Essays on Lakota History and Culture, Literature and Music

Selected Essays

Drama
Hanblecheya, The Vision

A Dream of Love Fulfilled

AN INTRODUCTION TO ROMANTIC OPERA AS LITERATURE

❧

AN INTERDISCIPLINARY EXPLORATION OF

La Bohème, Carmen, La Traviata

AND *The Rake's Progress*

WILLIAM WALLIS

A Dream of Love Fulfilled

AN INTRODUCTION TO OPERA AS LITERATURE

First Edition 2001, Second Printing 2004.

With gratitude to Martin and Rita Horn

Printed in the United States of America by
Delta Printing Solutions, Valencia, California

©2001, 2004 by William George Wallis

All rights reserved.

Library of Congress Control Number 2001 131012

ISBN   1-891135-02-3

Book design by Lynn Eames.

Preface

This book is for the person who wishes to begin exploring the vast and fascinating world beneath the glittering surface of opera. The first section is an introduction to the complex of elements—literature, drama, music and the visual arts—of which opera consists. Each of the four disciplines is then emphasized in the interpretation of a popular operatic work. *La Bohème* is discussed primarily for its literary values, *Carmen* for its dramatic qualities, *La Traviata* for its musical excellence, and *The Rake's Progress* for its visual aspects.

The complex of elements in opera offers a great variety of tools to develop believable character. Operatic portrayal of character is, in well-crafted operas, as effective as in any art form, including drama, film and the novel. In opera, however, music—the most esoteric of all art forms—plays a major role in character building. Music is not only the aesthetic glue of opera, but opera's primary element and the source of opera's most profound statements about human character and thought. Music rises out of the complex interdisciplinary weave of opera in performance to make most profound statements about human inscape and values.

In a broader sense, these essays were written to share an enthusiasm for *dramma per musica*, drama through music. Opera's surface is delightfully engaging with its symphonic elegance, spectacle, lovely melodies, and brilliant voices. Many of us embrace opera as children or because the child in us simply loves that beautiful surface. These essays attempt to show that, although we will hopefully never lose the child-like attraction to opera's obvious charms, there is much more beneath the surface if we wish to explore it.

This book may be read in conjunction with the *English National Opera Libretti*. The reader of this book will probably find it informative to read the bi-lingual text of each opera concurrent with this book—then listen to a recording of the opera, possibly with text in hand. The reader should then be prepared to enjoy the experience of a theatric or cinematic performance of these four—and any other—operas.

I wish to thank Philip Barranco, Betty Spradlin, Arthur Arny, Harold Thompson, William Taylor, Marjorie Lawrence, Robert Beadell, Lee Lemon, Pete Jenkins, John Zei, JoAnn Kimball, Dallas Williams, Kristi Limbo, David Landis, David Bell, Dean Tschetter, David Williams, Frau Ena Thiessen, Dorothea Thiessen, Max Lehner, Johannes Pichler, Julio Malaval, Vilmos Desy, Don Haggerty, Robert Chauls, John Harrison, and Kathleen Sullivan. I also wish to thank my wife Leslie, without whose love and forbearance this sequence of essays would not have appeared.

Los Angeles, January 2004   *William Wallis, Ph.D.*

A Dream of Love Fulfilled

AN INTRODUCTION TO ROMANTIC OPERA AS LITERATURE

IN MEMORIAM

Marjorie Lawrence

TABLE OF CONTENTS

Part 1

THE SOURCES AND ELEMENTS OF OPERA

Introduction

It is not surprising that romanticism, a revolutionary artistic-philosophical movement emphasizing emotionality, praising imaginative power, and espousing the rejection of traditional values should be associated with opera. That opera should also be associated with the Romance genre—melodramatic love stories—is also understandable. Opera evokes high emotions; it is sometimes a musical dynamo that moves the listener to emotional heights. The prevalent subjects of opera are themselves highly emotional in nature. The subject of many great operas is the success or failure of a passionate relationship—consider, in this regard, Othello and Desdemona, Tristan and Isolde, José and Carmen. And opera not only celebrates passion, it asks why such passionate relationships succeed or fail. Romantic opera is primarily concerned with the romantic obsessions of its characters and with the interlocking themes of eros and thanatos—sexual passion and death. Since the mid-19th century, opera has often concentrated on what might be called the psychology of character. Since the premiere of Verdi's *La Traviata* in Venice in 1853, a number of great, complex characters have emerged from operatic scores.

This first group of essays discusses how opera's four elements—Literature, Drama (including Dance), Music, and the Visual Arts—work in combination. Traditionally, the ability to understand a character's emotions and thought in theatrical art is based in language, so we will begin our discussion with opera's literary aspects. In opera, language is piggybacked on music to charge it emotionally. Visual aspects then round out the performance experience. My approach to understanding and enjoying opera is to read the libretto and any appealing ancillary materials about the opera, listen to a recording of the opera—text in hand—and then see a staged performance or view a video/film of the opera.

Music is primary in opera; music is opera's aesthetic glue, combining and changing its quartet of elements into a musical-dramatic whole. Literary elements are, however, essential in understanding the complexity of opera. And even though musical and visual elements (lighting, physical action, costume, dance and other aspects of spectacle) may help us understand a character, it is often through language—poetic dialogue or soliloquy—that a character continues to live in our minds long after the performance has ended.

The originators of opera sought, late in the sixteenth century, to recreate the literary and dramatic values of ancient Greece. Taking their cue, we begin our exploration of opera with the values of the Classic Greek drama described in Aristotle's recipe for poetic tragedy, *The Poetics*. Aristotle's concepts will help elucidate opera's complex beauty.

Greek poetic tragedies continually invigorate Western culture with their unforgettable characters and the depth and complexity of their plots and imagery. It is through our empathy for the suffering heroes and heroines of these dramas that we are drawn into the striking dimensions on the stage before us. Instrumental music was a small but crucial element in Greek performance art, but it was a mere complement to the universal and essential musicality of poetic language. The essential elements of Greek tragedy—character, plot and meaning—are language-based. This is rarely true of opera, in which music is the determining force. Opera and Classic Greek tragedy use the same elements in different proportions.

Opera allows us to vicariously experience the emotions of greatly diverse characters in extraordinary and sometimes exotic circumstances. That is one of opera's melodramatic charms. Early opera was based thematically in the essential ideas explored in ancient dramatic literature—mythic exploration/conquest, mankind's relations with divine forces, and historical events—but since the eighteenth century, opera has been increasingly concerned with obsessions like sexual passion and jealousy, and the psychology of human character under stress. This is the case with three nineteenth century masterpieces *La Bohème* (1896), *Carmen* (1875), *La Traviata* (1853) and to a lesser degree with *The Rake's Progress* (1957).

Literary Elements of Opera

Opera's dependence on literature is obvious and intimate. Most of opera's characters, plots and themes have literary sources. From the perspective of this book, the literary sources of opera are a matter of secondary, although fascinating importance. Many opera texts (*libretti*) are patterned after dramas, though many operas are based on novels, short stories, or narrative poetry. Giacomo Puccini's *La Bohème* is based on Henri Mürger's drama and novel *Scenes from the Bohemian Life*. Georges Bizet's *Carmen* is based on Prosper Méremée's novella of the same name. Giuseppi Verdi's *La Traviata* is based on Alexander Dumas *fils'* novel and play *Lady of the Camellias*. All these sources are readily available, and exploring them may cast light on the complex literary aspects of not only these masterpieces, but most other operas as well.

It is not necessary, however, to be familiar with an opera's sources to understand or enjoy a performance. *The Magic Flute's* plot was derived from a number of exotic tales, but enjoyment of this *Singspiel* ("play with singing" or "sung play") does not rest on that knowledge. Sometimes a libretto may have a more esoteric source; for example, the source of Igor Stravinsky's *The Rake's Progress* is a series of paintings/engravings by William Hogarth (1697-1764).

Sometimes, familiar literary/dramatic themes and characters become the property of opera for, as we will see in the following pages, opera has tended to imitate dramatic and literary forms from its birth and has continued to cultivate a close relationship with them throughout its evolution. For example, operatic form was greatly influenced by the nineteenth century's longing for the continuity inherent in prose narrative, i.e. the novel form. Most operas are based on narrative; they tell a story. Familiar universal themes and corresponding imagery patterns are constant in opera, tragic or comic; for example *the dream of love fulfilled* is a constant in the inner worlds of most Romantic operatic heroines. Romantic opera is female-centered and in general sustains the worshipful attitude toward female characters established in Renaissance culture, especially painting. Following Puccini, I refer to such idealized characterizations in opera as *luminous images*.

Most important for the purposes of our literary discussion, however, are the manifestations of the literary elements (1) *dialogue*, (2) *lyric poetry* and (3) *description* in opera, because all three are essential to the creation and performance of opera. My primary interest is in the chief elements of dialogue and poetry, since the libretto's use of description often appears as stage direction, which is to be read, not listened to. Let us consider how dialogue and poetry—including poetic description—play essential roles in opera. Both are usually chanted or sung in most operas.

(1) *Dialogue*, dramatized conversation, is an element of most literature. In nineteenth century opera, it is usually poeticized—written in rhythmic units, often rhymed—then set to music as recitative, chanted speech. Recitative has two forms, both of which have been present in opera from its inception.

First, *recitativo secco* is dialogue like its name—dry, non-melodic, and functional. It is accompanied by a keyboard instrument like the harpsichord. It moves the action along between musical numbers in most operas composed before 1850, but was still being used selectively by Puccini and other composers well into the twentieth century. It generally rolls along as quickly as stage dialogue would, sometimes faster. It finds its greatest fulfillment in Mozart's comic operas in the Italian (*opera buffa*) style, although Donizetti, Rossini and Verdi employ it later with great skill. Almost any scene from Mozart's *The Marriage of Figaro* (1786) provides superb examples of this type of operatic dialogue. Always fascinating, Igor Stravinsky—"the last great composer"—uses *recitativo secco* extensively in his masterful contemporary opera *The Rake's Progress*.

Second, *recitativo accompagnato (stromentato)* or "accompanied recitative" is another approach to setting dialogue altogether. This form of dialogue in opera is accompanied by full orchestra and may be melodic. Orchestral elements and the availability of melody make this form of dialogue expansive and allow the composer to make the opera's action flow seamlessly from one scene to the next. Gluck (1714-87) theorized about it in mid-eighteenth century: His aims were to "restrict music to its true office by means of expression and by following the situations of the story." *Recitativo accompagnato* was the means by which he made his musical-dramatic creations more fully continuous. In the capable hands of Giuseppi Verdi, accompanied recitative became a principle means of the uninterrupted flow of dramatic action so sought after in the post-Romantic period. Following Gluck, Wagner made his unique contribution to operatic form with the continual flow of the *Gesamtkunstwerk* (unified work of art).

The myriad possibilities of interaction between the engaged orchestra and the dramatic action of the stage's realm have yielded riches in musical-dramatic form. The entire first act of Puccini's *La Bohème* before Mimi's entrance, for example, is a flood of witty dialogue/*recitativo accompagnato*. Each following act was meant to be a ceaseless flow of musical drama. Composed forty years earlier, Verdi's first act of *La Traviata* is a stunning achievement of continual musical action.

(2) *Lyric Poetry* is the second major literary element. In most operas the text is a functional form of poetry in which rhythmic units of poetry called "feet" approximate music units called "measures;" and through the interface of these units, words and music are joined. The unit of the lyric poem—a short poem of an emotional, often contemplative nature—is especially important to opera, since it serves as the literary component for the *aria*, a crucial means of operatic characterization and a chief source of opera's unique appeal.

An aria is a song, generally of great power and beauty, demanding not only a performer with an extensive vocal range, but one with an understanding of the delicacy of dramatic nuance. It is accompanied by orchestra and contains melodic power representative of the character's emotional state. In opera, an art form in which music is the chief glory and the human voice the chief expression of that glory, the aria is a crucial element. It is the aria, composed of a unique combination of a lyric poem and the voice in melodic flight supported by full orchestra, that offers the listener the clearest picture of character inscape—the character's desires, fantasies, ideals, needs. Opera is about character.

It is the in-depth appeal of character that brings us back to opera, again and again, after the lights fade. A great aria contains all the emotional striving of the human soul for completion. The aria invites us, through its unique combination of poetry and music, into the intimate depths of shared human experience. An aria's melody may take our emotions soaring, but it is the fact that this melody represents an aspect of human *character* with which we can empathize that makes opera meaningful. The empathy we feel for an operatic character brings our own deeper emotions and thoughts into play during a performance. Poetry counts on music to achieve this effect.

The aria is the equivalent of a soliloquy in drama or a dramatic monologue in poetry; it is a revealing of the soul and generally stops the stage action or, perhaps better said, *internalizes* it. In an aria, we are telescoped into the inner world of character. At the end of *La Bohème*'s first act, Rodolfo and Mimi's arias do little to advance the plot; *such arias are primarily pure outpourings of character feeling and thought.* They demand the cessation of stage action—and a surrender to musical glory. Generally, crucial plot movement *follows* an aria. For example, the brief duet that immediately follows the two arias in *La Bohème*'s Act 1 determines the remainder of the story and action of *La Bohème*. It is an intense declaration of passion. The arias that preceded this duet are essential dramatic—and psychological—preparation for the duet; they help us understand Rodolfo and Mimi's later actions. The remarkably condensed lyric of the duet can do its work so quickly because the preceding arias have been so revealing of character qualities like loneliness, insecurity and desire.

As an aria's text, the lyric poem provides us with the narrative of the character's thoughts. Music then charges this thought to instill it with emotional intensity. Generally, poems that serve as aria texts do not stand alone as good poetry in the eyes of literary critics; a libretto is fulfilled only in partnership with music. There are, of course, exceptions to negative generalizations concerning the special type of lyric poetry of which a libretto consists; for example, portions of Auden's text for *The Rake's Progress* are lovely verses that stand alone as pure poetry.

(3) *Description* is an inherent part of lyric poetry and is, to paraphrase Aristotle, so obvious an element as to not need definition in dramatic context. Characters describe what they see or feel and we take it at face value. Whether it is the scentless lilies and roses Mimi sews or the cold wind that sweeps through Rodolfo's apartment, we understand that poetic description has deeper meaning than literal description.

Study of any opera should begin with its text. Generally, this is where the composer began to appreciate the librettist's skill, and we could do worse than follow in the footsteps of Giacomo Puccini, Georges Bizet, Giuseppi Verdi and Igor Stravinsky.

Dramatic Elements of Opera

Aristotle's *Poetics* points out classic drama's three great gifts to opera: character, plot (the arrangements of events) and thought (meaning or theme). One approach to character from the dramatic perspective is to discuss a character's *internal*, or *personality-driven forces* (desires, dreams, needs), as well as the more obvious *external*, or *plot-generated forces* that shape character. *Carmen* is an excellent opera to demonstrate opera's dramatic qualities. We will trace the patterns of force that shape both Carmen and José in Bizet's masterpiece.

It is the three minor elements described in Aristotle's *Poetics*—*melos* (music), *lexis* (poetic elements) and *opsis* (spectacle)—that are most likely to attract us to opera initially, but it is character and plot (and their musical representations) that bring us back. These are the two great elements that enrich our internal life. We sympathize with operatic characters initially because of the extraordinary power of music to portray character mood and emotion, but we grow to empathize with them because of the unique power of the word combined with music to represent experience and thought. The plot of an opera is the chief means by which a character is given the chance to change, to fulfill itself aesthetically: character change or growth is an important initiator of character depth and complexity. Such character development involves the audience's mind as well as their emotions.

Dance, primarily ballet and folk dance, functions in most opera as an optical decorative element, yet its abstract patterns may effectively enhance local color, echo plot and illustrate character. Operatic characters rarely dance, though Carmen and Salome do so effectively as an aspect of character. Dance generally functions as a part of the setting or local color, greatly adding to the atmosphere of a specific scene; e.g., in Act 2, scene 2 of *La Traviata* or the opening of *Carmen*'s second act. Ballet is one of the elements of opera that ties opera firmly to the tradition of folk dance, the source of most Western classical musical form.

Musical Elements of Opera

Music is the most essential element of opera, the voice the primary instrument. The aria is its most effective musical form in terms of creating character. Our interpretation of opera will be largely character-centered, but will also explore how each discipline is employed in the creation of character emotion and thought. Music complements to the furthest degree imaginable the amalgam of literary and dramatic elements already introduced. The major musical elements are (1) *the orchestra*, with its string, woodwind, brass and percussion sections, (2) *the chorus and the solo vocal artists* in all their uniqueness and diversity, and (3) *the musical-dramatic forms* of which opera is shaped.

The opera orchestra, whose initial role in performance was to accompany the singers, has increasingly encroached upon the singer's art—beginning with Gluck and, in fact, in part because of his theories—and has taken on additional duties: creating stage environment, even local color, and portraying character mood and conflict. This encroachment seems natural as we scan the history of opera. Still, it was a hard shock to audiences when Richard Wagner made the singing voice yet another orchestral dimension and formalized the symbolic power of music through musical motif structures (repeated musical ideas). With Wagner, subtlety in orchestral form became a great psychological tool and thus a chief means of characterization. Still, most critics agree that Verdi's skill in balancing the orchestra and voice in creating character in musical-dramatic flow in his final works is unsurpassed. The orchestra also portrays the inner world of character. This is one of its chief tasks.

As important as the aria is to character, the duet, trio, quartet and ensemble usually are to plot. When more than one character sings simultaneously, the action usually advances. As pointed out earlier, Rodolfo and Mimi's love duet at the end of *La Bohème*'s first act may appear outwardly static, but the rest of the opera's action flows from its dramatic consequences. Consider also the lovely quartet that closes Act 3 of *La Bohème*, in which Mimi and Rodolfo stand frozen in the emotional memories ruling their imaginations, while Musetta and Marcello act out their frustrations with life and each other.

Some of the most striking moments in opera come during ensembles in which most stage action ceases and each character withdraws into his or her own private world. Plot time ceases and as listeners we can relax and more fully appreciate the complex beauties of opera's unique musical forms. *La Traviata*'s Act 2 Finale is, for example, a remarkable union of literature and drama enhanced by musical form.

Opera's purpose is remarkably fulfilled to a great degree when one simply listens to, rather than sees an opera. Listening is, of course, not the final step in opera exploration and appreciation, but the informed *listener* is, perhaps, in a position to best appreciate the pure power that opera exercises over the imagination. Listening is the very rich and important second step in the full appreciation of an opera.

The Visual Elements of Opera

Of the visual arts, painting provides the large-form visual stage environment in the form of flats (very large paintings which are framed and fastened together), backdrops and cycloramas. (Both these terms describe large paintings used to approximate scenic background, e.g. a landscape.) These large paintings fill the background of the scene, while plastic arts are employed to shape smaller forms, such as trees, boulders and other natural or man-made objects. Costumers, wigmakers, jewelry and property makers, and make-up artists create the living statues that sing before us. Finally, light—that visual element sometimes indicative of the spiritual element on the stage and the aural equivalent of musical harmony—unites all the elements of the four disciplines mentioned above with its synesthetic power.

No other art form involves so many diverse elements as opera and no other art form integrates these elements so effectively in an aesthetic tapestry portraying human character. How does the person who is attracted to opera find an entrance into this brilliant castle? It so happens that the easiest way to become familiar with opera in contemporary society is not only simple; it also echoes the creative process of the librettists, composers and performers of opera.

First, begin with reading the libretto that is usually included in every opera recording. *Second*, listen to the opera—text in hand, if you can—and initiate the engaging, imaginative acts of consciousness that opera evokes in the listener. *Finally*, watch a taped performance or filmed version of the opera, or, best of all, see a live performance.

Each of us comes to opera possessing varying degrees of familiarity with literature, drama (and dance), music, and the visual arts, if only through the world of media—television, film and the computer. Most of us are novices in one way or another in most of the arts and media. This need not concern us in our desire to experience opera. Even if we have little experience in any of these areas, this approach is designed for the reader who will work at his or her own level toward a more complete understanding of opera.

Those who are more advanced in one discipline will work at learning the relationship of that discipline to the others that constitute opera. In this way, the reader's understanding of their home discipline will be enriched. The greatest challenge and fun is in discovering how two or more disciplines interlock to create a meaning more complex than any single discipline is capable of attaining.

Remember that these great operas were not written for the professional musicians who perform them, or for the designers or stage directors who make their performance possible. They were written for an audience and for the heart and mind of anyone who cares to open themselves to the experience of opera through reading, listening or viewing.

The Aristotle Connection

There is good reason for employing Aristotle's *Poetics* in discussing opera. There is considerable evidence that the creators of operatic form, among them a group of literary *dilettanti* who met at the house of Bardi in late 16th Century Florence, endeavored to recreate Attic drama in the experimental presentations which began to codify a new art form called "opera."

The works they produced were the forebears of opera. They were also a far cry from Sophoclean tragedy. These *dilettanti* did, nevertheless, envision *Oedipus Rex*, Aristotle's example for poetic drama in the *Poetics*, as sung or chanted drama. They may also have understood that the sole purpose of music in Sophoclean drama was to underscore and heighten the dramatic content of the dialogue. Whatever their understanding, desire or intent, the product of their efforts to recreate Greek poetic tragedy created a unique and complex art form ultimately dominated by musical considerations. Opera's unique interdisciplinary nature invites widely varied interpretive approaches.

Our approach to understanding and enjoying opera is built on structural considerations rather than more discipline-specific ones. There is more than one way to set a finely cut gem so that it may appeal to a wide variety of tastes, and so it is with appreciation of opera. Any of the four disciplines may serve as a gate to the realm of opera. This approach begins with literary considerations, but seeks a balanced interdisciplinary appreciation of opera's dramatic, musical and visual aspects.

In Classic Greek poetic tragedy, highly structured verse was chanted or sung by soloists and chorus. The performers were accompanied by a small ensemble of instrumentalists—a harp or lute, a flute and drums. Every movement of the chorus was probably choreographed, while the soloists had more individualistic freedom of movement and vocal expression. A performance was highly stylized, i.e. choreographed to the highest degree. The highly stylized verse forms imply this and what we know of Greek performance practice supports this theory.

The Florence group, also called the *camerata*, aimed at a performance genre they described as *dramma per musica*: "Drama *through* music" placed music at the center of the camerata's presentations. Partially because of their worshipful appreciation of the source of their inspiration, they often based their earliest efforts on mythic subjects. Peri's *Dafne* (1597) is considered the first opera. Out of the performance of the first operas came an emphasis the language-conscious Greeks would never have allowed: the musical element of melody combined with verse to create songs and choruses. The effect of this union was called *arioso*. In this form, music took command of the literary arts, which were supreme in Classic Greek poetic tragedy.

Musical sophistication in the new art form took a great step forward in 1607 with Monteverdi's *Orfeo*. This work made music the essential glue of the operatic formula. As sometimes happens in the development of artistic form, one gifted individual like Monteverdi may determine through his unique musical-dramatic gifts the development and the formulae of a major art form. The elements were uniquely combined according to his taste and gifts.

It may seem retrogressive to reach back to the eras of Aeschylus, Sophocles and Euripides for the terminology and definitions to describe a musical-dramatic form that emerged between 1580 and 1607 in Florence and Padua, but in fact the taproot of opera—and, indeed, almost all Western drama—is Attic in nature. In his *Poetics*, Aristotle (384-322 B.C.), an admirer of Sophocles' poetic tragedy *Oedipus Tyrranus*, gave Western Civilization an aesthetic recipe that provides terms and values that describe the artistic urge and structure constituting most literary and dramatic genres. Since opera is formally a dramatic portrayal of character, Aristotle's terms for the ingredients of tragic drama provide us with a general, flexible structure for an in-depth discussion of operatic form.

The terms he gives us define poetic tragedy as "the imitation of an action that is serious and complete in nature in itself." Here are the three major elements of poetic tragedy, in the order of importance Aristotle gives them.

Aristotle's Major Elements

(1) *Plot* is, according to Aristotle, the life and soul of poetic tragedy. It is the arrangement of incidents in the story according to probability or logic. The general structure of the plot is that of rising ("knotting up" or complication of action) and falling ("loosening" of action), such large-form structure, easily echoed in small-form elements like verse forms or melodic lines, with a predictable rise and fall, satisfies an inherent sense of balance in the audience.

Here, briefly, is Aristotle's description of the plot's structure:

The complication is the part of the plot from the beginning up to the point which immediately precedes the occurrence of a change [peripitae] from bad to good fortune, or from good fortune to bad; the denouement is from the beginning of the change down to the end. (XVII,2)

Aristotle's division of the plot into "constituent parts"—prologue, episode, exode, and choral song—has rough structural counterparts in opera's musical form, especially during the first 250 years of opera's development.

Aristotle distinguishes between plot and what we would call "action," including the literal gestures of character—for example, a sword fight. Such action might be caused by either a character's inner needs or by a character's reaction to a plot twist. By action, Aristotle means the flow of energy out of or in between characters caught within the plot's mechanism.

This is what Aristotle says concerning the primacy of action as a dramatic element: "Tragedy is not a representation of men but a piece of action, of life, of happiness and unhappiness." Character gives us qualities, but it is in our actions—what we do—that we are happy or the reverse. The best structure of tragic plot is "complex, ... one that represents incidents arousing fear and pity" in the viewer, which emotions are then purged through the plot's workings. Even the story of the plot alone, as is the case with *Oedipus*, should be capable of arousing fear and pity.

(2) *Character* is that which makes us ascribe certain moral qualities to the agents. According to Aristotle, character should be (1) "good," a quality shown when the character makes choices either through dialogue or action (Aristotle states that characters—"objects of representation"—must be either "good" or "inferior," as distinguished by their "ethical differences"); (2) "appropriate" or well-defined in terms of type, e.g. manly or womanly, without mixing character-istics; (3) "like," as in the traditional portrayal of a given character, e.g. Odysseus should not ever be portrayed as being stupid; "consistent" in action and dia-logue, or "consistently inconsistent." Further, a "good" character should have "some flaw [*hamartia*] in him," through which he falls into misfortune.

Aristotle is very clear where the motivation of a character is concerned. *Character is that which reveals the moral purpose of the agents,* i.e. the sort of thing they seek or avoid. As I have stated, the aria is one of the great means of devel-oping character in opera. During an aria, the character's inner world opens to us, and they often speak directly to us of their deepest desires, feelings and fantasies. As important as action may be in illustrating character, dramatic truth may emerge in brief, still moments of character emotion and thought. So it is with the aria. Aristotle compares the drawing of a character to a painting on canvas, stressing the necessity of clarity of form and values. The aria is such a literary-musical canvas.

(3) *Thought,* (meaning or theme) is all the character says when proving a particular point or enunciating a general truth, i.e. the power of saying whatev-er can be said, or what is appropriate to the situation. More importantly in terms of dramatic conflict, thought is "an argument that something is or is not."

> *Under the head of Thought come all the effects to be produced by the language. Some of these are proof and refutation, the arousing of feelings like fear, pity, anger and so on, and then again exaggeration, and deprecation.*

In summary, Aristotle places each of the three major elements in a formula which echoes his analytic approach to art.

> *Thought and character are the natural causes of any action and it is in virtue of these that all men succeed or fail—it follows then that it is the plot which represents the actions.*

In another sense, meaning emerges from a character's wrestling with her or his personal destiny, which is determined by the unique nexus of that charac-ter's internal forces (dreams, desires) and the external forces represented by the plot. Oedipus is manipulated by forces beyond his control. Aristotle collects such supernatural and natural forces within his concept of plot.

Aristotle's Minor Elements

Aristotle's three minor elements are *lexis* (diction), *melos* (musical ele-ments) and *opsis* (spectacle). He neatly summarizes his approach to these three elements. "We have, then, a natural instinct for representation and for tune and rhythm—for the meters are obviously sections of rhythms—and starting with these instincts men very gradually developed them until they produced poetry out of their improvisations" (IV,7). It is fair to say that Aristotle shared his master Plato's disdain for poets and artists generally; these great thinkers considered any copy of reality a dimension of shadows. Plato also addresses song in the following dismissive manner in *The Republic*: "You certainly, I presume, have a sufficient understanding of this—that song is composed of three things, the words, the tune, and the rhythm?"

(4) Diction (*lexis*) is "the expression of meaning in words, and this is essentially the same in verse and in prose"; further, it is the composition of the verses, the expression of the character's thoughts in words (in opera, the libretto). Specifically, Aristotle says that "diction" is "the metrical arrangement of the words; and a part of the process of 'song-making'" (*melos*). Books XIX,8 through XXVI, 16 of the *Poetics* are primarily concerned with diction, *lexis*.

(5) Music (*melos*) is song, the most immediate characteristic of which—melody—according to Aristotle, is too completely understood to require explanation and is the greatest of the pleasurable accessories in tragedy. *Melos*, as used here refers, as in the above quote from *The Republic*, to the unique combination of poetry, melody and rhythm that was the aural medium in Attic tragedy. Later, Plato says that "the music and the rhythm must follow the speech," an idea which we will discuss more later. We know that "melody"—now used in the sense of "tune"—became much more important in the post-Renaissance music which was used to set the first operatic texts.

(6) Spectacle (*opsis*) is the stage appearance of the actors and the dramatic setting that surrounds them. This includes scenery, costumes, make-up and masks. "Spectacle, while highly effective, is yet quite foreign to the art and has nothing to do with poetry." Aristotle's austere intellectualism insists that "The tragic effect is quite possible without spectacle, which is more a matter for the costumier than the poet." In short, the essence of poetic tragedy is for Aristotle in the words and the dramatic values that shape the plot, characters and thought inherent in the poetry—not in the staged performance.

These are the major and minor elements Aristotle gives us. In the following essays, these six dramatic values or constituents will be referred to in contemporary terms approximating their original meaning: plot, character, meaning, text (libretto), music and stage setting. Some philosophers say that most of the deep thinking of Western civilization occurred between 500 and 300 B.C. Others say that all Western philosophy is a footnote to Plato, Aristotle's teacher. At all accounts, Aristotle is our deepest dramatic-literary taproot, partially because we have (in relatively good condition) the play which Aristotle chose to use as the paradigm of classical tragedy, Sophocles' *Oedipus Tyrranus*.

Imagine the Greek chorus circling the orchestra—the circular area before the staired, pillared *proskene*—in graceful steps, their heads thrown back in controlled ecstasy as they move to the throbbing of the drum, linked invisibly by the musical web of lyre and flute. The great, meticulously trained voices are carefully modulated to the ensemble sound. Their form, when they slow, turn and cease their motion has the dancer's grace and expressive power. Their robes follow their lithe forms in the Aegean breeze, like shadows.

See them far below you in the great theater of Athens, moving as one in the September night. From a distance they are a shimmering necklace, their sung words somehow recreating, encompassing your awakening evening dream. This circle of flesh encompasses what was once an altar, representing the hero's crown—for where he stands, towering above the chorus in mask, robe and cothurni, you also stand. His voice rings out and their dance ceases. The old pain becomes new, the old secrets are again charged with the mythic divine.

We have, then a natural instinct for representation and
for tune and rhythm—   *Poetics, IV, 7*

Visualizing Structures—
REFLECTIONS ON LITERARY FORM IN OPERA

Moreover, in everything that is beautiful, whether it be a living creature or any organism composed of parts, these parts must not only be orderly arranged but must also have a certain magnitude of their own; for beauty consists in magnitude and ordered arrangement.

The Poetics (VII,8-9) brings up the matter of the organic balance of a work of art. The complex structures of opera, basic forms are easily visualized; for example, the flow of dramatic action in opera might be pictured as an arch. This balanced structure supports the weight of material over an open space. We might visualize an operatic plot as a masonric bridge, a bridge made up of stone blocks, each representing a scene in the opera's plot. Each part of both the arched bridge and the opera plot depends absolutely on every other part making up the bridge's arc or span, its "parts... orderly arranged [with a] certain magnitude of their own."

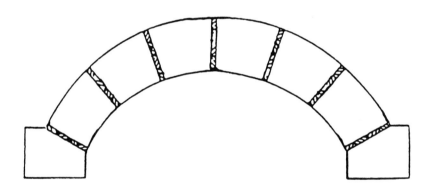

The opera's plot as the bridge or great arc represents the opera's musical-dramatic form, and diverse aspects of each of the four disciplines—Literature, Drama, Music and the Visual Arts—constitute sub-arcs of the great arc. The great arc consists of the plot's parts, the units or divisions of the opera's story: acts, scenes and musical numbers. These units are a unique amalgam of musical-dramatic forms that librettists and composers have developed through the centuries.

Sub-arcs consist of the literary, musical and visual elements as we might isolate them for purposes of discussion. Together, these sub-arcs create patterns of meaning built on the principle of association. The better integrated each sub-arc is, the stronger the great arc, the plot of the operatic work of art.

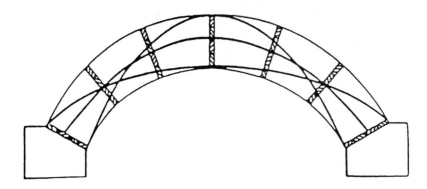

As we discuss each sub-arc, especially each musical sub-arc, patterns of augmentation (the building of action or intensity) and diminution (the lessening of action and intensity) will become clear. Here are some introductory observations about *La Bohème*'s plot to illustrate arc and sub-arc.

Balance of Plot and Character in *La Bohème*

La Bohème's plot and characters are formed from a remarkable blend of literary, dramatic and musical elements. Let us begin with the elements about which the librettist(s) and composer likely spoke in their first conversations about the opera.

Puccini places great weight on character, especially female character; his plots are character-driven. *La Bohème*'s plot consists of action caused by the internal worlds of the protagonists, especially by the desires and dreams of the heroine, Mimi. The two main characters are Rodolfo, who begins and ends the opera, and Mimi, who enters the opera late in Act 1 and departs before the end of Act 4. *La Bohème* is their story, the story of their short, passionate relationship. Rodolfo is a struggling writer with a dark streak of obsessive jealousy, Mimi a seamstress with romantic notions of being the mistress of a wealthy man.

Concentrate on gathering each character's back-story as you read and listen. The clues will emerge at unexpected moments. In *La Bohème*, hunger, loneliness and despair haunt the hero and heroine. Since the action of *La Bohème*'s plot is character-driven, the more we know about the major characters, the better. Operas like *La Traviata* and *Carmen* are more plot-driven, i.e. the characters seem at times to be puppets driven by forces beyond their control.

In *La Bohème*, we experience only a short span of these characters' lives: from Christmas Eve (Acts 1 and 2), through bitter February (Act 3) into April (Act 4) of the following year—perhaps four months altogether. The story begins in the dead of Winter and, ironically, concludes in early Spring. (The environment of this play is important, for Poverty is not only a theme but becomes almost a character, as it seems to influence event after event.) This plot is chronological, though with jagged leaps in stage time, e.g. two months pass between Acts 2 and 3, and then two months between Acts 3 and 4.

If the actions of Rodolfo and Mimi constitute the plot of *La Bohème*, then the actions of secondary characters or foils like Marcello and Musette constitute the subplot. The subplot enhances the plot by providing it with a parallel relationship for comparison and contrast. Later, you may wish to compare the elements of plot (arc) and subplot (sub-arc) to melody and counter-melody, especially when listening to Act 3 of *La Bohème*.

Patterns of Repetition in *La Bohème*'s Plot

La Bohème's settings make us aware of the keen role repetition plays in all aspects of operatic structure. Acts 1 and 4 are set in the same scene, "in the Attic," and this visual recurrence alone gives the viewer a sense of "return" (*ritornello*) or closure. If we look at the initial and final positions of those two acts in the plot's arc, we will see many structural similarities, all of which augments our sense of balance and closure as the action resolves.

Poetic and musical terms—"envelope" or ABA form—are used to describe the "return" to the beginning which gives the audience psychological closure. You may want to relate the idea of closure to Aristotle's term "catharsis," in the sense that both elements release emotional and intellectual tensions in the audience by engaging the memory of specific past events to elucidate the present dramatic situation, as the drama concludes.

Now let us consider the details of the dramatic action in Acts 1 and 4 of *La Bohème*. Each act grows in a crescendo of action from a conversation between Marcello and Rodolfo to horseplay involving all four Bohemians. In each act, the horseplay is interrupted: in the first act by the landlord, in the fourth by Musetta's adumbration of Mimi's entrance. In both acts, after Mimi's entrance, the stage action diminishes and musical intensity is augmented. With Mimi comes intimacy and revelation of character. After her entrance, the first act features the wonderful aria/aria/duet sequence that brings the act to a close, glistening with intimacy rather than action. The corresponding portion of the fourth act takes the form of an extended duet between the two lovers that reviews melodic material from the first act, in addition to offering new musical ideas of power and beauty. Clearly, in terms of the dramatic action—entrances, character interaction—the two acts are similar in general design. Unconsciously, this gives us emotional/psychological—musical/dramatic—closure.

Act 1 grows in musical power and intimacy as the lovers draw closer, just as the fourth act clearly grows in dramatic power as Mimi's death approaches. Themes of passion (eros) and death (thanatos) are unusually closely related in Romantic opera. Freud was a great student of the opera and I wonder that he never quoted from an opera in his work. (Doubtless that would have been too unscientific.) He would certainly have found many wonderful examples to illustrate his final great theory, an exploration of the close relationship between love and death in the unconscious.

Such contrasts typify opera. They strengthen the arc of plot with complexity, variety. No one understood better than Shakespeare how to use dramatic contrast, and Verdi greatly admired the bard of Avon. He learned a great deal from him about contrasting dramatic elements. Puccini learned from Verdi, whose *Aida* inspired Puccini to become a composer. Consider the contrasting endings of *La Bohème*'s Acts 1 and 4. Act 1 concludes—as does Act 3—with an empty stage and the lovers' voices filling the air from a distance. The final act ends with Rodolfo's cries of despair and the orchestral phrases that capture the anguish of the living struck by the final loneliness at facing the sea of death. Though the acts share a common setting and much common action and music, the endings of Acts 1 and 4 contrast powerfully in the emotions they elicit from the audience. This is dictated by the great arc of the plot, and the necessity of the catharsis inherent in Rodolfo's final cries.

For many listeners, the greatest subtleties of opera lie within the tensions between elements, e.g. Mimi dies in "the Spring of life." The subtleties of any work of art are more likely to become apparent when one is aware of operatic elements as individual entities, because understanding of the parts of the whole makes clear the unifying principle of a work. This understanding allows the listener to see the work as a balanced work of art, rather than a pleasing blur of action that elicits emotion.

Plot and Subplot in *La Bohème*

The subplot of *La Bohème* strengthens the plot by comparing and contrasting with it, just as secondary characters are meant to contrast with major ones. In a psychological sense, diverse characters may, when taken together, give the audience a sense of completeness, because singular characters may represent a single aspect of a personality.

The plot of *La Bohème* is as follows: in Act 1, Rodolfo and Mimi meet and a short time later she sings "*Io t'amo;*" in Act 2, they grow closer, despite Mimi's flirtations with a student; between 2 and 3, an obsessively jealous and guilt-ridden Rodolfo leaves Mimi; but they reconcile in later in 3, agreeing to separate in Spring; between 3 and 4, Mimi leaves Rodolfo for the "*Viscontino*" Rodolfo complained about in 3; in 4, Mimi returns to the attic to declare her love for Rodolfo before she dies.

The subplot of *La Bohème* is comic, and meant to contrast with the plot: in Act 1, Marcello mentions Musetta's "marble" heart; in 2, the fiery pair reunite publicly; in 3, they separate after a jealous spat; in 4, they reunite in a futile attempt to save Mimi. As Musetta and Marchello's relationship renews itself at the end of Act 2, they join Mimi and Rodolfo, who met perhaps an hour earlier. If we wish to compare the two relationships, we are given little time to do so.

We know much more about Mimi and Rodolfo because of their Act 1 arias. Our knowledge of Musetta and Marcello is slight, must be gleaned from remarks in ensembles. It is there, but must be gleaned. By Act 3's beginning, some two months later, Mimi and Rodolfo are at odds, while Musetta and

Marcello are still together. To make full use of both contrast and irony, Puccini has the couple reverse positions by the end of the Act 3—Musetta and Marcello scatter to the four winds, while Mimi and Rodolfo agree to stay together till spring.

When plot and subplot intertwine, things usually get complex and fascinating: knowing this, Puccini drew the inspiration for the magnificent quartet at the end of *La Bohème*'s third act from the diverse vicissitudes of love experienced by the two couples. The great musical dramatists sense when to create a musical form—in this case, a quartet—which not only captures the dramatic essence of the plot's flow at that point but augments the dramatic content by contrasting elements. The quartet in Act 3 is such a musical occasion and a lovely one. As Marcello and Musetta fly the coup, Rodolfo and Mimi settle back in their uneasy nest until Spring.

Act 4 of *La Bohème* nullifies both relationships and romance by introducing the element of death. It was the foreshadowing of Mimi's death that drove Rodolfo away from her and into the night earlier in Act 3. Mimi's death transforms the meaning of *La Bohème* from the hope of personal fulfillment to selfless sharing, for every character is moved to give what they can for Mimi's final comfort. Mimi recognizes this and attempts to show Marcello Musetta's deeper admirable qualities: "Marcello, your Musetta is so good." "It is true," he agrees. But their relationship is no longer the point. In fact, character itself is no longer the point. Aristotle was correct: plot (Fate) is supreme and has determined the heroine's destiny and, for the moment tainted every other character's. Fate, an arc, is universal and supreme; destiny, a sub-arc, is individual and relative.

Structural Similarities in The Plots of *La Bohème, Carmen* and *La Traviata*

As in *La Bohème*, the plots of Bizet's *Carmen* and Verdi's *La Traviata* are broken into four parts. The final act of each of these three operas is set where the opera began, *La Bohème* and *La Traviata* in the same room, *Carmen* in "a square in Seville."

La Bohème's entire action is confined—as if the characters were trapped in a cage of poverty—to Paris. In true Romantic fashion, the couples of the other two operas try to escape from the city into a natural environment. *Carmen* draws José *dans la montagne* (*to the mountains*), while Violetta withdraws to "a country house near Paris" with Alfredo to restore her health and to cultivate their relationship. Rodolfo and Mimi only make it as far as the *Barrière d'Enfer*, the gate to the city.

The plots of *La Bohème, Carmen* and *La Traviata* may be summarized as follows: in Act 1, the lovers meet and fall in love; in Acts 2 and 3 (2,2 of *La Traviata*) complication of jealousy or a third party tests the relationship; in Act 4 the affair ends with the heroine's death. Each final act also contains parallel literary, dramatic and musical sub-arcs (often consisting of patterns of repetition) which recall the first act or *Prelude* to support the great arc of action's scenic closure. We will discuss these patterns in much more detail in the case of each individual opera. For example, the marvelous *Preludes* to both *Carmen* and *La Traviata* provide suggestive music materials that will be employed in musical sub-arcs at crucial points in the four acts that follow them.

Beginning with our first opera, we want to strengthen our sense of plot, character and theme. Opera, like all Western art, is built on certain structural assumptions and from certain basic materials. Let us now discuss in more detail some of the literary building blocks of which opera is shaped, using *La Bohème* as our example.

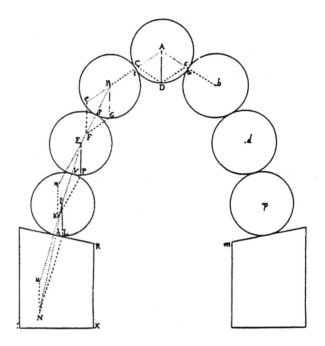

Literary-Dramatic Elements in La Bohème

MEANING, IMAGE AND CHARACTER

In great operas like La Bohème and our other three masterworks, a rich tapestry of visual images emerges from several sources: from the poetic text, from dramatic action, from music, and from the visual environment. Each of these four disciplines may make a strong symbolic statement. The great power of opera lies in the ability of the librettists and composer to unite these disciplines in spectacular moments that create luminous symbols of haunting and lasting beauty. We will look for and seek to appreciate such moments in each opera we discuss. We will look at aspects of meaning (theme), image and character common to well-constructed opera libretti.

Like much of post-Renaissance Western art, opera concentrates most of its meaning within a cluster of themes having to do with love or its absence and with love's success or failure. Tragic operas are usually about passion obstructed or gone wrong and death straightens out the issue in one way or another; while comic operas are about the temptations of eros and other human foibles, and marriage (or restored marriage) is usually the solution to the comic problem. Consider, in this regard, Mozart's *Figaro*, the greatest of all comic operas.

On an intellectual level, a surprising number of operas explore the tension between the sacred and the profane in a religious and/or philosophical sense. *The Rake's Progress* is such a work, as are *Nebucco*, *The Magic Flute*, and *Parsifal*. But the vast majority of operas work from a much more direct and human base. The most common tragic formula in opera results from the intertwining of eros (sexual passion) and thanatos (death).

Man and woman, usually young like Mimi and Rodolfo, are passionately attracted, but any long-range plans are destroyed by forces seemingly beyond their control. In the best tragedies, no single thing causes the catastrophe, but a balance of internal (character-based) and external (plot-based) forces cause the lovers to act and react in ways that shape their destinies.

Sources of Conflict in *La Bohème, Carmen,* *La Traviata,* & *The Rake's Progress*

Each of our operas carefully defines the forces that will destroy love. In *La Bohème*, a series of forces beset the lovers, among them squalid poverty, psychological needs amounting to character flaws in both lovers (Mimi's flirtatiousness and Rodolfo's obsessive jealousy) and Mimi's physical disease. In *Carmen*, it is José's descent into jealous rage, his psychosis exacerbated by Carmen's reckless passion and superstition. *Carmen* features a unique treatment of the idea of Fate or Chance, almost amounting to determinism. Ultimately, Carmen is violently slain by José in the street of Seville. *La Traviata*'s formula is similar to *La Bohème*'s, but occurs in the privileged demimonde of Paris. The hero's abusive jealousy is precipitated by the condemnation of the affair by Alfredo's father, who represents bourgeois respectability.

In both *La Bohème* and *La Traviata*, the heroine is claimed by disease, under extenuating circumstances: Mimi has had a tempestuous, exhausting Winter; Violetta is depressed and destitute. Both die penniless. Mimi, Carmen and Violetta are all victims of a unique combination of character flaws (internal forces) and circumstances (external forces.)

In contrast, Anne Truelove, of *The Rake's Progress*, is in many ways a modern woman. Her only weakness is her inability to recognize evil and to shield Tom from it; she is a decent individual in an indecent world. She may not ever find the happiness her ill-fated love for Tom promised but did not give her, but she will not allow herself to be dragged down by Tom's tragic weakness and his yoke of misfortune. *The Rake's Progress* is the only allegory of our four operas. This libretto has the best poetry of our four operas; W. H. Auden, the librettist (and one of the great poets of the twentieth century), has imbued his libretto with unique and diverse imagery forming subtle patterns of meaning, which evoked musical finesse from a great composer.

In all these great music dramas, the ascent and descent of the heroes and heroines are complemented by cycles of imagery featuring the seasons, the religious and social powers that be, and the inner lives of the major characters.

Literary-Dramatic Image in Opera

Three kinds of literary-dramatic imagery often occur in opera: (1) the image of presence or appearance; (2) image of specific action, as directed by the libretto, in mime or in conjunction with music, i.e. the dumb show (action performed in silence or to minimal accompaniment) that Puccini was so fond of; and (3) literary image, image of verbal gesture, that is such a strong element of poetry and poetic drama, of which opera is a hybrid.

Each of these images is most effective when integrated with as many other elements as possible; in opera, all of them are accompanied by music, which augments and directs their meaning. Needless to say, any of these images may take on the power of a symbol, acquiring meaning far beyond its initial, concrete appearance. Let me give examples of each kind of image in *La Bohème* and our other operas, and explain how each works within the unique musical-dramatic environment where we find them.

(1) Images of presence are a matter of basic recognizability. Many characters in comic opera are types taken from Italian comedy and dress in a certain kind of costume, but characters in more serious dramas generally dress typical to their occupation or station in life. For example, the comic characters of Benoit, the landlord, and Alcindoro, the aging lover, of *La Bohème* are not only social types, but were also minor (local) character types from Italian comedy, the *Commedia dell' Arte*, called *caratteristia*. Major characters in tragic opera are necessarily more realistically costumed and portrayed.

Mimi dresses plainly but attractively, as a *grisette*, a social type of her time: a flower girl with hopes of becoming a social fixture on the arm of a nobleman. Musetta has already made this transition, and dresses her success. The four bohemians are poor and dress their parts. There is a particular poignancy to Colline's farewell to his overcoat in his famous aria in Act 4 of *La Bohème,* for his *vecchia zimarra* (ancient overcoat) is a part of his identity. Both Violetta, the most celebrated courtesan of her day, and Carmen wear clothing that represents their social rank and expresses their values. (Remember that Violetta and Carmen only hold their rank in the demimonde.) Anne Truelove, a decent and well-to-do landowner's daughter, dresses accordingly.

Objects particular to a character may serve as unforgettable images: José's flower, uniform and sword—later, his knife, Mimi's *cuffietta rosa* ("pink bonnet") and many more. Occasionally, a character will have a particular characteristic or action that creates an image. In *La Bohème,* Mimi's hands are always cold—from *che gelida manina* in Act 1 to *mani riscaldare* in Act 4. Her hands become an on-going symbol, uniting intimacy of character, theme, and an environment of poverty and disease.

(2) A character's actions, both physical and verbal, are far more important than her appearance. Physical actions, whether accompanied by music or not, are powerful tools of characterization. Mimi's fainting spell soon after her entrance affects Rodolfo on different levels and his confusion is echoed in two very different remarks about her, *Che viso d'amalatta* and *Che bella bambina!* These two contrasting asides represent pity and passion, a unique combination and, to the wise, touching. Consider also the paradigmatic power of Rodolfo's offering Mimi a cup of wine soon after her entrance: Listen to how Puccini emphasizes this simple action musically when Rodolfo says *Così?* He imbues the mythic gesture with universality by his use of orchestral consonance and warmth.

More subtle and far reaching are the attitudes of role-playing assumed by Mimi and Rodolfo as Act 1 closes. Rodolfo loftily sings to her, *Dammi il braccio, mia piccinia...* (Give me your arm, little one) and she answers, as a grand lady might, *Obbedisco, signor* (I obey you, my Lord). Here each character fantasizes the future they long for and assumes that role, to the delight of the other. The failed writer and the failed prostitute assume the roles of a grand couple.

In fact, each fantasy feeds off the other. Just as, earlier, Mimi pretended not to see Rodolfo find her house key and hide it, she now takes his cue to become the "great lady" of his fantasy world. Such gestures are quite common, yet their resonance, considered in light of what we come to know of these people and the environment in which they live, can be quiet profound. Both these young people live in poverty and hunger: a rich fantasy world would be a great comfort to them. Puccini's music makes the fantasy world quite accessible to the audience, but careful attention to detail allows the audience to appreciate a richer, more complete picture of character and meaning in *La Bohème.* Ironically, in *La Bohème,* Fantasy blooms into tragic misery.

(3) Literary images emerge from the poetry of the libretto and are endowed with luminescent quality by musical setting and occasionally by physical action and environment. In the second part of this book, we'll look in detail at Mimi's aria, *mi chiamano Mimi,* which contains a plethora of images of

Spring, including flowers, light and, inevitably, the possibility of love. All these images climax in the lines *foglia a foglia la spio*—for, as Mimi describes the flower opening, her own character is opening before the audience like a flower. The unique power of the aria, with its union of lyric poetry and orchestral accompaniment, creates a rich nexus of meaning in which musical, literary and literal gestures combine to create a singular dramatic moment.

Characters—the Most Complex Images

How do we get to know a character? Let's examine the ways in light of what we know about people in general and in light of what we've discussed above. First, each character has a *back-story*, the life they've lived before we meet them. This story may emerge gradually from the text of the opera, or it may remain a mystery to us. We find out more about Violetta's past life in *La Traviata* than about Mimi, Carmen or Anne's lives in our other operas. It so happens that, if we look to the sources of the libretti for each of these works, Violetta still emerges as the richest figure in terms of personal history. The backstory of the character may help explain their motivation. It is important, it seems to me, that Mimi, Carmen and Violetta all came from backgrounds of poverty.

Second, we know a character by the way they appear, their costumes and make up. As we know from real life, to judge on the basis of external appearance can be dangerous, for a noble heart may conceal itself in rags. Third, we know them by the way they act and their actions—physical, literary, and sung gestures—and our understanding of the motivation for these gestures. We come to know very quickly that the gentle, romantic Mimi is also flirtatious and, in her own way, ambitious. In fact, it is the particular ambivalence she evokes as we look closely at her character that is one of her most powerful qualities. Ultimately, she is a very human being.

Fourth, we know a character by the way they *react* to the forces around them. The way one confronts misfortune is very telling. Each character of *La Bohème* reacts to Mimi's final illness and death in a distinct way, a way that tells us a great deal about them. Fifth, we may listen to what others say about a character, but be careful to consider the source in such cases. Marcello says only wicked things of Musetta, but we come to know her as a generous, gracious (if fun-loving) individual. On the other hand, it turns out that in Act 3 both Mimi and Rodolfo give Marcello accurate descriptions of the causes of tensions in their relationship. Ironically, he doesn't believe either of them. He, of course, has his own problems. Sixth, and very importantly, in music drama we know a character by the music assigned them. Many times we know a character's type or mood by the music that accompanies them. For the particulars, we usually have to consider the musical setting of the word. As the story progresses, the use of a repeated musical idea (*motif*) is a remarkably subtle tool for characterization.

If we begin to associate a particular melody with a particular character, emotion, or idea and this melody appears in a new context, it can be quite striking. As Mimi lies on her deathbed, for example, she and Rodolfo attempt to recapture the beginning of their relationship rather than consider the end of it. This is natural for two children of fantasy, faced now with despair and loneliness. Mimi's greatest fear is loneliness—in every act of *La Bohème* she sings the word *sola* over and over. So great is her fear of being alone that she pursues Rodolfo off into the cruel February night rather than spend the rest of the night alone. This reaction to being alone makes her one of the most needful and desperate of all operatic characters. I think she fears dying alone.

It is in the unique combination of all these elements—meaning, image and character portrayal—that the most powerful or synesthetic images are created. We will see later how each of our composers draws on the innate power of all these images to create truly unforgettable operatic moments. One such moment is when in Act 1 Rodolfo turns from shouting down to his friends to find Mimi bathed in moonlight he praised only moments earlier in the first few lines of his aria *che gelida manina*: *Ma per fortu—è una notte di luna, / e qui la luna l'abbiamo vicina*. Struck to the core with the halo of moonlight gracing Mimi—*o dolce viso*—before him, he sings, *O suave fanciulla, o dolce viso / di mite circonfuso alba lunar, ...* And their fates, for better and worse, are sealed. In this case, it is Mimi herself who becomes the luminous image, but this Mimi, the character which assumes such importance for Rodolfo, is being created by an interplay of many images of psychological power—literary, dramatic, musical and visual.

Let us now briefly consider the musical and visual elements of opera.

The Musical Elements

Musical performers of opera fall into two clear units: the singers (soloists and chorus) and the orchestra. The orchestra is a dominant factor in opera, for in most opera the orchestra is a near-full symphonic size so that the magnitude of its sound determines the size and quality of the voice required to sing any of opera's chief roles.

The uses of the orchestra in the operatic medium are many and vital. The manner in which a composer employs the orchestra is called orchestration and this is for the singer—and thus for the literary-dramatic elements—determinant. The skill with which the composer writes for the voice and supports vocal art with orchestral accompaniment is also a crucial element to consider. The orchestra's performance of musical form determines the great arc of most operas, because, in opera, plot—the arrangement of events—is parceled into musical forms. This is true of the greatest operas, which manage to combine all six of Aristotle's elements in musical form without drawing attention to the form itself, but rather making a profound comment on the human condition.

Orchestral music interacts with every literary, dramatic or visual sub-arc, or any combination of the three, throughout most operas. Opera is, it is always good to remember, *dramma per musica*, drama through music. Music is the essential element of opera and, despite the orchestra's central importance, the human voice is the chief solo instrument of musical expression. I will discuss the duties of the orchestra, the chorus and the soloists, then the musical elements and forms employed by composers in opera. This mere introduction must necessarily be both general and succinct, but do consult more specific books to augment what this approach offers.

Orchestral Duties

The first duty of the orchestra is to furnish stage environment, which is without music a discrete combination of setting and character vitality. Music adds an aural-emotional dimension which cannot be overestimated. *La Bohème* opens with the undeniable vigor of the first four young men we will meet and continues in a lively tapestry of their wit and play for 15 minutes. At Mimi's entrance late in Act 1, the orchestral mood and color change remarkably. It moves from the rambunctious physical to delicate strokes of emotion, from the dimension of the externals to the internal realm of dream and fantasy. In profound contrast to both these techniques of orchestral painting, the opening scene of *Carmen*, the orchestra paints in broad, warm strokes, echoing the warm, sunny environment and actions of the waking city of Seville.

Carmen's curtain also rises as the orchestra's ascending patterns echo the rising, drifting noonday heat of Seville, as well as the cigarette smoke of the girls who work in the nearby tobacco factory. In Act 1 of *La Traviata*, the curtain rises in Violetta's apartment, with the orchestra full of the frivolous energy of the demimonde in full swing. This infectious energy will not cease until Alfredo declares his love for Violetta later in Act 1. The opening curtain of *The Rake's Progress* reveals what we have already heard in the orchestra: the rich pallet of nature in rural England. The orchestra may also be used to describe local and natural events or conditions such as cold in the opening of the third act of *La Bohème* or the mid-day heat in the opening scene of *Carmen*'s Act 1.

Second, the orchestra accompanies singers, not only their voices but often their actions as well. Great and innovative composers accompany singers with remarkable variation. Puccini's approach to accompaniment is to use a lush orchestral sound, and often to use homophony—when a section of the orchestra plays the melody with the singer, especially on climactic passages. Puccini's orchestration ennobles his soprano heroines by having the French horn accompany their climactic phrases. This particular characteristic of Puccini's orchestration is one way he makes it clear that his heroines are the driving force and thematic center of his serious operas.

Bizet, composing thirty years before Puccini and deeply influenced by the French tradition, uses the orchestra descriptively, to create and augment local color, but also with dramatic facility and clarity, accompanying the voice richly and subtly while supporting it effectively in climactic passages. Verdi's art of accompaniment is complex and dramatically effective: in arias, he usually strips the orchestra to bare yet dynamic rhythm and exposes the voice above it. In this he is following the *bel canto* style he inherited from Bellini, Donizetti, and Rossini, all of whom wrote the kinds of deeply serious operas in which Verdi most fulfills himself. In *The Rake's Progress*, Stravinsky's art of accompaniment consists of his own unique amalgam of three centuries of operatic accompaniment technique. He borrows only from the best and sometimes burlesques them stylistically—even the great Verdi.

In general, the composers of the second half of the 19th century used the orchestra to make dramatic statements at the expense of the singer's freedom of vocal expression. Verdi and Wagner created operas in which the voice is, musically speaking, another important solo instrument. Comic opera has always used the orchestra as a means of dramatic subtlety, with Rossini leading the way in the early 19th century. By the time of Schumann's song cycle *Dichterliebe*, accompaniment was proving itself capable of being an equal partner with the soloist in serious dramatic expression. The innovations of Verdi and Wagner in the treatment of the voice revolutionized the dominance of orchestra as the ever-growing arbiter of meaning in opera performance. In Verdi's two final great operas, *Otello* and *Falstaff*, the orchestra rollicks and roars with laughter, a character in its own right.

Third, the orchestra may represent abstract dramatic elements such as death, and Fate (as in *Carmen*'s *Prelude)*, or social values such as religion or patriotism. Three themes are introduced in *Carmen's Prelude*, the first two united by martial vigor. The first theme will not reappear until the opening of the fourth act, the second early in the second act; the striking third theme is, however, a musical representation of the inescapable threat and power of the unknown in life—it is referred to as "*Carmen*'s Fate" theme—and will echo at crucial moments throughout the opera to signify danger. Its second appearance is in the brief orchestral interlude before Carmen throws the flower at José. Its final appearance is in the jagged, powerful utterances of the orchestra in the climactic duet of Act 4.

Fourth, the orchestra may represent character inscape—individual character mood, attitude, even thought—with a concreteness relative to dramatic situation quite apart from environment. The *Prelude* to *La Traviata.* is a musical portrait of the heroine, Violetta. Each section of the composition hints at an aspect of her personality and life. It begins with the ethereal qualities of the sick woman's state of consciousness, proceeds to the yearning of a gracious but lonely woman, and finally adds the decorative frivolity of the social life of the courtesan. Some of the musical material of the *Prelude* will be used later in the opera, most strikingly in the opening of Act 3 when we find a profoundly depressed Violetta awaiting death in her frigid apartment. It would be difficult to overestimate the effectiveness of Verdi's genius at orchestration and the portrayal of character in music drama through musical form.

The Opera Chorus

The *opera chorus* functions much as the Greek chorus in the poetic tragedy perfected in Greece between 500 and 350 B.C. The chorus represents mankind or, depending upon the opera, a particular society or class of persons within a given country. They are employed in a wide variety of ways by composers. In *La Bohème* the chorus represents the masses of Paris; in *Carmen* they assume a wide variety of roles, from guardsmen and townspeople to gypsy smugglers; in *La Traviata*, they are gay figures of the demimonde, lost in empty celebration; in *The Rake's Progress*, they are Londoners, passersby, bidders at an auction, inmates in an asylum.

In Act 2 of *La Bohème*, the chorus is part of a vast impressionistic musical tapestry that is Paris on Christmas Eve. (Compare Bizet's use of chorus in 4,1 of *Carmen*.) It witnesses the action of the major characters, comments on it, and serves in part as an audience on stage. The chorus in *Carmen* appears at times passively integrated into the setting and musical environment in the opening scene, but soon becomes involved in the passionate action of the main characters. Later in the first act, the female chorus, for example, divides into those who support Carmen and those who support the girl Carmen disfigured. *Carmen*'s chorus is used to great musical-dramatic effect in the final scene.

Verdi often uses his chorus as a facet of the orchestra, giving the solo voices reign in ensembles; see, for example, the *brindisi* in act one or the magnificent third act finale of *La Traviata*. Contrast Verdi's purely musical use of chorus there to the dramatic power of Bizet's use of chorus in *Carmen*'s third act finale. Stravinsky's use of chorus is varied and skillful in that chorus members are called on to portray a wide variety of character types. In each case, the chorus is an integral part of the dramatic power of that particular scene.

Aristotle's demand that the chorus always be considered a character—"The chorus too must be regarded as one of the actors. It must be part of the whole and share in the action"—is adhered to in most successful opera, certainly in our four masterworks. In addition to being character and commentator, the chorus is an extension of the aural and visual environments, representing from time to time universal qualities as well as local color.

The Solo Voice

There are so many different types of operatic voices that entire books have been written on the subject. I will offer here only a few generalizations. The higher voices—tenor and soprano—usually represent younger characters, while darker voices—baritones and mezzo sopranos—portray more mature characters; old age and wisdom are generally inculcated by the deepest voices: the bass and contralto voices. Mimi, Musetta, Michaela, Violetta and Anne are all sopranos; their lovers are all tenors. *Carmen*, a mezzo-soprano, leads the ranks of more sensuous heroines. Baritones, mezzos and an occasional soprano make up the characters of sub plots, while basses add local color and moral gravity. A voice's category is determined by its qualities, its color and timbre, and not its range.

The Musical Elements

The major musical elements will be discussed in detail when we reach *La Traviata*, but let's list them here, define them, and give some examples. The major elements are: *rhythm* (and *tempo*), *melody, harmony, vocal form*, and *orchestration*. Each of these plays a major role in an operatic performance, but is so integrated into stage action that, generally speaking, they are unnoticed except to the practiced ear, in the musical-dramatic performance.

Rhythm is that aspect of music not concerned with pitch but with the distribution of sound—notes—in time and their accentuation. This beat or musical accent coordinates melody and harmony. Although Puccini is one of the great melodists of music history, *La Bohème* is a masterpiece of rhythm.

Generally, rhythm has two sources: musical rhythm emerges from the body in basic patterns of duple or treble rhythm, while language-associated rhythms emerge from speech rhythms. Musical rhythm is generally dominant when words and music combine and is measured from accent to accent in pairs, threes or compound units of these, the first beat of each unit being accented the strongest. The duple rhythm is deriving from walking, the treble from dance movement. The rate of speed of a composition is referred to as its *tempo*.

Rhythm is, in a broader sense, a far-reaching concept underlying all artistic expression. It is essential in conceptualizing interdisciplinary explorations like ours. Rhythm defined as it is above, that is within the context of music composition, is a small form element—an element contributing to local effects. As it will be used in reference to plot and total music-dramatic framework, it is a large-form element. We began to explore the large-form aspect (arc, sub-arc) of rhythm in our operas in Essay 2, above.

Melody is a succession of notes varying in pitch and having a recognizable musical shape. As we think of it today—as a tune—melody depends on symmetries of harmony and rhythm that seldom occurred in Europe before 1600, except in folk music. In its most primitive state, melody requires rhythm but can develop without the aid of harmony. Greek melody, as Aristotle experienced it, was not based on a harmonic system and was rhythmically tied to the word rhythms it accompanied. It would hardly seem tuneful to our modern ears.

Melody works by involving the listener in an immediate dynamic. In terms of acoustics, melody is a linear development of sound through time. It also has a roller coaster effect on our emotions in that it involves us more as it goes higher, and we relax at the effect of gravity on the musical phrase. For most of us, melody is the most immediately recognizable and enjoyable element of opera. It is sometimes called a *theme* and as such—even more as a *motif* (a repeated theme)—may acquire specific dramatic meaning in a musical-dramatic context

Harmony is the simultaneous sounding of tones in a way that is musically significant. Harmony, in its most basic function, is the multi-voiced accompaniment of melody. Harmony works indirectly, deeper in a psychological sense—vertically, in a visual sense—than do melody and rhythm in creating environmental or character mood. If melody is the surface of musical form, harmony is its depths, and the inextricable orchestral web of harmony and orchestration combined turns the deeper keys of musical meaning. Harmony is to classical music what texture and color are to visual art.

Musical Form

Art form generally and musical form specifically work in patterns that augment and diminish visceral tension. As the rise and fall of these tensions form patterns, for example in an aria, a scene or an act of *La Bohème*, they form structures characterized by the rhythm of their patterns' recurrence. In drama, tension is created by dramatic conflict, as characters struggle with their own natures and Fate; in music, harmonic colors and changes generally move us from concord to discord and back again. This movement is one of the major structural devices of *musical form*.

Although harmony has a linear aspect in that its many voices do progress toward tension or the resolution of that tension, and may even form several diverse melodies simultaneously (polyphony) in its flow, harmony's maximal expressive power lies in its vertical—simultaneously sounded—aspects, the layering of sound as clouds are layered about the earth's surface. Time is stopped when harmony sounds; time is defeated when more than one note sounds at once. The aural-visual frame of reference becomes multi-dimensional as the listener's mode of thought becomes relational rather than fixed on a single idea or image. Harmony's effect on us may be one of slight wonder.

Vocal form is, structurally, used in most opera as a musical counterpart to plot—the artful arrangement of scenic action. (I am using the term vocal form here to denote a musical number—any musical form — featuring the voice.) In many cases, opera has invented vocal forms to approximate dramatic units, for example scene 5 of *La Traviata*'s first act is described in the libretto as *Recitative and Aria.*

We have discussed recitative, secco (declamatory) and accompanied (melodic), and the aria (complex song form) above. Duet, trio, quartet, etc. are all self-explanatory common terms. The *ensemble* is musical number which does what no other dramatic medium except opera attempts—express the thought or emotion of many characters simultaneously in a structured way. The *chorus number* involves the voices of the chorus as it participates in, comments on and serves as background to the opera's action. *Carmen*'s chorus is used exhaustively, fulfilling every function of which a chorus is capable.

In terms of vocal form, it is fascinating to see how each composer strings together the four elements of recitative, aria, ensemble and chorus number within plot structure. The better integrated the chorus is into the dramatic-musical structure of the opera, the less need for a grand finale (closing scene of the opera) to serve as the musical climax of the opera, as in Bellini's *Norma*. In *La Bohème* and *La Traviata*, the chorus is not even there for the final scene of the opera; in *Carmen* it is off-stage. It is there, with haunting effect, in *The Rake's Progress*. Such masterful use of the chorus places the musical-dramatic emphasis on individual character and meaning in these four operas, rather than on effect.

Other Musical Tools

Although none of our four operas uses one, the *Operatic Overture* is instrumental music composed as an introduction to an opera, oratorio, or stage play. Following Gluck, the operatic overture was a musical argument of the drama to follow. Mozart's overtures to *Don Giovanni* and *The Magic Flute* were among the first overtures designed in the sonata style to anticipate the musical essence of the ensuing operas. Initially, overtures were in part employed to get the audience in their seats and quiet before the curtain went up.

Dance music is of two types: social dancing, as in the first scene of *La Traviata*; and ballet, as in 2,2 of *La Traviata* or the opening number of *Carmen*'s second act. Dance rhythms play a great role in *Carmen*'s music and the title character's musical portrayal. Contrast the basic, evocative role of dance rhythm in *Carmen* to Stravinsky's highly intellectual—sometimes parodic—employment of rhythm in *The Rake's Progress*.

On- and off-stage music has a realistic effect, as in the climactic finale of Act 2 of *La Bohème*, the changing of the guard in Act 1 of *Carmen*, or the first act of *La Traviata*. Verdi in particular had a genius for creating spatial, as well as musical effects with this tool, as in the first acts of both *La Traviata* and *Rigoletto*. *Carmen*'s use of castanets in Act 2 is one of the most famous uses of on-stage, non-vocal musical effect in opera.

Off-stage singing is used strikingly in all four of our operas and is quite common in opera. It can be used in a variety of subtle ways dramatically. In the first and third acts especially, Puccini uses it to great effect, leaving the stage full of an ethereal atmosphere. In *Carmen*'s second act, Bizet uses the two verses of José's tavern song to measure the character's approach to Lillas Pastia's tavern. It also heightens the tension of the Gypsies' departure and Carmen's expectations. Later, in the opera's final scene, the off-stage chorus is an effective and vital influence on the on-stage events. In *La Traviata*, Verdi uses off-stage singing to great effect in the first and third acts; in *The Rake's Progress*, Stravinsky uses it effectively in Acts 2 and 3.

Dramatic Mime or *melodrama* must be very carefully used in modern times. Puccini is a master of these devices. Mimi's death is an example: an *sfz p* chord in the brass (*pp* in the woodwinds) signals her last breath, but none of the characters on stage notice it for some time. (Compare this effect with a similar one at the beginning of Rodolfo's aria, *che gelida maninia*, in Act 1: these chords signal the beginning and end of love in Mimi's stage life.)

Orchestration is the composer's means of coloring the stage environment and exposing the interior worlds of his characters. Orchestral color is a matter of mixing and matching instrumental sound from the string, woodwind, brass and percussion sections. Mozart and Wagner, among opera composers, may be classified for the remarkable effect of their "dramatic orchestration;" that is, their strikingly innovative ideas as traced within the history of instrumentation. Verdi, too, made enormous advances in coloring character through orchestration in *Rigoletto* (premier Venice, 1851) before beginning work on *La Traviata* (Venice, 1853).

In Part 4, which concentrates on musical elements in *La Traviata*, I will discuss orchestral and vocal contribution to opera in much more detail, but as you listen now, consider a few of the following observations. Brass instruments are initially very important in creating the dynamic rhythms of *La Bohème*'s first act, while Mimi's entrance is heralded by a rising sequence of chords in the string section. Open harmonies in the strings create the slow vibrations that somehow perfectly conjure the frigid nature of a bitterly cold February morning in the opening of Act 3. Notice Puccini's use of vibrant, percussive chords to begin and end every act of *La Bohème*, reminding us always of the vigor of bohemian life, which not every character can survive.

The Visual Arts in Opera

Aristotle's decision to allocate music, versification and spectacle to minor status in his *Poetics* was a decision based on deeply held intellectual, critical, and philosophical convictions. The arts for Aristotle were one aspect of civilized man's desire to know himself, so naturally art at its greatest should give insight into man's *character*, the *meaning* of his thought concerning human existence, and *plot*, man's action defined within the limits of time and space.

Music, poetry and visual effect were for him functional minor elements in achieving these intellectual goals. While the visual aspects of opera are crucial to an aesthetically fulfilled operatic performance, the essential material for understanding plot, character, and meaning of any opera are there for the appreciative listener.

We live in the century of ever increasingly sophisticated auditory and visual recording and need not rely on the availability of live operatic performance. Still, it is in live performance that opera fulfills itself most completely. This accounts for the prodigious efforts of innumerable persons to produce and perform operas on both the amateur and professional levels.

Dimensions of the Stage

When we look at the stage, we see within and behind the proscenium a vast living picture, featuring large painted surfaces, framed or hung, representing natural and man-made settings; plastic representations of such natural things as rocks and trees; living statues (characters) which are painted, costumed, wigged and shod; and hand-held objects of exaggerated proportions, like swords, called properties. In addition, all these visual elements are blended into an integrated visual surface by stage lighting. The stage itself exists in a building, a "theater," and the design of these facilities and their acoustical properties are crucial elements of performance art in themselves.

When any single element of opera draws attention to itself, it is not functioning in proper aesthetic balance with opera's other elements—this is especially true of visual, as well as musical elements. Yet an ingenious stage design is a thing of beauty, lovely costumes are a joy to behold, and excellent lighting can make or break a production. In fact, in any of the four areas of opera, every element, however small, makes a crucial, desired contribution to the performance. This contribution, however, is functional; it is the servant of plot, character and meaning.

Opera at its most basic needs only two elements: a singer and a stage. Opera has tended to Attic spectacle involving mythic plots, gods as well as mortals, choruses as well as soloists. Greek theaters were vast, open air arenas built into hillsides, but opera has from its beginning prospered in proscenium theaters—theaters which function as if a fourth or northern wall had been removed from a great room into which the audience may peer and where settings recreate natural and man made environments with great technical finesse.

I would like to present a brief introduction to the technical aspects of theater. Those already familiar with the basic elements of technical theater should see Darwin Payne's *The Scenographic Imagination*, illustrations from which I use here with the gracious permission of the author and Southern Illinois University Press.

A stage is usually positioned in an architectural structure especially designed to contain it. Regardless of the building's structure or the complexity of the stage mechanism, the relationship of the audience to stage in the proscenium is as shown below.

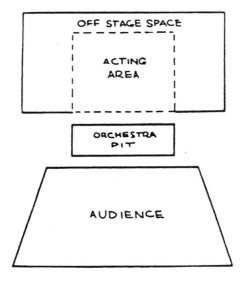

The stage designer fills the general background with scenery, light and properties dictated by the operatic score, the production's needs and the stage director's desires.

The scenery is usually created in large geometric units called flats that consist of canvas stretched over wooden frames then treated and painted much like a large oil painting. The flats are reinforced and braced by metal strips, by which means the flats are attached to the floor and to each other. Rope is often used to hold sets together when a show has many sets and when the theater does not have the capability of moving whole set units on rolling platforms.

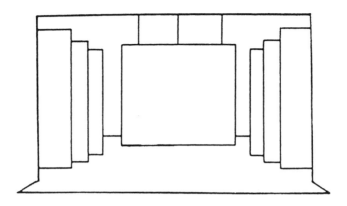

To this basic setting, once it is painted, are added furniture and other smaller scenic pieces—then light, characters and properties.

For a more complete picture of the proscenium theater's elements, on the following page is Darwin Paine's illustration and the corresponding definitions of the stage elements by number.

1. Proscenium arch
2. Stage floor — (A) Trap in stage floor, opened here, closed when not in use
3. Apron
4. Off-stage space (wings)
5. Orchestra pit (In some theaters, it is slightly recessed under the stage)
6. Back wall of theater
7. Grand drape
8. Main curtain (Can be lowered, or drawn from the side)
9. Second portal
10. Gridiron (A number of supports suspended from the ceiling of the stage house which allow scenery to be flown up and out of sight)
11. Fly gallery (Usually suspended some distance from the stage floor and where the lines attached to the flown scenery are manipulated after it has been counterweighted)
12. A cloth drop suspended from the gridiron
13. A cut drop suspended from the gridiron
14. Cyclorama
15. Scenic unit (composed of flats, platforms, steps, all built on a movable wagon)
16. Ground row
17. Footlights
18. Light batten suspended from gridiron
19. Front of house lighting portals

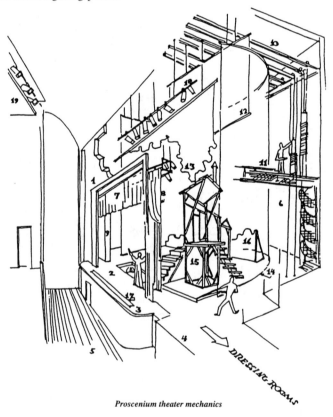

Proscenium theater mechanics

Costumes are also scenic elements and must be carefully coordinated with scenic design, especially as to texture and color. Costumes and properties are extremely important to the actor, much more so than any other scenic element.

In *The Dramatic Imagination*, Robert Edmund Jones makes several points about costume design.

> *A stage costume is a creation of the theater. Its quality is purely theatrical and taken outside of the theater, it loses its magic at once. It dies as a plant dies when uprooted.... Each separate costume we create for a play must be exactly suited both to the character it helps to express and to the occasion it graces. We shall not array Lady Macbeth in pale blue organdie or Ariel in purple velvet. Mephistopheles will wear his scarlet and Hamlet his solemn black as long as the theater continues to exist.*

Two Perspectives

I would like to consider the stage picture from two perspectives at this time: that of the scenic designer and then that of the stage director.

The scenic designer deals with space and surface to create a three-dimensional environment for living stage figures. Each of the illustrations of the stage settings in this section indicates the area where the scene painter may practice his art, employing the same general elements—color, texture, line, design—as the oil painter on a canvas, but on a massive scale. Unless a scenic backdrop is involved, the surface features of a stage stetting are strictly limited by the perspective of the stage area itself. This area contains the visual realm of the performers who fill the set with dramatic meaning.

In creating the stage setting, the scenic designer must foresee the fluid patterns of action within the stage setting. He and the stage director must consider every relevant aspect of movement and tone within the stage picture, which is framed by the proscenium opening, and the stage area, the three-dimensional space in which the characters will move.

The designer's concern with the stage area is both architectural and painterly. The surface areas, usually consisting of painted canvas and wood flats, must be arranged to create and preserve perspective. The colors, textures, and shapes covering these surfaces and their arrangement in the stage area create an enclosed environment, often giving the effect of a room with a fourth wall missing. Within this enclosed area, the set designer must imagine each individual action and reaction; he must run the opera like a film in his mind as he creates his design. He knows his work is functional and must not draw attention to itself after the opera performance begins. The most successful stage designers and directors are the least visible in performance.

Opera receives special treatment from the scenic designer, especially where light is concerned. Of all the abstract elements of opera, music is closest to light in nature, and thus seeks its visual complement. The intermarriage of light and harmony can lead to visual poetry. Opera is a special challenge for theater technicians: they must think in terms of large spaces because opera choruses generally require voluminous stage space. Yet every opera has intimate scenes and in these more intimate scenes, this same total area must somehow be used and lighted without dwarfing the soloists. (Verdi's *Aida* is a special challenge in this regard.) Grand opera is, spatially speaking, big opera.

Together, the scenic designer and stage director create the living painting that opera becomes. The stage director is, among other things, the actor's guide in the creation and portrayal of character. The director gives the actor specific movement (blocking) which always has one of two sources of justification: the score, or the motivation of the character. Similarly, the director is responsible for emphasizing the opera's meaning through working closely with the speech, singing and motion of each actor, as well as the chorus. It is the realm of the music director (conductor) to perform the superhuman task of coordinating all the visual, dramatic, literary and musical aspects of the performance, but if the stage director and stage designer have done their work well, the conductor's task is as much a joy as a challenge.

The stage director is also responsible for maintaining balance and clarity in the stage picture at all times. He is concerned with the balance of all technical elements and the interplay of these elements with those contained within the permanent art work—in this case, the score—and its stage space. All visual elements combine to create the stage picture. The stage director arranges the stage figures into patterns that form a composition pleasing to the eyes of the audience and logical in dramatic function. There are other kinds of audience-stage relationships, such as the one in the following illustration, called a "thrust" stage. One famous example of such a stage is the Mark Taper Forum in Los Angeles, another the Tyrone Guthrie Theater of Minneapolis.

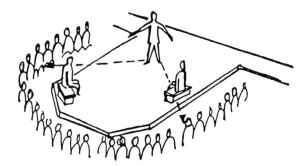

Where more than two characters are involved, the balance is reached by arranging characters in patterns based on geometric principles. The simplest and most important of these is the triangle. In Part 5, when we study the paintings that served as the basis for the *The Rake's Progress*, we will see that the basic form for painterly composition is the triangle within a rectangular frame. Two characters should be directed to play subtle variations on the fluctuating plane that the linear dimensions of their figures define in relation to the audience. The single stage figure defines this plane of action with the planes of his body and his face. The actor's eyes and hands are his most important visible tools, and, as such, determine the planes that he manipulates in relation to the audience's picture.

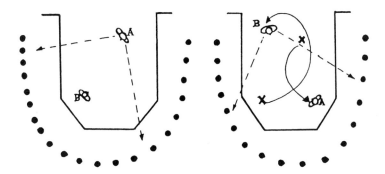

The stage director must always concentrate on one crucial thought where visual aspects of the production are concerned. Unless the script specifies otherwise, the audience's focus in the stage action should always be on one specific point at a time. Just as in a well-composed painting the viewer's vision is directed to begin at one focal point, so the drama should emphasize one visual-musical-dramatic point at a time within the flow of action. For this reason, actors generally move only when they speak or sing—in short, when they wish to capture the audience's attention. Usually, the invisible hand of the stage director moves through a staging, placing characters here, moving them there, seeking to maintain a balance pleasing to the eye, as well as to retain a dramatic tension pleasing to the mind.

All these elements are functional and must answer not only the needs of the script, stage director, and the production, but the individual performers as well: an awkward costume, bad make-up, stage doors that do not open properly, or poor lighting cues are just a few of the technical pitfalls potentially limiting the success of a production. Every technical aspect, every technical effect can be of vital dramatic importance.

Let us go on now to a more concentrated discussion of the literary elements of *La Bohème*, but not at the expense of what we now know of the other three disciplines—Drama, Music and the Visual Arts—we have begun to discuss in the essays above. In each of the following parts, I will focus on one particular opera and the discipline I have chosen to associate with that opera, but still bring to bear, in a general sense, any elements introduced earlier in this book.

I recommend that you first read, then listen to and only then view the opera being discussed in each part of the book. At least read the opera's text and listen to it once before reading the part of this book dedicated to that opera. Part 2 is concerned with literary elements—dialogue (recitative), lyric poetry (arias, duets, ensembles), and description—and their roles in the creation of character, idea, and environment in our first masterpiece, *La Bohème*.

Part 2

PUCCINI'S *La Bohème*
OPERA AS LITERATURE

La Bohème and Literature

Most listeners are originally attracted to Puccini's *La Bohème* by the rambunctious musical power and attractive melodies that typify its scenes, but they continue to return to it because of the joys and sorrows its characters share through the wit of their dialogue and the depth of their confessional poetry. In opera, poetry and dialogue are the verbal gestures that reveal the thoughts and feelings of character. The literary elements allow the characters to describe their feelings in a specific way that both charms and informs us. When words mount music and ring out as song, they acquire a heightened emotional content.

Whether it is Mimi shyly baring her soul to Rodolfo as she describes her lonely room and the works of her hands in Act 1 or Rodolfo pouring out his fear and pain to Marcello in Act 3, the characters in *La Bohème* live initially from the words with which they describe their circumstances, ideas, dreams and desires. We find most literary characters believable because of the unique mix of words spoken and action described. Dramatic characters use appearance, words, and actions spontaneously in live performance. Opera greatly expands—and to some degree, simplifies—the means by which we know a character in drama by adding music to the repertoire of verbal and physical gestures.

The process of creating an opera is complex and sometimes lengthy adventure. It is instructional to remember that in the process of an opera's creation, the text comes first; Puccini began composing *La Bohème* by studying roughly the same text we hear Mimi and Rodolfo sing. Thus there is a virtue in reading an opera's text before listening to it. The opera's text serves as the basis for both the creation and appreciation of opera.

Clearly, music is opera's primary element, but opera without words is an inauspicious mime show set to glorious music. The composer piggybacks words on music, and we may, when inundated by melodic splendor, initially discount and then forget the original literary-dramatic structuring of the opera. But words—especially the visual images poetry and poetic description evoke— deserve our attention in good or great opera. This section is about the literary component of that structure and the art of the librettist that inspires and complements the composer's art. Your choice of a libretto and introductory materials can be important. At the risk of repeating myself, let me remind you that reading the libretto and listening to the opera once before beginning to read this text will make the entire experience more rewarding in terms of developing the visual and auditory aspects of your imagination.[i]

❦

Operatic characters and stories come to us from all forms of literature, but I can not stress too often in the early stages of our discussion that opera's initial source was Classic drama's portrayal of mythic character and story in poetic tragedy as defined by Aristotle in *The Poetics*. Not until the primacy of prose fiction in the Romantic Era (1790-1830) did opera really begin to imitate the characteristics of literary forms other than myth, legend and poetic drama, i.e. the novel.[ii]

There are few books concerned with the art of the librettist, which is to transform the essentials of the literary source into that remarkable blend of poetry and play that the libretto must be to inspire compositional greatness. The libretto's words must inspire and complement the musical form with poetry that both advances plot and reveals character.

Giacosa and Illica took roughly three years (1893-96) to ransack Mürger's episodic novel, *Scenes of the Bohemian Life*, for the materials they shaped into the text for Puccini's *La Bohème*: (1) a series of settings that contain an ecstatic, pained love affair in bohemian Paris; (2) a remarkably disjunct plot tied together only by the emotional roller coaster of the affair; and (3) obsessive characters that are—when successfully drawn, as Mimi is—sometimes amalgams of diverse characters from the novel. Mimi (Lucia) is, for example, an amalgam of the actions and attitudes of several female figures in Mürger's novel—Mademoiselle Mimi, Seraphine and Francine. (4) Giacosa and Illica also adapted to the stage a plethora of images from the novel, including images of presence and specific action. These images are of a literary nature. The images the librettists chose to cultivate are particularly adaptable to the operatic medium, not only in that they are universal in nature but also in that they resonate in an interdisciplinary environment. Among these images in *La Bohème* are the flower, Spring, the sea, and diverse articles of clothing including a bonnet and a coat.

By literary image, I mean an image that depends upon the meaning of words—however much this meaning may in opera be augmented by music—for its resonance. Imagery is a term used to signify all objects (and qualities) of sense perception referred to in poetry or other literary genre, i.e. the libretto and all description, allusion, and figurative language in it: in literary description, for example, Mimi's lilies and roses "speak to her of love" in Act 1; by allusion, Rodolfo calls Marcello "Loiola," in Act 4, inferring that he is hiding his true feelings; metaphorically speaking, by Act 4 Mimi's love has become, in her own words, "as great as the ocean." This powerful image springs from Mimi—a wellspring of images in the opera—in a crucial moment and will have profound consequences for Puccini's final orchestral statement in *La Bohème*.

When Mimi sings *il primo bacio dell'aprile è mio!* (Spring's first kiss is mine) in Act 1 of *La Bohème*, we are naturally affected by the musical setting—featuring Puccini's melodic gift and his enchanting orchestration—of the words; but buried within this phrase is an essential image so common and evocative that it is second nature to us: in Spring comes renewal, rebirth and, on the personal level of Mimi's character, the promise of love and fulfillment. The images and image clusters involving Spring and the related ideas of love fulfilled are the chief expression of a major theme of opera: *the dream of love fulfilled*. *La Bohème* is saturated with seasonal imagery and images of natural growth. The presence of imagery in this opera's text is so omnipresent that imagery patterns clearly complement all three major dramatic elements: character, theme and plot. This kind of formal integrity can be expected only in the very finest operas. Each of our four operas has this integrity.

Here is a brief map of what will follow in Part 2. The next essay is a study of large-form patterns of repetition in Acts 1 and 4 of *La Bohème* and the way in which these patterns complement, even embody an essential subject of romantic opera: the intertwining of eros (sexual passion) and thanatos (death). The third essay is a detailed discussion of the poetry of Mimi's *Mi chiamano Mimì* in preparation for more complete, multi-disciplinary discussion of aria and vocal form. Literarily, as well as musically, the aria often provides the essence of character. The fourth essay concerns the idea of character as symbol and the corresponding creation of the *luminous image*, the idealization of characters like Mimi, when Rodolfo sings *o soave fanciulla,/o dolce vision di mite fuso alba lunar* ("O lovely girl, sweet vision in moonlight") to her.

The fifth essay will discuss how Illica and Giacosa wrestled a libretto from Mürger's novel *Scènes de la vie de bohème* over three difficult years. The techniques of the librettist can teach us a bit about opera. The libretto is a literary map of the *drama per musica*, the musical-dramatic tapestry of opera. *La Bohème*'s libretto is unusually ambitious in a number of ways, some of them distinctly literary in nature, i.e. this libretto cultivates distinctly non-dramatic imagery and poetic elements, such as language sound patterns that reward a close textual reading.

In the following essays, remember that the term *large-form* refers to larger units of a musical-dramatic work of art, like the whole plot, or the action or atmosphere of an entire act. The next essay is concerned with large-form considerations. It discusses the similarities of Acts 1 and 4 of *La Bohème*. The third essay of this part, on the other hand, is concerned with *small-form* matters, like variations in form and content of a more particular or local nature, i.e. within a particular musical number or scene. It involves the use of specific material in a specific context, e.g. an image from an aria, or a *motif* (a recurring image or idea). When literary, visual or musical images become attached to a specific situation, action or idea in one scene, then reappear in a new context later, they bring with them memories of the previous scene. With awareness of such patterns, we can begin to relate small form considerations to large ones.

The next essay will discuss how Act 4 of *La Bohème* consists in part of the repetition of diverse material previously introduced in Act 1 after Mimi's entrance. In general, the greater awareness the listener has of repetition of literary—as well as dramatic, musical and visual—images, the richer and more rewarding their operatic experience will be. Let us begin with literary elements and go on to the other three in the third, fourth and fifth parts of the book.

The Sources of Opera in Literature

IMAGE AND IDEA, THE DREAM OF LOVE FULFILLED

The literature and art of the bitter 20th century has been shaped by irony and game playing. Consequently, the range of poetic imagery has contracted to a narrow playing field, and then further constricted by the mechanics of academic philosophy espousing the inhumanity of civilized man and the irrelevance of mankind's higher facilities. At the same time that the very basic values and principles of Western Civilization are under fire, the canon of western art has often being discounted as an extension of an empty, destructive ideology. We have only to glance at a scenario of the horrific highs and lows of this century to understand the basis for this intellectual despair in mankind's abilities to create an environment where humankind may prosper and artists create. The music critics of this century, especially those specializing in music drama, have been among the most condemning of what they saw as mediocrity, ever narrowing the canon of acceptable operas and punishing those that, in their opinion, do not measure up.

The canon of Mozart (certainly the greatest of all composers), Verdi (the greatest composer of Italian opera), Wagner (the revolutionary musical-dramatic genius), Berg (the cynical intellectual's favorite for his dark vision and musical complexity), or Britten will hardly be threatened by Puccini or Offenbach—nor should they be. They are the best, when evaluated according to the criteria of Western aesthetics. They are the very finest wine Don Giovanni so longs for at his orgies. Yet not everyone can afford, longs for, nor finds meaning in the finest wine. The presence of greatness does not appear in a vacuum, and much of what created the milieu from which such greatness emerges is also worthy.

These five composers are indeed among the very best, but the greatest works of these composers are, for most of us, not always accessible in the way Puccini or Offenbach is. The very reasons the magnificent masterpieces of these geniuses are so critically praised is the elegance derived from the integrity with which the complex operatic elements are combined. This complexity is the very reason in most cases why they will not necessarily win new audiences for opera—certainly among the young. The works—like *Figaro, Otello, Tristan, Wozzek* and *Peter Grimes*—are the turrets of the castle.

These works are quite wonderful aesthetically, even as distant architecture, but most of us enter the castle of operatic repertoire through the lowly and sensuous gates of melody and character crisis, unable to immediately appreciate the lofty relationship of theme and plot to musical form. Once admitted, we proceed gradually up toward the turrets. The intellectual and aesthetic heights will always be there for aficionados and critics to scale. Critics who condemn all but the heights sometimes discount opera's age-old appeal as popular culture. One key to winning new audiences for operas has always been the accessible beauty of melody and poetic text. At any rate, this book seeks to appreciate accessible beauty, the beauty of a time before bitterness and cynicism contracted the fields of poetic endeavor and melodic elegance.

In opera, one essential source of this beauty is a literary image that, heightened in opera by musical and visual elements, allows the listener to exercise rare creativity by imagining the environments of operas and by entering into the worlds of the characters that inhabit such environments. Complex art forms like opera or film work most successfully when complex, i.e. interdisciplinary images combine to represent aspects of character or action.

We are naturally attracted to those elements that empower us, allow us to share the vision of the characters appearing before us on the stage. Images of presence (and appearance), specific action and purely literary content appear in the flood of information that the libretto opens for us. Assigning value to such images is an unavoidable and rewarding activity of the empowered opera reader and listener. May I assume now that you, dear reader, have read the libretto to *La Bohème* and have it before you as you read this book ? Such effort, while time-consuming, gives admirable integrity to your study of opera.

The Uses of Imagery

Imagery is an effective literary tool for characterization. In good poetry, every image represents an aspect of character, action, idea or environment. In this century, some critics argue that character is most successfully cultivated in lengthy prose form, especially the novel where the multiplicity of detail—captured, in part, by imagery—and protracted time framework describe the psychology of human change, especially emotional growth, in great detail. Sensing this, many librettists have adapted novels to the operatic stage. They then build upon the ethos already established by the novel's reputation. Because opera almost always uses many fewer words than either a drama or novel, and because the particular tone and form of a libretto is more poetic and abstract in nature, we must give especially the literary aspect of opera its due. The poetic aspects of opera text are rewarding to explore. The sub-arcs of poetic image and idea often relate intimately to the great dramatic arcs of plot and character in good operas.

Let us now begin to explore *La Bohème*'s libretto for images, some purely visual (dramatic), but most tied securely to character and meaning. The connections between image and character make *La Bohème*'s environment capable of sustaining believable, sympathetic characters. Consider, for example, the character of Mimi—described as a flower in several scenes in Acts 1 and 2—trapped in the environment of Paris's dreary Winter. Every successful opera has patterns of imagery recognized as universal. Generally, these images relate directly to character—we will concentrate primarily on Mimi in *La Bohème*—and to environment, the scenic atmosphere of the work.

La Bohème's Patterns of Imagery

In *La Bohème*, one paradigm of imagery dominates: the seasons. Images cluster around the contrasting ideas of Winter, with its aspects of cold, darkness (Acts 1 - 3 occur at night) and Spring (Act 4), with its warmth and light. And there is the theme of the difficulty of passage from one season to the other, creating patterns of contrastive imagery, in which irony and dramatic tension thrive. Imagery of nature adds its accessible plethora of images to this poetic arc. Winter's chill and wind make rooms prison cells containing jealousy and despair. Winter itself is, like the stove of Act 1—as well as Benoit and Alcindoro— described as an aged man (*vecchio*),[iii] while Spring's lightness and warmth bring dreams and sweet fantasies to Mimi's room.

Ironically, the Spring Mimi has dreamed of all Winter contains not the love fulfilled she has dreamed of, but her death. So thoroughgoing is the irony of *La Bohème* that Mimi dies in April in the same room where her passion for Rodolfo began four months earlier—and where she sang, *il primo bacio dell'aprile è mio!* The gap between the Winter and Spring—as between reality and dream—is very great for *La Bohème*'s Mimi. So the general design of the imagery of *La Bohème* is the tension-filled movement from Winter and passion (eros) to Spring and death (thanatos). This is also the imagery design, with some variation, of *Carmen*, *La Traviata* and *The Rake's Progress*, though *Carmen* and *The Rake's Progress* play subtle variations on the seasonal theme. *Carmen*, the least self-consciously literary entity of our four masterpieces, offers the greatest subtlety and dynamism of imagery.

This is the prominent pattern of literary image in our four works and in many other operas besides. There are also many images of appearance and action that are of paradigmatic importance—for example, the offering of a cup in Act 1 of *La Bohème. A lei!*

Imagery and Character in *La Bohème*

Let us now consider the literary imagery of *La Bohème* and how it relates to character—especially the character of Mimi—and plot. Acts 1-3 occur in Winter, the Winter of the lack of artistic inspiration, of hunger, and of loneliness. As Act 1 opens, Marcello refers to himself as *un freddo cane*, a frozen dog. He and Rodolfo desire warmth, not only from literal flames—*che lieto baglior*—but the flames of passion found in the "stove of love": *l'amor è un caminetto*. This image adumbrates all love affairs in *La Bohème*, which are both brilliant (*vivo*) and brief (*ma dura poco*). With a touch of cynicism and unintended irony, Rodolfo adds, concerning matters literary and amorous, *la brevita, gran pregio* ("but brevity is praised"). Once Schaunard arrives, a fire is started in the stove. We are reminded again of Winter's cold only after Mimi enters and Rodolfo takes her chilled hand: *che gelida manina*.

With Mimi, images of darkness, night and the moon and its light appear. Mimi awakens Rodolfo's senses to the environment. But the darkness of this apartment contains warmth—*segna vicino al fuoco*, Rodolfo begs Mimi—and moonlight is more than sufficient to light the lovers' way, even after the Winter wind has blown out a candle or two. Rodofo's great aria moves quickly from images of cold and moonlight past "castles in the air" to the light of Mimi's eyes, from Mimi's hand to her beautiful eyes and to Rodolfo's hope (*speranza*).

Mimi's answering aria is a treasure of images of Springtime: flowers (dreams and fancies of a poetic nature… *di sogni e di chimere, / quelle cose che han nome poesia…*) and the sunlight (*il primo sole*) are hers. Mimi has brought the imagery of Spring with her and it is clear that when she describes the opening of the rose in her aria (*foglia a foglia la spio!…*), she is herself the rose, opening for Rodolfo, and for us. But in the final moments of her aria, she sadly contrasts the flowers she crafts to those she envisions. The remainder of Act 1 develops the imagery so far introduced by Rodolfo and Mimi. Rodolfo is ravished by Mimi in moonlight (*O soave fanciulla, o dolce viso / di mite circonfuso alba lunar*) and they are enfolded in the dream of love: *in te, ravviso / il sogno ch'io vorrei sempre sognar!*

These literary images establish a universal sub-arc for *La Bohème*, but images of presence and specific action also add variety and, as often as not, humor. Each of the bohemians is surrounded not only by the argot and imagery of his profession, but each is typified by distinctive images of presence to add spice to the image stew of the opera. Marcello refers to Musetta's heart as a block of marble, Rodolfo's drama returns to heaven when it is burned, and Schaunard's musical skills are employed to produce the death of a Socratic parrot. In Act 1, Marcello often throws out titles: Rodolfo is "author," Benoit "a canon," and Colline "Bear!" As a group, the four have their collective argot. They constantly refer to antiquity, even quote from and ad lib in ancient languages, as in the world of their student days. Western Civilization itself is in peril—*è Roma in periglio*—as they burn Rodolfo's play.

Images of specific action in Act 1 are also very important. They complement, even emblemize the emotional contours of the lover's relationship. The image of ascent and the offering of a cup both enliven Mimi's sphere of action in Act 1. She has ascended the dark steps to Rodolfo's attic door and this ascent has been a struggle toward something previously desired or denied (or both)—in this case, passionate love. In Act 4, Mimi will once again ascend these steps. Her first ascent was to find love, her second to die in her lover's arms. Operatic heroines are haunted by the unique combination of eros and thanatos, by "the song of love and death."[iv]

Additional Images

In addition to these images, there is the imagery of the fancies and imagination of characters. These are characters trapped in the cold world of poverty who sometimes see themselves as being someone else, someone better off. In Act 1, Mimi becomes Rodolfo's *piccina* (dear girl), he her *gran signor* (lord and master). The failed poet and the *grisette* (flower girl) play the grand lord and his beloved amidst abject poverty. They live "a gay life, yet a terrible one!"[v] Earlier in the act, Rodolfo has pretended to be a the lord of "castles in the air." In Act 4, Colline will pretend to be the minister of finance.

Acts 2 and 3 offer each character a chance to develop the imagery assigned them in Act 1. Rodolfo refers to Mimi in Act 2 as "poetry itself" and to the words of his found poem as "flowers" inspired by her. Surely he is remembering her *giglia e rose* from the attic. Not only a man of words, he has bought her a bonnet "trimmed with roses," which Mimi says has opened her heart to him. Love is, according to Mimi, "sweeter than honey," an assertion with which Marcello violently disagrees.

In contrast to this flow of romantic imagery, the witty bohemians create a biting repartee at a café table in Act 2. Their multi-lingual wit and wordplay is joined by the beginning of Musetta's spunky war on the idea of marriage, as she advises the crotchety Alcindoro not to play "Bluebeard" with her. She will not go obediently to her room for eternity like an obedient wife. Musetta not only uses literary allusions, but attracts several from the men around her. This may be because she is more literary and dramatic type than real flesh-and-blood, stage character. She is the direct descendent of Manon and, long before Manon, of Roman Drama's *Caritas* (Charity.) In Act 2, Marcello refers to Musetta as *casta Susanna* (the epitome of false modesty and lost chastity) and "blood thirsty raven," continuing the animal imagery of the bohemians, while Schaunard and Colline label the entire event "a stupendous comedy." Finally, all of Act 2's imagery is swept away in the symbolic *tambur maggior*, the Drum Major, representing the warrior of old, as the changing of the Parisian guard at midnight on Christmas Eve becomes a parade of conquerors.

Act 3 provides a new dramatic context for established images, though the characters are still gripped by the dark chill of Winter. It is perhaps two months later. Some images become more specific: Mimi's "beautiful eyes" are blue and her tendency to flirt has centered on a single person, a certain *viscontino*. This flirtation has driven Rodolfo to jealous rages.

Other images change: the fires of passion from Act 1 are now burning in Mimi's feverish brow and in Rodolfo's jealousy. Poverty has put out the fire that burned in Act 1's stove and the fire of Rodolfo and Mimi's passion is also in jeopardy. The Winter wind that put out Mimi's candle now howls through their apartment. Most striking is Rodolfo's description of Mimi again as a flower, but this time as an exotic flower wasted by cold and in need of more than his love can give.

In this case, imagery complements plot, for we know that Mimi's condition has worsened: she coughs almost constantly now. This is effective use of visual motif: Mimi's flower bloomed before us—perhaps too early—in Act 1 and is now wilting in Act 3. It is not only the Winter chill that is causing Mimi to diminish, but her advancing disease and the approaching death of a relationship.

As Mimi turns to leave Rodolfo in Act 3, she creates a list of images. In her aria, *D'onde lieta*, there are her prayer book, the "lifeless flowers" from Act 1, and "the pink bonnet" from Act 2. This is too much for Rodolfo and, overcome by memories, he initiates a duet that, literarily speaking, amounts to a descriptive exploration of Spring. In this lovely duet—which develops into a quartet with Musetta and Marcello's entrance—Mimi and Rodolfo revive and develop images of April's light and flowers and add lovely detail, painting a dream world for themselves:

Al fiorir di primavera	The flowers of Spring
c'è compagno il sol!	Accompany the sun
Chiacchieran le fontane . . .	The chattering fountain...
La brezza della sera	The evening breezes
balsami stende sulle doglie umane.	spread balsam over the earth,
Vuoi che aspettiam la primavera ancor?	when Spring comes again.

Flowers, fountains and breezes are celebrated; they will calm sullen sorrow. Should they stay together until Spring, when the beauties of the season will comfort them for the loss of a lover?

It is clear now, as they sing in the falling snow of February, that their Spring is entirely a Spring of words, an internal, literary Spring—the Spring of dream and of the hope of love fulfilled. In fact, their closing words offer the ironic conclusion that they will part when Spring comes. *Niuno è solo April*, says Mimi: "I'm not so lonely in April." Notice, also—as you listen—that, though they are not mentioned, birds flutter through the orchestra throughout the latter part of this act. (These orchestral flutterings will be given names in Act 4.) And so ends the third act of *La Bohème*'s Winter—full of the dream of Spring and love fulfilled.

Patterns of Repetition in Act 4

Imagery patterns create complexity and, if they are used carefully, integrate themselves with plot and character to the enrichment of both. This is certainly true in *La Bohème*. Act 4 cashes in on most previous imagery through patterns of repetition amounting to what is sometimes called extended, implicit metaphor in literary analysis.

First, the opening patterns of the bohemians from Act 1 are repeated, echoing repetitions of character thought, dramatic situation, environment and plot. Once again Marcello envisions Musetta as he paints, but this time in greater detail—her bright eyes and lips haunt him—to the final effect that his heart is burning for her—fire and ice. Matching Marcello in their duet (almost a double aria), Rodolfo praises Mimi's hands, fragrant tresses, forehead; and he clasps her bonnet to his lips. Each man has an object to symbolize his lover and his passion.

After the entrance of Colline and Schaunard, the bohemian quartet's lively nonsense degenerates into a fake duel, Mimi again ascends to the attic, this time not to be reborn by love but to die. Now Puccini and his librettists come fully into their own, through repetition and the introduction of new imagery.

We know from Schaunard's remark that Mimi is close to death, so every reminiscence will be colored anew by that knowledge—the present Spring cannot help but be a false and ironic one. Mimi complains again that her hands are cold and, even though she is no longer alone, she longs for her hands to be warm just once. It quickly becomes clear that her cold hands have now become a symbol of approaching death. Even Rodolfo's *che gelida manina* must now take on a new gentle irony. This motif from Act 1 becomes rich in meaning in Act 4.

Faced with her death, Mimi is given two images with which to paint life—her love for Rodolfo—and death: the ocean and an Autumn sunset. Then she and Rodolfo relive their meeting in Act 1, adding the darkness, the key, and Mimi's cold hands. *Rondine e cinguetta* have been fluttering in the orchestra since Act 3.

Rodolfo began the review of images by producing Mimi's bonnet. Musetta now enters with a muff for Mimi's frozen hands and, as Mimi finally feels her hands begin to warm, she dies—and with her dies the dream of Spring and love fulfilled, even though, according to the stage directions, "A ray of sunshine falls through the window upon Mimi's face," reminding us that "April's first kiss [was hers]!" Mimi's dream of love and Spring is over.

In the following three essays, we will explore how the images surrounding Mimi complement plot and character to the degree that characters may themselves become images of surpassing beauty and symbolic power. In ironic contrapuntal movement of imagery in relation to plot, the early-blooming flower representing Mimi has wilted and died just when it should have been opening to the Spring's rays during the movement of the seasons. The power of such imagery is visceral and immediate. We can recognize what we can visualize; more importantly, we can empathize with what we feel we know. Knowledge comes from the familiarity of shared images of universal resonance: love, life and death, survival.

Acts 1 and 4

IMAGERY PATTERNS THAT COMPLEMENT PLOT

Serious opera is often concerned with illicit love and its punishment. Tragic opera is a moral medium, whose plots—admittedly, often the least logical aspect of opera—involve the exploration of passion and that passion's death at the hands of society, or a jealous lover, or simply through the machinations of Fate. Though jealousy does play a role in Mimi and Rodolfo's relationship in *La Bohème*, it is Fate in the form of a disease that really determines the destiny of the heroine. Superstitious Carmen's "Fate" is written in the cards, but her destiny is brutally determined by her reckless lifestyle. In *La Traviata*, Violetta feels condemned by society itself, that society being represented by Germont. Poor Tom Rakewell never seems to have a chance in *The Rake's Progress*; it all seems to have been predetermined by the forces of evil. In the finest musical tragedies, as is the case with Verdi's *Otello*, a character like Iago may simply become a destructive machine, an "unmotivated malignancy," that determines the destinies of heroes and heroines.

The tensions of tragic plots are eased in death, sometimes in transfiguration, while the tensions of comic plots are seemingly erased by marriage. Some great comic operas may well portray marriage grown old (*Figaro*), or threatened by green-eyed jealousy (*Falstaff*) or the results of dissolution (*The Magic Flute*). There are of course political operas (*Don Carlo*), religious operas (*Moses and Aaron*), and operas of personality (*Boris Gudonov*) where passionate love plays a secondary role. There are also operas that mix all these themes, like *Otello*. Passion, if not obsession, still plays a role in such operas, but the passion may be political or ideological in nature. Many operas—*Don Giovanni, Figaro, La Bohème, Carmen, Otello, La Traviata, The Bartered Bride, Tales of Hoffman, Eugene Onegin, Tristan, Tannhäuser, et alia*—maximize the powerful emotional possibilities of music by personalizing them through characters who experience the ecstasy of love and terrors of death. Other themes piggyback on passionate love, for example social justice in *Figaro*, but passion is, finally, both precipitant of most action and thematically the essence of opera. In opera, passion is emblematic of life itself.

For some, opera's formulas seem extreme, even sensationalistic. I find that great opera uses passion as a vehicle to introduce themes that allow the creators of opera to portray human character successfully. Aristotle taught us that characters must be tested, and the most difficult test is to deprive a character of the love that must grow from passion. This is when truly great themes emerge from literature. The greatest theme of opera is, it seems to me, the metamorphosis of passion to compassion. This is the theme of *La Traviata*, Verdi's most cohesive and accessible great opera. The compassion that Violetta exercises in the final scene is almost heavenly in its power. Mimi has some of this power about her in Act 4 of *La Bohème*. But I am getting ahead of myself.

In the last essay, I listed the major imagery patterns of *La Bohème* and how they helped flesh out character and theme; in particular, the theme of love is fulfilled in relation to Mimi. The element of irony is very strong in *La Bohème*, and rises from the contrast of things as they are desired—represented by the dream of love fulfilled—and things as they are and can be. Mimi's dream of love fades to dust in *La Bohème*'s fourth act. The next essay will address how imagery and poetry generally work in aria form to offer the essence of character to the reader and listener, but in this essay, I would like to show how imagery patterns in Acts 1 and 4 of *La Bohème* complement plot—the arrangement of events in a story—and signify the overwhelming theme of tragic or serious opera: the death of illicit love, a form of the tragic intertwining of eros and thanatos.

Images gather about Mimi and portray her inner world in Act 1; she draws us into the lonely room of her soul. By the fourth act, she is still clinging to the dream of love fulfilled, but mortality has given her only a little more time—just time enough to say good-bye to Rodolfo. To contrast with Mimi's vulnerable personality and fragile dreams, Puccini has given us the robust world of the bohemians, who are given their own patterns of imagery and themes. They are, despite their poverty, comedians worthy of a *comedia dell-arte* troupe, and their dynamism prances in effective contrast to Mimi's slow, inexorable movement toward death.

Sub-arcs of Imagery in *La Bohème*

Sub-arcs of imagery support the great arcs of plot and character development. The plot aspect of *La Bohème* is fragmented, but practically all other elements are strong—environment and character relationships chief among them. Characters and their relationships bolster the fragile sequence of action in *La Bohème*, which is only loosely anchored in time and causality. Characters like Mimi are made unforgettable by their personalities and by the imagery that reveals lyric aspects of personality.

Let me demonstrate. Images are the principle literary means by which we recognize and understand character; they may indicate a character's values and thus how she might act and react. Several images make Mimi an unforgettable character. She is, poetically speaking, her beautiful hands, which are always cold. She seeks the warmth first of love (Rodolfo), then of wealth (the *Viscontino*) to alleviate this discomfort, but achieves this wish only immediately before death. The image of Mimi's frozen hand grows in crucial importance in the opera until in Act 4 her hand falls from the muff, signaling her death. The pink bonnet is bought at the beginning of Act 2, but reappears at important points in Acts 3 and 4, representing the gift of love. These two literary/visual motifs accentuate Mimi's actions and *La Bohème*'s plot. They span the whole arc of action of the plot and strengthen it. These image clusters are literary sub-arcs that complement big form elements of character, plot and idea.

Every great character changes essentially in the course of a plot, and images may signal such changes in character. Mimi begins as a "neighbor," but becomes "a sweet vision" before the evening is over. In Act 2, Rodolfo crowns her queen of flowers with a *cuffietta rosa* and calls her *poesia*—poetry itself. In Act 3 she is "an exotic flower" destined, Rodolfo fears, for death in wintery Paris's bitter garden. In Act 4 she becomes the swallow returning to her nest. Rodolfo begins as a poet and is called a "professor" of love by his mocking friends in Act 2, but is finally simply the object of Mimi's love, which by Act 4 has grown vast and deep as the ocean. In the face of lost passion and Mimi's impending death, Rodolfo can only bow his head to Mimi's destiny and rage against the dying of her light. Mimi also performs certain acts of a symbolic nature, which stress her vulnerability (she coughs) and insecurity. She flirts, for example, first with Rodolfo, with students in Act 2, and constantly with the *viscontino*, whom she leaves in Act 4 to die in Rodolfo's arms.

You can see that we could catalogue images and group them according to their function, but that is not my purpose. I simply want to make you aware of their presence, so that you may begin to consider literature's contribution to operatic form and imagery's role in augmenting plot and character. These patterns of imagery are a part of the integrity of the literary aspect of the greater work of art. The images mentioned above are universal in Western literature. Many of them occur in myth. We saw how the plethora of Spring images and the images of nature typify the movement from Winter to Spring in the last essay. We can now, it seems to me, draw the conclusion that Mimi, emblemized by flowers of Spring, light and warmth, also represents for us that which she so desires to constantly experience: the dream (of Spring) and love fulfilled. In this desire, she becomes memorable as a very human being.

Mimi's dream and our dream for her are not to be fulfilled, however, and here lies the tragic rub of *La Bohème* and tragic opera generally: eros is always accompanied by thanatos. Cupid's arrow not only awakens but wounds. In Aristotle's terms, the protagonist of a poetic tragedy must fall, and the greatest fall is death.

Patterns of Repetition and Plot in *La Bohème*

La Bohème uses special devices of repetition to emphasize the conflict of eros and thanatos in its plot. The repetitions involve setting, plot, character action, and theme. Both Acts 1 and 4 occur in the attic, which gives us a feeling of closure visually—in terms of setting. Both acts begin with Marcello and Rodolfo alone on stage. They are joined by their friends, Colline and Schaunard. Note that the action in Act 4 is more compressed than in Act 1, though in each case food is brought on the stage and good-natured horseplay is created to contrast with the serious matters that follow.

Many small actions also unite the acts; for example, in Act 1 Colline is trying to hock something, while in Act 4 he succeeds in selling his coat. Other considerations of formal balance are also apparent. During the first section of Act 1, Schaunard has an arioso; slightly after Mimi's entrance in Act 4, Colline is given a little aria.

The most effective patterns of repetition featured in Act 4 are those established in Act 1, developed in Acts 2 and 3, then repeated in Act 4, where they are augmented by new images such as the swallow and the sea. (The latter image is thundered magnificently in pure musical power at the opera's close.) I want to review the patterns of repetition that are used primarily in Acts 1 (Christmas Eve) and 4 (a day in April). Turn in your libretto to the scene in Act 4 beginning after Colline's aria. Mimi begins with the image of the sea, and follows it by gently rebuking Rodolfo's "sunrise" compliment with a reference to "sunset." So far all the imagery is new (sea, sunrise/sunset).

But now Rodolfo attempts to cheer her by producing the bonnet that he purchased for her in Act 2. This triggers a repetition of literary poetic and musical images from the latter part of Act 1. The lovers relive their initial meeting, of when Mimi "by chance" entered Rodolfo's life. They relive the darkness, the key—a resonant literary image of the 18th and 19th centuries used by James Joyce so effectively in this century in *Finnegin's Wake*—Mimi's *gelida manina*, and the warmth of love before Mimi's spasm interrupts their dream-like reminiscences. Both now see these actions and images as the beginning of their interlocking personal destinies. Fate—as distinct from destiny—has plans for Mimi, as we will soon find out. These pattern of repetition and the new images help us sense the tragedy to come. Mimi is correct; her sunset and final darkness approach.

Such a repetition of images from Act 1 creates patterns of comparison—we relive Act 1's eternal enchantment in a final scene ripe with intimations of mortality—and contrast in light of all we have learned of these characters' imperfections, the metamorphosis of their relationship, and Mimi's health. The repetition is effective and gives the story a great deal of closure, while the new images continue the development of Mimi's character and help bring the plot to a logical conclusion.

Elements of comparison and contrast abound in Act 4, with the repetitions based in Act 1 providing a pleasant echo to contrast with the grim realities of Act 4. So, while Act 4 maintains a striking "orderly magnitude of its own" through new images (as well as action, idea and certainly music), it contains striking patterns of repetition in imagery and plot structure (and accompanying scenery and music), which serve to give emotional closure because they summarize that which came before and hint at that which is to be.

Rodolfo's watch by Mimi's bedside in Act 4 is a visual image of great paradigmatic power and echoes visually the precious but passing moment in Act 1 when Rodolfo bends over Mimi, who sits comfortably but expectantly by the fire, to offer her a cup. And from this cup flows the wine-red sea of passionate love that Mimi relives in Act 4. But his watch may also remind us of Mimi's complaint to Marcello in Act 3 that Rodolfo watches her obsessively, even as she sleeps.

The theme of poverty underlies both these acts, and many other operas. Can love prosper under such conditions? Too often then, as now, eros and thanatos intertwine in an unsympathetic environment. On a lighter subject, the next essay explores Mimi's remarkable aria *Mi chiamano Mimi* and begins to examine one of the chief sources of character—the aria.

The Poetic in Mi chiamano Mimi

ARIA AS ESSENCE OF CHARACTER

This aria's text is very effective dialogue in that it involves Rodolfo—and the listener—with its revealing qualities, but it is much more than dialogue; it is poetry, self-consciously rhythmic and rich in images. Such poetry is natural in the world of opera, for opera is an image-creating dynamo.

Mimi's aria is all about her character—her desires and dreams. Mimi's aria is a study of both confessional naiveté and calculated ingenuousness. As such, it indicates character depth. Mimi is not the most complex of characters in opera, but in this aria we see into her depths. She poeticizes simple things, yet there is calculation in her naiveté, for example she is careful to inform Rodolfo three times that she lives alone in lines 3 and 7 of stanza 2. (This is the first time Mimi mentions the word *sola*, ["alone"], but she will sing it a great many times before her hands finally grow warm in the final scene.) This aria has the poetry of a genuine personality about it. It is a confessional poem and has the unique power of visionary utterance. There are clear points at which the speaker of the poem opens utterly—almost as in a dramatic soliloquy—to Rodolfo like a rare flower. She unselfconsciously bares her soul to us. This is meaningful drama, in part because it is charged with the emotional power of lyric poetry.

Clearly, Rodolfo's outpouring of poetic fancy in his previous aria has affected Mimi, and his compliments have not been lost. Her lovely eyes have robbed him of his "castles in the air," but also filled him with hope. Although Rodolfo is a poet, his words are less affecting than those he evokes from Mimi. As in many arias, we enter into the charged inner world of the character.

In this form of poetic utterance, symbols and other images will indicate the complexity of the character's internal world, involving desires, needs, hopes, and fears. Although it is impossible to separate the verbal and musical constituents within the aria form—so inseparably are they welded as sung text in opera—it is possible to discuss the aria's text as poetry and to point out the role of the purely musical aspects in approximating the density of sound pattern and imagery native to lyric poetry.

Elements of Lyric Poetry

The text of Mimi's aria constitutes a lyric poem of a very special kind, one designed to complement the rhythmic units of music, as well as the singer's art. It is made up of two verses, the second verse of which is irregular; having an additional six-line unit that approximates the rhythm and the content of lines 9-13 of the first verse.

Note also that each verse is closed by a line or two of dialogue uttered in secco recitative. The form of these verses is certainly dictated by considerations of musical form—this passage might well have been written after Puccini composed the music—yet the verses have a certain power as poetry. This power emanates from its images being integrated into musical form. The successful union of imagery with music in dramatic context creates recognition of character or idea, i.e. a sense of dramatic truth.

The elements of a lyric poem are as follows. (1) The persona, or speaker of the poem gives us the point of view of the poem. Mimi's poetic utterance is dialogue that grows into heightened dramatic monologue. (2) A lyric poem may have a line of action that approximates a plot, but it certainly has an emotional contour that moves toward a high point and then away from it. The emotional contour of the poem will be complemented by figurative language, rhythm, and rhyme; these poetic elements in combination constitute the literary equivalent of a melody complemented by harmonic and rhythmic patterns. (3) The theme or meaning of a poem is its emotional truth, intellectual point, or moral significance. (4) Figurative language consists of images, especially metaphors and symbols. The density of figurative language may be compared to harmonic complexity and/or orchestral web, the multiplicity of colors furnished by the orchestra.

(5) Rhythm is the pulse of the poetic unit, with the poem dividing itself into stanzas, lines, phrases, and metric "feet." These feet can constructively be equated to the musical rhythmic division of "measure." Phrases and stanzas also have relatively exact musical counterparts. (6) Rhyme consists of patterns of sound repetition, especially standard (end) and internal rhyme, but also alliteration, which is when patterns of sound recreate the rhythms and sounds of the thing described or evoked. An example is *chiacchierna le fontane…* which sound patterns imitate the "chattering" of fountains. Musical harmony is approximated by the interplay of sound patterns like assonance (patterns of vowel sounds) and consonance (patterns of consonant sounds), though in single phrases the flow of a particular sound pattern might approximate counter melody. (7) Mood is the emotional feeling we derive from a poem. It is a product of the interplay of the poem's images in our minds with the total effect of the poem's sound tapestry on our emotions.

Interpreting the Poem

Remembering that music will alter most of these elements considerably, let's look at *Mi chiamano Mimi* as lyric poetry. First, note that the poem is in first person and is confessional in nature. Mimi begins with the simplest act of self-definition: she names herself, twice. There is a candid quality about how she reveals her real name, Lucia. Mimi is her nickname.

She then describes where and how she lives, then quietly moves through verbal gesture in an almost distracted manner toward the complex image of a flowers—particular flowers, the lily and the rose, which she fashions with her hands—then to the natural flowers of spring. It is here that Puccini's melody lifts her (and the listener) onto a higher emotional plane. In particular, the image of the rose is developed in such a way that it comes to represent her inner life, her self. Having begun to create the idea of spring, with its light and dreams, Mimi pauses to ask Rodolfo if he understands what she means. Moved, he answers simply, *Yes.*

Mimi continues, perhaps a little nervously, for verse two begins exactly as verse one, then after continuing a moment in the same chatty manner as in verse one, offers still more ecstatic intimacy. As the second verse progresses, Mimi describes her sensuous joy in Springtime's light and warmth and in the fragrance of flowers, not once but twice in ascending melodic lines. The first ascent is an account of how she claims Spring as her lover: "April's first kiss is mine!" she exclaims ecstatically. Then for a second time, she—as in the last six lines of stanza one—withdraws into the chambers of her mind and shares the ecstatic visions of her lonely, hungry soul with Rodolfo.

In stanza 1's brief passage (lines 9-12), she personifies the flowers she creates, as if their voices were the voices of kindred souls, their faces and visions her own. Lines 14-19 of stanza 2 are graced with a similar music treatment and are even more revealing. Her ecstasy with the natural beauty of an opening rose is wonderfully captured in Puccini's setting of the lines *foglia a foglia la spio!... / Cosi gentil / il profumo d'un fior!* (Petal after petal unfolds, / a lovely thing—the flower's fragrance!) The unfolding of the rose petals is revealed in *foglia a foglia la spio*, in the poet's subtle combination of rhythm and alliteration. Puccini captures the triple rhythms of the words (dactylic feet) in duple measures, creating a lovely tension hinting at Mimi's final, melancholic observance that the flowers she creates with her hands have no fragrance of their own. She sadly contrasts the fragrance of the natural blossom to those scentless ones she creates with her hands. The works of her hands are poor imitations of the natural essence. She cannot create Spring; she can only dream of it, then create an imitation of it with her cold hands.

Mimi here voices the essential French Romantic doctrine: Nature ennobles and completes mankind. In her longing for Spring's light and her appreciation of nature's beauty, Mimi is, in terms of the poetic imagery given her, the essential Romantic figure. Puccini's rapturous orchestral settings raise the emotional level of the poem appreciatively.

Poetic Elements at Work

Here is how the poetic elements work in the poem. (1) The persona is a character in a drama, who begins in the dialogue mode but quickly moves to a much more poetic, confessional mode. (2) The poem's action or plot is descriptive, emotional and revealing. Mimi describes how she experiences simple pleasures and performs simple tasks. (3) The theme, the meaning of the poem is the descriptive truth of Mimi's existence. She is at first calculating and conscious of what she says, but quickly moves into a personal and momentarily unselfconscious revelation of her fantasy world. (4) This poem establishes the image patterns of Spring, with its vital ancillary images of light, warmth, and flower fragrance. It also associates these qualities with Mimi's character. The complex image of Spring creates an image cluster that clearly signals the character's state of mind. Further, the interplay of figurative language and melody creates complex images descriptive of Mimi's inner world.

Metaphoric density is complemented, if not replaced in this—and most—arias by orchestral web, i.e. in terms of orchestration and harmonic complexity. (5) One has only to listen closely to the aria to hear the perfection of the rhythmic properties of this poem for musical adaptation. Generally, a musical phrase requires two poetic lines in this libretto, except in the climactic, stretchy phrases where heightened emotion justifies the melodic expansion of phrase. (6) End rhyme sometimes unites consecutive musical phrases, but as often as not occurs within a musical phrase. It may also help tie musical phrases together. The flexibility of Puccini's compositional technique allowed him to accomplish a subtle interplay between the units of the poem and his musical phrases.

In general, music's melody, harmony, rhythm, and other formal considerations complement poetry rhythm and rhyme so effectively as to almost replace them for the listener. Melody, rhythm and orchestral color can vivify an image, as in Puccini's subtle, repetitive setting of the phrases *che han si dolce malia* in stanza one and *foglia a foglia la spio* in stanza two, each preceding the build up to the climax of each stanza: the musical/poetic ecstasy of *di primavera* in stanza one and *il profumo d'un fior* in stanza two. The subtle turning of the notes in the *foglia* phrase accents the melodic unfolding of the rose, already inherent in the poetic rhythm of *foglia a foglia la spio*. (7) The mood, the emotional content of the poem is shaped largely by the music, though the combination of imagery with that music is a powerful synesthetic tool. Just as musical considerations have usurped some poetic elements (complex rhythms, sound patterns, the weave of metaphor and symbol), the images, action, theme and mood of the poem will be augmented by melodic, rhythmic, and harmonic intertwining.

Although density of word sound is not unusual in good opera (see Rodolfo's text in the Act 3 quartet), the poetic effect of this device, when sung, is minimal and, from the standpoint of the singer and listener, not necessarily desirable. Consonants interrupt the pure flow of vowels from which the stream of legato vocal line lives, and beauty of vocal line may be preferred in some cases to perfect projection of text. Melody lives from assonance as in lines 9-15 of Mimi's second stanza. Too much consonance may intrude on vocal line and projection.

Clearly, poetry and music function to complement dramatic purpose. Poetry is more precise in specific matters—imagery, description of detail, and subtleties of character development—while music is more immediate in the presentation of emotional states and shades of character, as well as of environment. It is largely through music that we understand the emotional depths of character in operatic performance. This is nowhere clearer than in *La Bohème*'s first act duet, the highly compressed but dramatically logical result of two successful arias.

PUCCINI'S *La Bohème*

Character as Symbol

MIMI AS LUMINOUS IMAGE

In *La Bohème*, one of the reasons the use of melody is so effective as a tool for characterization is because it represents the emotions of character inscape, with its dreams, reflections, and reminiscences. Character accounts for much of opera's content, and dreaming expresses a character's desires, wishes and ideals—as in both Rodolfo and Mimi's Act 1 arias. The aria reveals a character's desires and visions. Within this interplay of lyric poetry and musical structure, each character creates a dream world where the soul can unfold in fragile dimensions of emotional meaning. Each character's internal world is a poetically charged environment based on real circumstances, but rising far above this reality through flights of the imagination.

The aural environment—in poetic terms, the atmosphere and mood—that harmony and orchestral color do so much to create in opera, may form a rarefied character inscape where the dreaming figure is immersed in image and idea, like a fossil within the earth's strata. The listener's orientation of time and space is removed for stratified moments created by poetic and musical forces; and during these moments we enter into the harmony of a character's vision. Musical elements augment the empathy, the emotional recognition we establish with a character like Mimi through her words and actions. Music furnishes us with an emotional shortcut to dramatic truth.

But we are here concerned with the contribution of literature to opera. The literary and dramatic images that emerge from the written and sung word in the libretto complement the visual aspects, the plot, and most importantly the characters. What occurs in the visual imagination as we listen to opera is of vital importance. The listener's ability to experience the essential visual/emotional world of the music-poetic component of opera provides the fundamental dramatic setting.

Once this setting, together with its atmosphere, is established in the mind and emotions of the listener, subtleties of contrast begin to appear. Consider that there is often a tension between the imagistic content of an aria and the stage setting and atmosphere in which the aria is sung. For example, Mimi's Act 1 aria describes the luminous glories of Spring as she sits in a frozen hovel. Art lives from such contrastive relationships between elements: atmosphere is created, then character is revealed and realized, plot is developed, and the power of an image is intensified as motif. In Act 4, Mimi will recall every detail of Rodolfo and her meeting in Act 1.

The brief duet that follows Mimi's aria is of such emotional and musical intensity that we, like Mimi and Rodolfo, are overwhelmed by it. Let us glance again momentarily at Mimi's aria to understand how it, as a primary instrument of character development, prepares the way for the following duet's brief but profound appearance, not only as continued character development, but as a strong unit of plot.

PUCCINI'S *La Bohème*

Mimi's Aria as Preparation for the Duet

Mi chiamano Mimi has two sources of power: from a literary standpoint, the text contains a resonant complex image; and, musically, the aria is a marvel of rising melodic phrases, the climax of each verse being an ascending orchestral phrase that frees itself from literary context and symbolizes the ecstasy of love's appeal. These rising phrases seek to express the mysterious nature of love, and of the human soul. The aesthetic high point of the aria is here, where music has the power to make its own symbolic statement above language ennobled by the images of the aria text. Music's particular power manifests revealed essence of character in this heightened dimension of music drama.

But Mimi's character lives from poetry as well as music; her poetic metaphors tie the stark reality of her life to the ephemeral hope of her dreams. She contrasts the odorless roses of her creation as an seamstress to the real roses that she keeps in her room in Springtime. As she embroiders the two-dimensional cloth flowers, she watches the scented roses bloom in the sunlight. In this way, she maintains her hope through the hours of tedious work. Her handwork gives her pleasure because her flowers represent nature and speak to her "of love, of Springtime."

Puccini's Mimi is a fully romantic spirit struggling for survival. It is no wonder that Mimi sincerely praises the poet Rodolfo, for artists—like Mimi at her embroidery—strive to capture their dreams and visions in their work. (In romantic literature, the artist is the most admired and idealized type of person.) Mimi tries to recreate nature, but in her own eyes fails: "But these flowers, sadly, have no fragrance." No character in *La Bohème* succeeds in fulfilling their dream before the curtain falls, but—in aesthetic terms—Mimi achieves something no other character does: she grows into a three-dimensional character. One reason for this is the imagery that she is given. Primary among these images is the crucial image of light: for Mimi, it is the sun. For Rodolfo, it is the moon. It is moonlight that creates Mimi as luminous image at the beginning of the duet.

As Mimi closed the first part of her aria, she was careful to qualify her poetic dreams as what "only poets know" or "what is called poetry," not only in deference to Rodolfo, but to appear sympathetic and appreciative. In the second act, he will summarize what both these arias have cultivated: I am the poet, / she is the poetry." Rodolfo's exploration of the flower imagery inspired by Mimi's aria continues throughout the opera.

The suggestiveness of the rose as symbol is made infinitely more touching in this context because of the interplay of the musical and visual elements with the purely literary ones. The image mounts Puccini's melody and ascends, taking Rodolfo's breath away and giving us reason to believe that these two characters could genuinely care for each other.

Musical Gesture as Symbol

Music is by its very nature symbolic and, when a rising and expanding melody is combined with the visual image of an opening rose (as well as the thought of its fragrance), the result is a moment of extreme emotional content, the kind Puccini loved to create. This synesthetic, ambient rose foreshadows in its intensity the climax of the first act of *La Bohème*. Music depicts emotional states and sensory experiences in an abstract manner; it does not represent literal or specific visual examples. Music needs words or visual counterparts to function with any degree of literal dramatic specificity in performance.

After Mimi's aria ends quietly and is followed by a brief comic interlude involving offstage music, the rhapsodic duet occurs. Remember the importance of contrast in dramatic form: between the ecstasy/depression of Mimi's aria and the ecstasy of the duet comes a brief comic episode, perhaps to remind us that laughter and romance often go hand in hand. Note that the comedy involves recitative and little orchestral support. This contrasts with the lush orchestration that typifies Mimi's presence and emotional state.

Image gives music the specificity it needs and a symbol like the rose is actually made more specific to Mimi by Puccini's use of melodic idea. A symbol, unlike a metaphor or simile, has no clear reference; the meaning of the rose as symbol must be created by each listener individually. That is the nature of a symbol. When it comes to assigning meaning to Mimi's symbolic rose, a cluster of possible meanings exist: love, renewal, Spring, Rodolfo, the art of poetry, the soul, life itself. But all these possibilities refer back to Mimi herself—or the presence of all these things in Mimi.

Mimi is both poetry and rose; Rodolfo makes this clear in Acts 2 and 3, as does the text generally in Act 4. As Mimi sings her aria, she is in a dingy garret, not unlike the one where she lives and sews her unscented flowers. Moonlight shines through the window, but she is not yet standing in its beam. She has no movement during the aria—oh, perhaps she rises as she sings and the spotlight follows her, echoing the Spring's first light that she so loves.

There is only her voice in melodic flight, the slow blossoming of the rose-as-symbol in the aria from its literary base into the atmosphere of a musical garden, and then into the audience's imagination. Finally, there is only the flute's spiral of ascending melody accented by a shimmering moonlight cymbal, symbolizing perhaps the emptiness within that Mimi wishes to fill with her love for Rodolfo.

Mimi as Luminous Image

But in the duet, as Rodolfo discovers Mimi standing in the moonlight streaming into the attic, his soul bursts forth as does Stephen Dedaelus's in Part IV of James Joyce's *A Portrait of the Artist as a Young Man*: "—Heavenly God! cried Stephen's soul, in an outburst of profane joy... Her image had passed into his soul forever... Her eyes had called him and his soul had leaped at the call... A wild angel had appeared to him, the angel of mortal youth and beauty." (Joyce, a gifted singer, knew opera well and is in his own way creating a luminous image of the opposite sex, just as Puccini does in most of his operas.)

Puccini centered his operas around female characters whom he found to be "luminous:" Manon, Tosca, Sor Angelica, La Fanciulla del West. Mimi is such a character, one with whom we can empathize. Such a character must acquire a great symbolic power before becoming "luminous." Luminosity is established by Puccini and his librettists by bringing every element of opera to bear in a brief ecstatic moment in that singular character's stage life.

We have seen how Mimi's poetic text associates aspects of her character with universal imagery and we can easily hear how music complements and augments the meaning of such images. In this way, each character, so to speak, may acquire his/her own constellation of imagery, which as the plot develops amounts to a motif. Remembering that allows us to examine this duet in terms of its literary and—more generally—dramatic, musical, and visual qualities.

Rodolfo is the commanding presence in the duet—he begins it alone and vocally he overpowers his partner—and, as musical strains of his aria begin again, he returns to the image of moonlight he mentioned earlier as his aria began. Like any poet, Rodolfo gathers the images of his poetry from the setting around him. But he now envisions Mimi in "a dream that he wants to dream forever." He then describes his feelings as the sweetest extremity of the spirit to the music in his aria with which he earlier praised Mimi's eyes. That which earlier enchanted him now possesses him. Mimi, for her part, surrenders to "love's command." Rodolfo has entered Mimi's dream of love through her "lovely eyes" and now her form, bathed in moonlight, approximates the buried idealization he carries for the opposite sex.

It has been theorized that this luminous image is for most of us based on an unconscious level in a parent, then metamorphosed into ecstatic hope of romantic happiness in adolescence, then buried deep in our adult psyches. Elements of religion, or worshipful urges may also be involved, especially for Catholic-educated artists like Joyce and Puccini, for their religion involves the worship of human beings as divinities, e.g. the Virgin Mary. But in the universal and perhaps literary/psychological sense, there is a profound part of each lover and beloved that longs to worship their partner in the sense of opening utterly to them, to share their deepest thoughts and dreams with them,... even for brief moments giving our soul into their care. Such worshipful appreciation of the luminous image in literature is clear, from the quasi-religious tradition of Courtly Love in the Middle Ages, through the worshipful studies of female subjects by a thousand painters during the Renaissance, down to the literary contributions of Puccini and Joyce. Woman as divine vessel is an essential part of nineteenth century literature and art. Mimi, Violetta and Ann Truelove are such luminous figures. Even Carmen, after her own fashion, is the object of worship of the men who surround and plead with her for love.

Dramatically, this duet is traditional: Mimi is momentarily overpowered and obeys "love's command"—although immediately afterwards she becomes her playful self again, resisting her lover's kiss and negotiating a meal at the Café Momus. Still, she murmurs "with abandon," *Io tamo* just before she and

Rodolfo depart to join the bohemians.

Mimi is also musically overpowered in the duet, her voice joining Rodolfo's only after his initial, resounding poesia. Obviously, the ecstasy is mutual, but Rodolfo, both dramatically (he crosses to her), literarily (he sings the first four lines), and musically overpowers Mimi. (The same thing is true, we will see, in *Carmen*'s Act 3 Finale and in *La Traviata*'s Act 1 duet.) In scenic terms, Mimi is "bathed in moonlight," her hair forming a halo about her face.

It is in the union of all these elements, focused in the character/stage figure of Mimi that Puccini's luminous image for *La Bohème* is created. We will see that Bizet, Verdi and Stravinsky do much the same thing at crucial moments in the three operas before us. Luminosity usually occurs in a duet, as in *La Traviata*'s first act, but also in arias like *La fleur* from Act 2 of *Carmen* and in extended dialogue form in Act 4 of *The Rake's Progress*.

The luminous image is a striking aspect of opera and has strong counterparts in both the painterly and literary worlds. Puccini knew its primal and aesthetic power. Its special power in the music-dramatic form is one of the major accomplishments of opera. It is responsible for two of the primary themes of opera as literary form: the primacy of the female character as spiritual presence, and the worship of woman as the vessel of human passion.

The Art of the Librettist:

FROM MÜRGER'S NOVEL TO LIBRETTO

Henri Mürger's novel was serialized in *Le Corsaire* between 1845 and 1849. It was dramatized in 1849, emulating the stage version of Dumas *fils'* *Camille*. It was published as a novel, *Scenes of the Bohemian Life* or *The Latin Quarter* in 1850. Its metamorphosis from novel to libretto is something of a miracle and well worth exploring. There are two phases to the librettist's work. In the case of *La Bohème*, each task was completed by a talented individual. The librettists of *La Bohème* are Illica and Giacosa. The first phase is primarily concerned with plot as large form and involves the principles of selection and compression of scenes and action of the larger work. The second phase is concerned with small form—versification, selection or creation of image—and involves the principles of selection and augmentation.

Phase One: Illica

The first phase—the "Illica phase"—is concerned with plot, the formulation of the action into a scenario which tells a story and embodies dramatic values, i.e. the design of the great arc of action of the opera. The arc of action is usually taken from the source, greatly compressed.

In the formulation of rising action between the crucial characters of Mimi and Rodolfo, which was always foremost on Puccini's mind in dramaturgical considerations, Illica would also have formulated the sub-plot of Marcello and Musetta's relationship for purposes of comparison and contrast. He also would have cultivated the secondary figures as foils—characters which reflect and elucidate the central characters.

Did Illica and Giacosa discuss how the chorus was to be used: as local color, to comment on the action, to represent the values of current society? Should the design of the rising action feature the classic values of Plautus and Terence, or follow the more sensationalistic lines of melodrama? Can Mimi's death—clearly the climax of the opera—occur anywhere other than the very end of the opera? And if it does, what of the falling action, the denouement? Such questions face librettists, even before they face demands of the composer.

Phase Two: Giacosa

The second, or "Giacosa phase" is concerned with selection and augmentation. Some of the burden of the extensive description of the novel form must be assumed by the poetic text of the opera. The librettist must carefully select images like Mimi's hands.

He must also create characters by versifying lyric thought. Every word of dialogue or poetry he writes must satisfy the composer's need for small-scale, phrasal rhythmic continuity, especially in arias; and he must use words in such a way as to allow the singer to pronounce them clearly while producing a sung tone. Together with the composer, he must create literary and visual images of accessible beauty to complement character, plot and thematic content.

The Rodolfo-Mimi scene closing Act 1 economically illustrates such literary and dramatic sub-arcs to support the great arc of the plot and to establish character growth that will continue throughout the remaining three tableaux of the opera. Each character sings a revealing aria, then their voices join in a duet.

Details of the aria-aria-duet sequence rewards close examination. Their recitative after the duet—*E al ritorno? / Curioso!*—is witty and revealing. Mimi's hands and key have been introduced as images of touching power and will return in Act 4 to give closure. Mimi's hands will become the single most striking literary and visual image in the opera because they tie together tragic character and hostile environment.

Examples of Compression

In adapting the novel to libretto, Illica compressed the source tremendously in terms of the number of scenes, the amount of action in scenes and the content of those scenes. First, the lines of each character must be selected from diverse locations throughout the source and compressed into a compact dramatic sketch.

Description of environment, atmosphere and character in the prose source, which may assume more than half the volume, must now be assumed by technical aspects of theater, principally by stage setting, orchestration, and occasionally by action. Puccini delighted in what is called "dumb show," i.e. action mimed to music. An example of this is when Rodolfo sprinkles water on Mimi's face in Act 1, or offers her wine in the same scene.

Sometimes, an operatic character will describe something at length, as Mimi does her room (her Act 1 aria), the objects she left in Rodolfo's room (Act 3 aria), and the ocean of love she feels (in Act 4), but all speech taken from the source must be poeticized and shaped into lyric phrases, i.e. phrases that complement musical setting and can be sung.

Metamorphosis of Character

Mimi is the lasting image of *La Bohème* and whatever internal complexity her character loses in the transfer from Mürger, it regains in elegance from the images of Giacosa (discussed in the essays above) and in sentiment through the music of Puccini. The result of the adaptation is four tableaux characterized by elegance of form and verse, each section of which is pungent and full of wry wit, touching sentiment, effective imagery, and felicitous wording where each characterization is concerned. Each character lives through his own language; each speaks particularly as him-/herself. This libretto is economic and finely crafted.

Mimi is in many ways the essence of *La Bohème* and her image should be, in Puccini's words, "a single, luminous figure that dominates the action." Each act adds a new dimension to Mimi's character. In Act 1, she is both vulnerable invalid and flirtatious *grisette*; in Act 2, she is poetry itself as she is overwhelmed by Rodolfo's passion; in Act 3's early morning bitter cold, she is in her own eyes "a poor little thing;" and in Act 4 Musetta repeats Mimi's earlier appraisal: *poveretta*.

Mademoiselle Musette's character is clearly described in Mürger's brief chapter bearing her name and, after reading the brief excerpt below, there is little to say about her birth in the novel. We have only hints of Mimi—"a beautiful girl" (111) who is "hospitable" and whose relationship with Rodolfo (143) disrupts for a time the infamous "four musketeer" gatherings at the Café Momus (112)—in Mürger until page 149 of *Scènes*, where the character of Mimi appears finely etched and full-bodied:

> She was small, delicate, arch... her features, of a certain delicacy and
> sweetly illuminated in the depths of her clear blue eyes, took on in certain
> moments... a suggestion of almost wild brutality which a physiologist
> might call a sign of deep selfishness or a great insensibility... But more
> often it was a charming head with a fresh young smile, with tender
> glances or full of a lordly flirtatiousness. Her youthful blood ran hot
> and quick in her veins, and colored with rose tints the skin, transparent
> in its camellian whiteness. This unhealthy beauty seduced Rudolph. (152)[vi]

We do not meet this Mimi in the opera. This Mimi has an inner fire in common with Musetta and Carmen.

After eight months together with Rudolph, she leaves because she has a new conquest (155). Just as Verdi—indeed, as Dumas *fils*, the playwright—chose to underplay less refined aspects of the prose heroine of *La Dame*, Puccini choose to ignore the "wild brutality" of Mürger's Mimi and to emphasize the "tender glances" and simple nature of the girl who remarks to herself, "Heavens, how learned the man is," when Colline accosts her with an absurd account of the history of coffee (146). Puccini has invested his Mimi with a fake Victorian formality in Acts 1 and 2, which prompts Marcello's teasing in Act 2.

Yet Mimi retains some of her wit at moments. The source of both her wit and sensuality is suggested early on (117) in *Scènes*, and is typical of Mürger's wit.

> "For me," said Mimi, fondling Rudolph with a glance. "I prefer
> beaune, in a little basket."
> "Have you lost your mind?" asked Rudolph.
> "No, I wish to lose it," Mimi responded, upon whom beaune had
> a special effect.
> Her lover was overwhelmed by the thought.

When we read pages 149-65 of *Scènes*, we see how the vain, sensuous Mimi has been softened, romanticized by both word and music in the metamorphosis to *La Bohème*. In compressing the action into four tableaux and attempting to develop so many (6) secondary characters, plus a strong subplot in less than two hours, Puccini does not give Mimi enough opportunity to develop. Verdi did not make this mistake with Violetta, though dealing with fewer characters and slightly more time, in *La Traviata*.

Shaping Other Characters

Violetta is always the absolute center of the action in *La Traviata*, while

Mimi must compete with a fiery Musetta, the comic antics of the bohemian quartet, and a partner who is at times given as much inner turmoil—depth—as she. Her stage figure is further weakened by theatrical convention: she conceals herself and overhears Rodolfo's confessional outbreak in Act 3 (theatrically speaking, only weak characters resort to self-concealment); and her Act 4 entrance is announced by Musetta, reducing its power.

In the selection and compression process of the transfer from novel to libretto, Marcello and Rodolfo become less complete as individuals, and at times seem almost different aspects of the same character. The same might be said to a lesser degree of Musetta and Mimi. In the quartet ending Act 3—a number approximating the peripitae, the motivational turn of the opera's plot—the introversion of Mimi-Rodolfo and extraversion of Musetta-Marcello might easily be melted into a single couple.

Such coupling or twinning is not at all unusual in literary and dramatic art. Individuals often form relationships often complement each other by offering what the other seems to lack. Remember that Musetta and Marcello are foils, secondary characters meant to contrast with leading characters. The off-and-on, tempestuous relationship of Musetta and Marcello is meant to contrast with the brief, singular one of Mimi and Rodolfo. Somewhere between the clinging obsession of Rodolfo and Mimi and the stalwart independence of Musetta and Marcello is a workable relationship, but this of course is not what opera is about. *La Bohème* is about extremes.

Rudolph's character in *Scènes* is given its only true depth through Mimi's description on 249-52. She says to Marcel,

You have no idea, you haven't, what kind of man Rudolph was, a disposition ruined by anger and jealousy, who was killing me bit by bit. He loved me—I knew that well—but his love was dangerous as a firearm and what a life I have led for fifteen months!

In these few pages she sketches the cruel jealousy and ecstatic passion that tied her to him for over a year. The content of this episode from *Scènes* finds its way into *La Bohème*'s Act 3:

Rodolfo m'ama e mi fugge,	Rodolfo loves and frightens me,
il mio Rodolfo si strugge per gelosia,	My Rodolfo struggles with jealousy,
Un passo, un detto,	A step, a gesture,
Un vezzo, un fior lo mettono in sospetto	any little thing makes him suspicious,
Onde corrucci ed ire.	corrupts him with anger.
Talor la notte fingo di dormire	Even at night when I sleep,
e in me lo sento fiso	I sense his stare
spiarmi i sogni in viso.	On my sleeping face—.
Mi grida ad ognhi 'stante:	He stares and cries out,
'Non fai per me, ti prendi un altro amante!'	'You're not for me, take another lover!'
Ahime! Ahime!	O God, what shall I do?

This is astute condensation. And what follows it is no less impressive. Rodolfo's narrative describing his and Mimi's life together summarizes several scenes and many elements of the last half of Scènes. At *La Bohème*'s Act 3 ensemble's climax, Mimi appears—*Mimi de serra a fiore*—but her image has already been foreshadowed many times in Acts 1 and 2. Then follows in short order Mimi's aria, evoking the flower image again, but this time only of the *finti fior*, the "lifeless flowers." It is still Winter and flowers are not yet in bloom.

Illica chose to compress the numerous garret episodes of the novel into two scenes or "tableaux"—Acts 1 and 4 of his libretto—but the researcher must search the twenty garret episodes of *Scènes* to find the events and characters of Acts 1 and 4 of *La Bohème*.

Act 1 is a miracle of compression. The first 31 pages of the prose source provide the descriptive mode and wit of dialogue and establish the individual character types of the male bohemians, but the action of Act 1 is derived from bits and pieces carefully selected from the entirety of pages 1-166. Act 2, on the other hand, is plainly sketched between pages 115 and 120; and the essence of Act 3 on pages 164-65, although there is no exact scenic counterpart for the Barrier (Act 3) in *Scènes*, as there is for the Café Momus (Act 2).

Illica's decision to present the plot of the opera in four—originally five—tableaux, rather than in a procession of more fluid scenes, gave a unity to the kaleidoscope of Parisian scenes in the loose run of *Scènes'* action—though *La Bohème*'s plot is hardly cohesive. This choice of plot structuring also gave the poet and composer a unity of scene and action for the accomplishment of their stunning success. Puccini, who always insisted on extreme economy of all literary and theatrical elements, as well as carefully-orchestrated, rising dramatic action, actually eliminated the fourth of five tableau, much to Illica's disappointment.

Images and Plot: Determining Character Action

To further demonstrate Illica's contribution to *La Bohème*, a brief description on 172 of *Scènes* is the basis for the duet opening Act 4, and within this duet he and Giacosa have gathered visual images (Musetta's ribbons, Mimi's bonnet) widely scattered in *Scènes*. This lyric look in the hearts of both men here in *La Bohème* does not derive from Mürger directly, but is rather a creation of Illica, Giacosa and Puccini as they answer the special and specific needs of the operatic formula. Description has become twin soliloquies; image has been augmented into verse.

It has been argued that *La Bohème*'s brevity, large number of characters, and concentration on surface detail cannot allow ample development of a complex character such as Mimi, as compared to those of Carmen and Violetta. Mimi and Rodolfo may finally be too literary in nature to be believable dramatically. They sing of being violent and jealous, but we never see them act that way with each other. A libretto should give the chief characters many opportunities to act and react violently in moments of crisis. Mimi and Rodolfo have only two such opportunities and both are precipitated by Mimi's health, rather than by their passionate affair. Mimi and Rodolfo fail to act and—from a certain, critical per-spective—are held back in their development by both complex metaphors and by Puccini's lush melodies.

Greater character depth and differentiation might have resulted from a dif-ferent selection of material from and manner of compression of Mürger's *Scènes*. The plot and character material of the chapter called "Francine's Muff" is very slight but proved irresistible to the librettists, and so the characters of Francine and Jacques are merged with the original Mimi and Rudolph to create a tone of idealistic romantic sentiment. This had a ripple effect through the opera, so that in Act 1 Mimi is flirtatious rather than sensuous, in Act 2 Mimi's delight in her bonnet rather than her flirtation is emphasized, and in Act 3 her abject illness and need, rather than her strength of character, is obvious. One might argue that the level of sentimentality in that one chapter of *Scènes* comes to dominate the entire literary, visual and musical nature of Mimi and Rodolfo's relationship in *La Bohème*. Mürger's highly romantic portrayal of a high-principled young sculp-tor and his ill-fated, simple mistress in a single chapter of *Scènes* comes to assume a role of inordinate proportions in *La Bohème*, dominating the vibrantly realistic aspects of the Rudolph and Mimi found in the original prose work.

Some other details of *La Bohème*'s carefully managed surface are worth mentioning. The brilliant, two-dimensional characters are shaped by literary con-trast and wit. From their interaction emerges an irony that does not ring empty—as irony often does—but rather combines with a gentleness to give us a brief glance at the playful, if not manipulative side of the bohemians, e.g. in Act 2 Mimi is teased but never injured for her social pretense. Mimi's charm in the face of death is also playfully ironic. In the final scene, Musetta and Colline sac-rifice their possessions in the mirage of hope, but their actions offer affecting glances beneath the surface of these characters.

Sub-plots are beautifully integrated in Acts 2, 3, and 4: no character besides Rodolfo has a deep relationship with Mimi, yet everyone cares for her. Tonal description is used to enhance stage actions like tearing manuscripts, sprinkling water, etc. Atmosphere is created, distilling time and weather in the opening of Act 3. Authentic melodies are also used, as in the march at the end of Act 2. Puccini's orchestral world is varied and always engaging. There is also the influence of Verdi's *Falstaff* (1893), which premiered as Puccini was begin-ning labor on *La Bohème*; a rapid pace of pure action and musical ideas of Verdi's comic masterpiece typifies the first half of Acts 1 and 4 of *La Bohème*.

The Versifier: Character Depth through Image

The versifier's role appears at first glance to be less complex. He must sat-isfy the poetic and imagery needs of composer and the need for verbal felicity of the singer. Rarely will a line be sung directly from the source; everything but stage directions must be versified unless it is to be spoken. Often the poem of an aria springs from the slightest hint buried in the prose source or from a process of pure deduction on the versifier's part—as is true of Rodolfo's aria. Mimi has two arias in Act 3, a short one to Marcello before Rodolfo's entrance and a substantial one to Rodolfo after his long descriptive/confessional passage to Marcello.

Both arias have their roots in the long confessional monologue mentioned above, which Mimi addresses to Marcello from her deathbed in *Scènes* (249-52). This passage is too long to quote in full, but this episode is the fitting climax of the book. After it and the continuance of Mimi's story in the final ten pages of the book, Mimi shines in the reader's memory, creating the strongest impression of character found in *Scènes*. Like *La Bohème*, *Scènes* is ultimately a lady's story. Like Violetta, Mimi dies in part because of a broken heart, more so in *Scènes* than in its operatic counterpart.

We can illustrate Giacoso's skill in meeting the technical requirements of a versifier by examining his interpretation of two passages adapted or derived from the episode in 249-52 of *Scènes*. The first passage has been quoted above with regard to Rodolfo's jealousy. Even with the translation you can see that Giacosa's adaptation features strongly rhythmic, rhymed verse shaped from the forceful prose of his source. The rhythmic unity of the lines is essential; the dense rhyme is a bonus which only the greatest composer can emphasize without appearing trite. Giacosa expands the dialogue he took from this part of *Scènes*. Lower on 249, Mimi says, "He told me that he didn't love me any more, that I must take another lover." This approximates Giacosa's "You're not for me. Go find another lover." (88) Mimi and Marcel's dialogue on 251 is faintly echoed late in *La Bohème*'s third act.

Mimi describes to Marcel her second and final parting from Rudolph in a lovely prose passage on 251-52. This episode is condensed into the last five lines of the Mimi-Marcello duet of Act 3; it inspired Giacosa to image making. Consider Mimi's Act 3 aria to Rodolfo. The first seven lines are functional sentiment, but the second seven lines contain a list of objects—a poetic element, having a naturalistic effect—echoing the cluster of packages holding Mimi's things in *Scènes*. (Rudolph has hidden these parcels behind a parasol so he will not have to think of Mimi's leaving.) It is from one of these packages that Mimi takes the bonnet to wear—at his request—on their last night together. Giacosa takes this opportunity to begin building a sub-arc of images. He has Mimi mention *la cuffietta rosa*, which Rodolfo purchased for her in Act 2 and will serenade at the opening of Act 4 before producing it later for the dying Mimi. In this aria a literary/visual sub-arc was born. In *Scènes*, Rudolph removes Mimi's scarf and asks her to wear "the little striped bonnet, for tonight" (251). In *La Bohème*, Mimi sings, *Bada, sotto il guanciale c'e la cuffietta rosa. / Se vuoi... se vuoi... serbarla a recordo d'amor!* (Listen, among my things is the pink bonnet... if you wish, keep it as a memento of our love.) In *Scènes*, it is Rudolph who is sentimental; in *La Bohème*, it is Mimi. Mürger's Rudolph is, however, accurately represented in Act 4's opening duet when Rodolfo serenades the bonnet, regretting his beloved's departure and remembering her fragrant head and dainty ivory hands.

The most important task of the librettist is to create character through image and action. This inspiration is what the composer initially requires—word craft must then follow. In their letters, both Puccini and Verdi speak of needing a luminous image, or an essential visual idea about which they can center the dramatic action, and upon which they can ground a musical universe. Passion is the essence of the music of *La Bohème* and *La Traviata*, and the chief image of these two operas is a luminous lady of flowers: Mimi and Violetta. Both these figures are variations on the figure of Manon Lescaut and the literary figurines who preceded her. In contrast, Bizet and Stravinsky chose subjects that allowed them to concentrate on the figure of the classical hero, Oedipus. They created José and Tom Rakewell to explore themes associated with that famous descendent of the house of Laius.

NOTES:

[i]I recommend the *English National Opera Guide* libretti, which are readily accessible in English-speaking countries. Their introductory essays, illustrations, thematic guides, good bi-lingual editions of text, and discography/bibliography are admirable. These guides are one-volume treasures. There are many admirable recordings of *La Bohème*, but my own preference is Seraphim IB-6000, which is conducted by Sir Thomas Beecham, and features Jussi Bjoerling and Victoria de Los Angeles. Remember to buy recordings with libretti included, even if you own a libretto like the ENO edition. My favorite video recording of *La Bohème* is the striking Zeffirelli production taped at the Metropolitan Opera January 16, 1982, starring Teresa Stratas and José Carreras. There are, of course, a huge number of auditory and visual recordings to choose from. Some viewers will prefer taped stage performances, like the Zeffirelli *La Bohème* or the English *The Rake's Progress*, others the filmed adaptations of operas, like Zeffirelli's *La Traviata* (1982) or Rosi's *Carmen* (1984). Special in its vision of the intimacy of universal values is Ingmar Bergman's visionary interpretation of *The Magic Flute* (1979) in cinematic form. All quotes from the libretti of our four operas are from the ENO editions of the original language text.

[ii]Peter Conrad's discussion of this in *Romantic Opera and Literary Form* is a worthy dissertation on the subject and points out the apex of this tendency: Debussy's setting of Maeterlink's short novel, *Palleas and Millesande*. (See also Conrad's *A Song of Love and Death: The Meaning of Opera* (Simon & Schuster, 1988) and Gary Schmidgall's *Literature as Opera* (Oxford, 1977), both rewarding works. Robert Donington's *Opera and its Symbols* (Yale University Press, 1990) is also a good discussion.) There are many fine books about opera, far too many to mention here.

[iii]In his Act 4 aria, Colline also refers to his coat as *vecchio* (old man).

[iv]The cycle of ascent and descent as mythic paradigms are rooted in the Orpheus cycle, which was explored early on in operatic traditions, most successfully in Gluck's *Orfeo ed Euridice* (1762). Offenbach's satire, *Orpheus in the Underworld* (1858), does its best to ridicule Gluck's classical values and is good for a charmed chuckle. Mythically seen, a character will ascend or descend in search of something essential, then return with knowledge to renew their previous life. Mimi's ascent, like Cio-cio-san's in Madame Butterfly, is modest in nature, though the ultimate result is the same: the death of the heroine on a lonely height.

[v]Henri Mürger, preface to *Vie de Bohème*.

[vi]All quotes here are from the 1930 Hyperion Press edition of the novel, translation by E. W. Hugus.

Part 3

BIZET'S *Carmen*
OPERA AS DRAMA

Introduction to the Dramatic Elements

In *The Poetics* the three central dramatic elements—plot, character, and thought—are described by Aristotle as more vitally important than the minor ones: music, visual elements, and poetic elegance of form (rhythmic and rhyming elegance, density of sound pattern, and intensity of tone). For Aristotle, effective portrayal of character is the essence, plot is the essential mechanism by which character is shaped, and meaning is the product of character's interaction with plot. Everything else exists only to serve the creation and portrayal of a complex character and the plot that will force that character to change.

In opera, character still rules, but the means of creating that character are quite different. Aristotle's minor elements come to the foreground in opera. Music replaces language as the principle means by which character is exposed and developed. Poetic form, while essential, becomes the basis for a musical elegance that indicates depth of character; literary elements are the beginning, but also the necessary platform for musically-inspired depth of character. Plot, while still important in opera, is not necessarily the logical machine that Aristotle describes as supreme in Greek Tragedy.

Music is supreme, visual aspects are often spectacular (as they strive to meet the splendor of orchestral music), and poetic imagery—often augmented by musical motif—often emerges as emblematic of the music drama's meaning. A coat may denote both generosity and poverty (*La Bohème*), a flower love (*Carmen*), a letter hope (*La Traviata*), and a machine both miracle and tragic destiny (*The Rake's Progress*). As we have seen, certain images—seasonal, natural, elemental—emerge as central to serious opera's inherent thematic and aesthetic values in *La Bohème*. The same will prove true for *Carmen*, *La Traviata* and *The Rake's Progress*, though each librettist-composer team will arrive at image values unique to their particular creation.

Review of Imagery's Usage in Music Drama

We have already noticed that a musically-charged image will often acquire symbolic qualities in relation to a character—Mimi and the images of light and Spring—and plot: Mimi sickens and dies, as a diseased flower might, long before her time. We will see that the librettists of *Carmen* give the image of the flower different values from those cultivated in *La Bohème*, values more integrated with the interplay of internal and external action. Mimi describes lilies and roses in Act 1 as delicate presages of Spring and hope. In Act 1 of *Carmen*, the heroine literally throws an acacia flower—instead of herself—at José. (In Act 2, this same blossom, when wilted, will represent for Jose the dark fire of his passion for Carmen.) Thus, in the first two acts of *Carmen*, the image of the flower will come to represent diverse qualities of different characters. For Carmen the acacia bloom is a tool, like her sexuality, while for Jose it comes to represent his passion for Carmen. The image of the camellia is used in still different ways in *La Traviata*. For Violetta, the camellia indicates her availability as a mistress, and when she gives it she gives her person. Each heroine uses the flower to express a dream or desire, thus indicating an aspect of her character. Carmen uses it literally, almost as a weapon, and thus most dramatically of the three.

Literary elements are the initial source of the visual imagery from which opera lives. Especially important is the study of literary image in relation to the essential dramatic elements described by Aristotle in his *Poetics*: plot, character and theme. We have also noticed how the desire for contrast in the interaction of literary and dramatic forms can be employed to develop irony in opera: Mimi dies in Spring, her favorite season. The death scene in *La Bohème* occurs in Spring, the season of rebirth. We will see how Carmen is murdered at the peak of her social ascendance— the Spring of her life. In *La Traviata*, we will see how Violetta dies crying out for the joy of the freedom whose excesses have hastened her death. In *The Rake's Progress*, Tom dies believing himself in Paradise instead of Bedlam. The descriptive medium of poetry intensifies the contradictions inherent in tragic obsession.

Romantic obsession plays an important role in opera in that it does not allow for the social necessities of personal freedom or rebirth, powerful and constant themes opera borrows from both lyric poetry and drama. Romantic characters become prisoners of the very source of their sensual and spiritual awakening. Thus the tragic formula thrives in opera. The intertwining of eros and thanatos often results from obsession. So Mimi pays the ultimate price for her obsession with Rodolfo, as will Carmen for toying with Don José, Violetta for indulging Alfredo, and Anne for trusting Tom Rakewell.

Imagery also makes a special contribution to the environment of an opera by interacting with the setting. In death, Mimi—a *grisette* in Paris's demimonde—becomes, symbolically, one of the scentless flowers she describes to Rodolfo at the conclusion of her Act 1 aria. The contribution of poetry to operatic text—to the aria and, often, the duet—indicates that the libretto is, historically speaking, the true shadow of the texts of the Greek poetic tragedies, which consisted entirely of highly-structured verse meant to be chanted or sung. The lyric poetry of an aria or ensemble should elucidate character inscape.

Enhancing visual images by unique combinations of literary, dramatic, musical and scenic elements is one way in which opera appeals to the heart of the mind. Among the plethora of image clusters produced in opera are two primary ones: The Dream of Love and Spring, and The Luminous Image. The latter image indicates to the primacy of the female figure opera, even when a male— José—is clearly a protagonist of classic proportions.

Visualizing Opera's Elements

I have offered visualizations by which we might organize the diverse elements of opera, e.g. comparing the great arc of a masonry bridge to the plot of an opera, as well as referring to literary, dramatic, and scenic patterns as sub-arcs that support and augment the aesthetic stability and meaning of the action of the plot. The following essays will examine *Carmen*'s plot, with each of the first four essays dedicated to an act's characters, plot and theme. The final essay of this section will discuss yet another of opera's unique elements, the ensemble, drawing on *La Bohème*'s Act 3 quartet and diverse pieces from *Carmen*. We will also begin looking forward to *La Traviata*'s extraordinary literary, dramatic and (especially) musical qualities, which yield superb ensembles.

We will explore *Carmen* as music drama. In *Carmen*, music's translucent powers release the dramatic qualities of *Carmen*'s characters to work at maximum efficiency. Music's power to symbolize the abstractions of internal and external forces is used wonderfully. Internal forces, you will remember, are forces generated as a function of character, e.g. desire for liberty (Carmen), or jealousy (José); while external forces are those generated as a function of plot, e.g. Fate, the brutal, glorious distraction of the bullfight in Act 4 of *Carmen*.

Bizet's use of music demonstrates that music skillfully employed never detracts from the essential story; it fulfills its multifaceted purpose without drawing attention to itself. To reiterate: Music (1) provides atmosphere (aural environment), even local color; (2) accompanies singers and action effectively with musical form; (3) elucidates character inscape; and (4) creates musical symbols that elucidate character conflict, turns of plot, etc. Bizet performs all these functions admirably, especially the last. Let us consider the dramatic qualities of the first music that we hear in *Carmen*—even before the curtain rises.

Carmen's Prelude

Carmen's *Prelude* provides musical material not only to evoke powerful emotional response, but gives the listener auditory images to define setting and character. These motifs—repeated musical patterns—will be woven as sub-arcs of image and idea throughout the opera in support of a powerful and logical plot. The *Prelude* offers three musical themes to represent two of the brilliant images inspired by Mérimée's novella.

The three musical ideas are arranged in a manner reflecting mastery of musical form and dramatic purpose. (1) The prelude begins with a celebratory march that will introduce Act 4. This is then contrasted with (2) the refrain from Escamillo's Act 2 aria, a second stirring march. The initial march is then repeated, constituting an ABA form for the first part of the *Prelude*. Then, after a brief pause, (3) the striking "Fate" motif is sounded *fortissimo*, darkly scored in brass—the instrument of public ritual. This descending melody is identified with Carmen's Fate, but also her fateful effect on José's life. This pure orchestral motif is used strikingly in each of *Carmen*'s four acts. It is Carmen's major musical symbol, as well as a musical structural devise.

Musically, in the *Prelude*, the bright public figure of Escamillo wins Carmen's affection, leaving an enraged, threatening José. So, from the very beginning of *Carmen*, even before the curtain rises, we are preoccupied with the music of characterization and conflict on an unconscious level. Such a *Prelude* is a dramatized reduction of an operatic overture, which originally introduced the opera's melodic content. The *Preludes* to *Carmen* and *La Traviata*, however, do far more than provide a map of the approaching musical world—they are distinct designs meant to indicate character depth and the conflict inherent in the plot of the opera to follow.

How We Know a Character

Great opera is about great characters—Mimi, Carmen, José—with whom we may develop a deep empathy. Let us briefly review the means by which we know a character in a dramatic performance. Moving from the external to the internal, we must consider how a purely literary and dramatic creation evokes our investment of empathy.

(1) The setting in which we find the character may indicate her circumstances and hint at what we may expect in the way of action, e.g. the sultry warmth of Carmen's Seville, or Rodolfo's freezing attic. The setting also includes stage properties (hand-held set pieces), such as Micaela's letter, or *Carmen*'s acacia bloom in Act 1. (2) Lighting provides not only visibility but atmosphere and may reflect the mood of an individual character. The depression of *La Bohème*'s characters in Act 3 is perfectly captured by the bitter gray of a February dawn. Remember that moonlight is vital to the finale of *La Bohème*'s Act 1. (3) A character's costume and make-up reflect social and physical well-being, taste and even mood. Mimi is pale and slight, *Carmen* dark and lush.

(4) Action, including physical gesture and choreographic movement, indicates internal values and emotional state. Some gestures, when repeated, become visual motives and have the same function as repeated literary or musical ideas: to create depth of meaning through repetition in varied context. Single actions of a paradigmatic nature may become symbols in themselves. (5) Character thought is expressed in verbal or musical gesture and, most effectively in opera of course, in a unique combination of the two—especially in recollection, imaginative flight, or in reaction to crisis. (6) Mood, as reflected in pure musical form, especially through harmony and varying rhythm, and in the unique interrelations of these elements, is a powerful musical-dramatic tool.

We may experience Carmen and José's passion and deepest fears; across the aesthetic distance between the work of art and ourselves, we will experience pity for their struggle and terror at their violent end. The power of Bizet's musical drama will allow us to purge ourselves of these powerful emotions to some extent as the curtain falls. The Fate of the two lovers in *Carmen*, like the Fate that traps Oedipus, seems determined by forces beyond the power of mere mortals to see or control. Jose is straight-jacketed as the final curtain falls. He can only utter, "Arrest me. I am guilty." His life seems short and brutish. Unlike Jocasta, he does not flee in horror and kill herself. Unlike Oedipus, he does not bid life as he has known it farewell. A mournful chorus does not weep at the protagonists' fate, but stands mute as José surrenders his life, as he has already surrendered his honor, to the mechanisms of Fate.

One might argue that both Carmen and José are victims—as are Oedipus and Jocasta—of Fate, but also of their *hamartia*—a fatal character flaw, an essential blindness of personality that leads to destruction. Carmen grows blind to danger in her passionate and prideful pursuit of Escamillo, and in her superstitious stubbornness insists that she must be utterly free to love whomever she chooses, whenever she chooses. José sinks into the blind fury of violated obsession, approximating Oedipus' overweening pride. Obsession never seems to yield personal happiness, but the depiction of it inspires great art.

The great theme of *Carmen*, as of all great drama, is human nature itself. Culture also plays a role. In a form approximating Naturalism, cultural values—Carmen is a Gypsy and adheres to Gypsy cultural values, in contrast to Micaela—to some degree replace religious values in *Carmen*; and the balance of internal and external forces is so fine that the characters appear to be the puppets of their own emotions (José) and superstitions (Carmen). In *Carmen*, our catharsis is a direct result of our ability to understand the characters and their struggle. Bizet's art makes this possible; the following essays will explain how he does this.

The Essays of Part 3

The next essay will discuss Act 1 of *Carmen* in detail, emphasizing the title character's entrance aria, with its imagery of liberty and danger, its absolutely true portrayal of character, and its foreshadowing of action. Remember the contrastive function of secondary characters, or foils, like Micaela, the first character we meet in Act 1 of *Carmen*. Micaela's entrance into Seville is careful preparation for the introduction of the title character, i.e. Micaela anticipates Carmen's entrance and contrasts utterly with her. *Carmen*'s second Act also employs a similar plot device: Escamillo's initial entrance and aria precede José's entrance and off-stage song. Similarly, in *La Bohème*, Musetta's bright extroversion in Act 2 contrasts with Mimi's coy introversion in Acts 1 and 2. The arts of adumbration and contrast go hand in hand. In *The Rake's Progress*, there could be no greater contrast to Anne Truelove in Act 1, scene 1 than Mother Goose in Act 1, scene 2, for each represents a specific environment—country and city, respectively. To portray rural environments as positive is a characteristic of romantic literature. *Carmen*'s first act—remember *La Bohème*'s first act—ends with a decisive duet, the *Seguidilla*, which begins the rising action of the plot. The *Seguidilla* also begins Carmen and José's relationship.

The third essay will explore Act 2 as rising action, with José's great aria, striking in image and idea, as its centerpiece of dramatic characterization. José's aria also acquires emphasis because it is delayed, as well as plot-driven—that is, precipitated by events of the plot. In contrast, both Carmen's and Escamillo's entrance arias are not plot-driven; they are essential exposition. José's only aria is essentially dictated by inner struggle between passion and duty. José's character inscape is craggy and perilous long before he follows Carmen to the mountains of southern Spain. Aristotle's definitions of the tragic hero or protagonist fit José well enough. Like Oedipus, he descends to a cruel end dictated by a unique interaction of his own flaws and Fate's machinations. Like Oedipus, he has killed pridefully. We will begin to trace his descent from the end of Act 1 through the final fierce gestures of the Act 4 Finale. Ironically, his descent is matched by Carmen's ascent. *Carmen* is about character: its dramatic and musical themes are all about the conflict between character interiority and the mechanisms of Fate.

The fourth essay will discuss Act 3 as the turning point of the plot, with its dark turn from eros to thanatos. As Carmen begins her ascent through José to Escamillo, José continues his tragic plummet into the loneliness of psychotic rage. The towering Act 3 Finale gathers together all the forces of José's situation, and their alignment reveals the tragic vision of his and Carmen's violent relationship. After this, José is driven to his fated destination, as he gradually loses all that was of value to him: rank, occupation, respectability, social position, his fiancée, his mother, and finally the thing that cost him all these things—the object of his passion, Carmen herself. We do not witness it, of course, but after the curtain falls he also loses his life. He follows his mother and Carmen into "that undiscovered country," leaving Micaela alone.

The final essay discusses the final stages of José's descent into hell and how he pulls the fatalistic Carmen down with him. The extraordinary final confrontation of the lovers involves the revival of earlier themes (*Carmen*'s freedom, José's passion and jealousy), imagery (of appearance, action and of a literary nature), and plentiful musical material in tension-building juxtaposition, as well as new ideas. All these elements are woven into an innovative, organic music-dramatic tapestry. The patterns of imagery have acquired complete and powerful meaning by the final scene of Act 4, as the off-stage public sports ceremony is more than matched by the struggle of passion and death in the private arena in the street just outside the coliseum walls: two sacrificial victims are claimed in this scene, one on-stage and one off-stage.

It is worthwhile to return to Essays 2 and 3 of Part 1 to review the dramatic elements explored in the following discussion. And listen to a good recording, preferably one featuring Jon Vickers or Placido Domingo as José. The title character is the heart of *Carmen*, but José is its soul. José's fall is seminal to the tragic power of this magnificent opera. The theme of unrequited love adds a powerful twist to the pattern of eros and thanatos inherent in serious opera. Jealousy and despair are powerful instruments and their effect on José is awesome in its power to destroy. His actions, internal and external, are strengthened by the patterns of imagery—in some ways similar to Rodolfo's, but more deeply tied to guilt and thus moral conflict—and the thematic designs that surround him. Carmen's death at José's hand is the tragic result of José's fall.

Great in suffering and jealous fury, José is a character that can truly evoke pity and terror in those who watch his struggle with the forces of Fate and the flaws of his own character. Overpowered by José's fury, Carmen is folded into a volume of history that is short, brutish and forcefully silent.

Character and Plot Exposition in Carmen's Act 1
Habanera AND *Seguidilla*

With the abstract power of the *Prelude* ringing in the audience's ears, Act 1's exposition subtly centers on the characters of José Lizzarabengoa, a corporal in the Sevilla regiment, and of Carmen, a Gypsy prostitute and smuggler who works days in the Sevilla tobacco factory. José is a common man from Navarre, a passionate athlete and brawler who has found a place for himself in the military's discipline. We also discover, if we read and listen carefully, that he deeply loves and respects his widowed mother and embraces her plans for him to marry the 17-year-old orphan, Micaela, and to assume a respectable life. We learn this during José's conversations with his new commanding officer, Zuniga, and from his duet with Micaela in Act 1. Back-story is vital.

We also find that José is vulnerable; he has an explosive temperament and a problem with control. By the end of Act 1, Carmen will have found her way through his military facade into his passions, and there she will remain, a trace of the chaos he has sought to erase from his early life. José, we sense, is an open book to us. Carmen is, in comparison, sphinx-like. Her depths are only hinted at in Act 1, and never exposed in the entirety of the opera. The one exception might be her feelings for Escamillo and her public declaration of love for him in Act 4. (This event is extremely brief, almost perfunctory, and carefully confined by musical form. It is also surrounded by a plethora of scenic and musical elements so that it tends to appear and disappear like a flame in the wind.) Also, the careful listener can scarcely fail to hear the powerful musical commentary that follows it. If this new passion of Carmen's is real love, as she swears to Escamillo, it is clearly a leaf in the hurricane of Fate enveloping her.

Act 1 shows us that Carmen is not a character who finds words necessary. Indeed, she does not seem to trust words. When around men, she sometimes resorts to nonsense syllables rather than words. She prefers physical gestures and dance to words. But she honors her verbal contract with José: in Act 2, she will keep the promise she made to José in Act 1—not just because she likes him but because it is Gypsy law, a matter of ethnic honor. But a greater law of Carmen's Gypsy nature is the law of freedom, personal liberty, and it is Carmen's absolute insistence on this law that will conflict with José's violated sense of duty and cause an irreparable schism in his character.

The secondary female character, Micaela, has two appearances in Act 1, both of which establish a youthful, bright and naive character meant to contrast with Carmen's dark maturity. José appears before Carmen in Act 1, and is at first passive, then gruffly vulnerable. There are clear hints at the power Carmen has already established over him when he and Micaela sing their duet, but his collapse into Carmen's arms late in Act 1 is clearly the beginning of the opera's rising action.

Habanera

The essential exposition of the Act 1 is contained in three musical numbers: Carmen's *Habanera*; the idyllic duet between José and Micaela; and *Carmen*'s crucial contract with José, the *Seguidilla*. José's actions in Act 1 also prove to be telling: he picks up the flower Carmen throws at him and places it next to his heart. Later, when she points this out before the *Seguidilla* and promises him an ecstasy he has never known, he quickly yields to temptation and is lost—though he cannot know it yet. The rest of *Carmen*'s plot is a record of José's fall and Carmen's ascent.

Following the *Prelude*, the opening chorus introduces the sleepy rhythms of Sevilla at mid-morning. It may be important that the first perspective we receive of Sevilla is the commentary of the listless, off-duty soldiers: this is José's world, and military duty will be José's last hope of resistance to Carmen's spell in Act 2. Micaela, José's intended and a crucial secondary character, appears to demonstrate both her innocence and cleverness. *L'oiseau s'envole* (the bird has escaped), murmur the soldiers, as Micaela slips through their fingers, establishing the image of the bird of freedom Carmen will later mention. They also mention *on fume*, smoking, an image conducive to atmosphere, the setting of the cigar factory, and, indirectly, to the lack of clarity in vision that will afflict José.

Local color abounds in scene 2, even before the changing of the guard. As in Act 2 of *La Bohème*, the military provides stirring local color, including children (urchins) mocking the military formality. As in *La Bohème*, children are attracted to the change of guard and mimic it with their voices. This is the same trumpet that represents duty and will attempt to pull José from Carmen's arms in Act 2. As the hero is introduced to us, his actions are mimicked by street urchins. In a few moments, Carmen will refer to love as *enfant de Bohème*, a Gypsy child, wild and free, untamable. The *femme fatale* is always part child herself. The role of the child, as image and collectively, is important in *Carmen*, and in opera generally. Consider the social statement made by the mere presence of children in Berg's *Wozzek* or the striking character of Miles in Britten's *Turn of the Screw*.

Scene 3 is a conversation containing important background on José. He left home after killing an opposing player in a fight after a *pelota* match. Note that we receive no such background on Carmen, other than, according to her Gypsy associates, she has always managed to mix love and business. She also manages this with José.

The girls of the cigar factory enter in 1,4, bringing with them the cigars for their admirers to smoke. They compare the rising, disappearing smoke to the words of love men offer them. This scene has a dreamy quality in its warm, ascending orchestral lines, and celebrates a quiet youthful passion and serenity. A good stage director will not fail to add subtle choreographic movement to this and the following scenes to give a visual dimension to youthful courtship and to perhaps remind us that folk dance and ceremony are a wellspring of classic musical form. The cigar workers adumbrate Carmen's entrance.

This reverie is interrupted by the demand of the soldiers to see Carmen, their favorite. When she appears the young men ask her when she will grant them her favors, she teases them, saying, perhaps never, maybe tomorrow, but certainly not today. *L'amour* is obviously a social tool for Carmen, a game. Realistically speaking, her sexual appeal was the only effective means of advancement open to a woman of her background and education in that society. We will also see that sex is her weapon.

Two musical instruments characterize Carmen in her entrance aria, the cello and flute. The cello introduces the sensuous rhythms of her entrance aria. The aria's themes are clear and Carmen's values never vary from those she reveals here. Carmen describes love with two images: first, a gypsy child that toys with affection; second, a bird of freedom. Passion is illogical, often combining unlikes. Carmen longs for *l'autre*, the unusual choice, the one man who doesn't talk, feigns indifference to her. She has already seen José working on his weapon nearby, ignoring her. He is just the challenge she needs. Carmen is an outsider, likely to choose the odd man out.

Carmen's values and qualities become clear in the *Habanera*. While revealing nothing of her inner world, as Mimi so clearly did in *Mi chiamano Mimi*—though obviously Carmen's circumstances in this scene are much different here than Mimi's—Carmen lets us know that she loves freedom of every kind. She is candid, flirtatious and independent. She is self-knowledgeable and, we sense, manipulative. She has a powerful sensuality, an allure, perhaps best captured by the enticing rhythms of the celli and the color of the flute in the lower register.

There is also something threatening about Carmen: she is dangerous, a trace of chaos—and so is the bird of free love she celebrates in her aria. Her character openly warns of the threat of all-consuming passion. Eros, she warns, is not something to be defined or contained; it must remain free as a bird or it will disappear like smoke. And in its need to be free lies danger: you cannot choose it, and you cannot make it stay. Carmen's "love" is elusive, playful, anarchic and— as José will find out—subject to Carmen's ambition and will. Carmen's greatness as a character lies, in part, in her will to be free and self-determining.

Carmen is a true operatic heroine, emblemizing not sentimental love and social commitment, but eroticism and freedom. It does not surprise us, then, that immediately following her aria, Carmen commits a playful act fraught with inherent emotional violence. She "attacks" a warrior, "piercing his breast" with a flower. She throws an acacia flower into José's chest in a mock challenge. She wants his attention, in part because he appears to not notice her. (Remember how Marcello tries to ignore Musetta in Act 2 of *La Bohème*?) As if in warning, the orchestra echoes the Fate motif from the *Prelude*.

Micaela and José's Duet

Carmen contrasts in every way with the naive and respectable Micaela, whom we get to know in the next scene. Micaela's duet with José features gorgeous melodies and luminous orchestration. It is also important exposition of José's character and introduces an invisible character of great importance in *Carmen*: José's mother.

This duet also introduces the idea of sentimental love, which is inevitably tied to nature and rural areas—José sings, *mon village*—in romantic literature and in opera generally from 1800 on. *Carmen* also features an ancillary theme of opera: the defeat of sentimental (socially acceptable or proper) love—represented by Michaela—by passionate (erotic, profane) love, which is represented by Carmen. But, before its defeat by Carmen's erotic charms, sentimental love is momentarily celebrated by these two. And from their engaging duet emerges the opera's first luminous figure, José's mother.

There are notable symbolic acts in this scene: first, Micaela comes as messenger, bringing only good things; second, the hero receives a kiss symbolizing forgiveness from a very clever mother. Although this scene is intimate, it also advances the plot considerably. During his strophe, José mentions that his mother will defend him from the charm of "that demon," Carmen. Clearly, José has been deeply affected by Carmen; she is on his mind.

José may also be, in his own way, as superstitious as Carmen is—although that has not been established yet. José will call Carmen demon, sorceress, devil, and Carmen will not shrink from the final accusation. "Are you the devil," José asks her in Act 3. "Yes, just as you have said," she answers. Certainly, both Carmen's actions—physical and verbal—are violent in nature: she throws a flower at José, cuts Manuelita, a fellow-laborer in the cigar factory; she delights in describing the "tortures" she expects while imprisoned. Later in Act 4, she will hurl a ring at José and this will somehow trigger his final rage and her death. Perhaps José on some level recalls the first object that she threw at him and this plays a role in his loss of control. At that point Carmen is hurling both objects and insults at José.

To create a striking contrast, this soft and sentimental reminiscence between José and Micaela is immediately followed by a whirlwind of public violence. As Micaela shyly runs away, girls rush on from the factory yelling of how Carmen has injured a fellow-worker. Carmen has cut an X—a Christian symbol, representing Christ, a sacrificial figure; also a symbol for the name of a person who can not write—in the face of a girl, disfiguring her and, perhaps, meant to serve as a warning to others. Note that Carmen has performed a violent act and shows no regret whatsoever. Most importantly, the act involved a knife and, although weapons are common in *Carmen*, a knife will appear only in two other places: in Act 3, when José and Escamillo duel; and in Act 4, when José stabs Carmen to death. Further, Carmen's playful, even mocking description of the treatment she expects in the military prison is of violent torture: *coupe-moi, brule-moi* ("Beat me, burn me"), she says, "I'll brave all your fire and steel." She is sentenced by Zuniga to jail, which would be death to a Gypsy. She must find some way to get away; she may have planned every bit of what follows.

Seguidilla
Left alone with José in the jailhouse, she first lies to him in an attempt to gain freedom. She claims to be from his homeland. Then, caught in her lie, she

claims it was meant as a compliment. Then, she plays her trump card: she saw him hide the acacia flower in his tunic earlier. She begins to sing, offering him sexual favors if he lets her escape. In her famous *Seguidilla*, she seduces José with the promise of sexual ecstasy at Lillas Pastia's inn, on the outskirts of Sevilla. Although he resists her as best he can, the very words he first objects to as the duet begins are what he is living for when the brief duet ends. Her nearness and the dream of love fulfilled she paints break down his resistance and his will collapses into her arms.

Carmen is in her own way genuinely attracted to José, as well. We will quickly see, however, that there is an extreme difference between these personalities. Carmen feels she can control herself in any relationship with a man, while Jose blindly leaps into love. He has more than met his match in Carmen; his emotional life hangs in the balance from the very beginning. For Carmen, José is a temporary amusement, as well as a step up from her usual partners. The *Seguidilla* is, however, not only an outright seduction of José; it is a contract: Carmen promises sex for freedom. This is a very serious matter for Carmen, and she will stick to her words. Blind to the greater danger, José agrees to Carmen's contract. Though Carmen will keep her bargain, which Jose mistakes for personal commitment, it is initially strictly to fulfill a verbal contract on her part. José may not understand this at all, just as he does not reckon with Carmen's criminal personality. With such a one, it is impossible to come away clean. Ultimately, it may be José's naiveté, his blind faith in sentimental love that elicits Carmen's disdain in Acts 3 and 4. Like Musette, she mocks the idea of a husband.

Act 1 ends with a reprise of the *Habanera*, reminding us that love is a Gypsy child, and containing the words *je t'aime* pointed at José. He hears only these words and not the phrase that follows them: *Si je t'aime, prends garde à toi!* Clearly, this reprise of the *Habanera* gives closure to the first act of *Carmen*. The repetition of the child image in Carmen's reprise has echoed the appearance of children in scene two. It has re-introduced the themes of her entrance aria and reminded us of her character's wild freedom and willingness to use love like any other tool at her disposal—among her tools, she now finds José. She has made a contract with a "naïve" and "dumb" soldier, and she will honor it.

In Act 2, she will attempt to add an improvised addendum to her contract with José: she tries to seduce José to the gypsy life on a whim. Carmen will fail to capture José's soul, but he will be forced to join the gypsies anyway. He is not as "gallant" as she had thought, but they will make the best of necessity as their encounter at Lillas Pastia's inn ends. Contrast the realistic irony of their situation at the end of Act 2 to Rodolfo and Mimi's poetry-driven fantasies two acts into *La Bohème*.

To fully appreciate the artistry of Bizet and his librettists, consider that Carmen's entrance aria is both an essential diagram of the title character's qualities and a design of *Carmen*'s plot: in the plot, we move through passionate game-playing to danger. Carmen's initial motivations for awakening José's passion are quite possibly a mixed bag: first, he is a challenge and she throws the flower at the indifferent José to evoke a reaction. Second, she desires freedom (*Seguidilla*). In Act 2, she will take him to her bed, initially, because it is Gypsy law: Carmen pays her debts. By Act 3, her attraction to him is over, negated by José's need to control Carmen.

But José is also an attractive, athletic man and, socially, a step up from the soldiers, the Gypsys or factory-worker lovers always available to her. The seed of Escamillo is, however, already planted in her desires. Escamillo is yet another step up, a big one, possibly a final one. Carmen's motivations are clear, but her inner recesses remain hidden. Because we do not ever see into her depths, the images she uses gather less dramatic or musical resonance about them than Mimi's do. From another perspective, they become more important as symbols with a high degree of mystery about them. She remains a teasing mystery, attracting and enticing, but never allowing certainty of knowledge.

One thing is certain: after Carmen initiates the relationship by throwing the flower—representing her self, perhaps symbolically her sexuality—at José, she seems much more in touch with her powers and her self than José is with his. From the moment José loosens Carmen's bonds during the *Seguidilla*, he begins a painful process toward self-knowledge, a peregrination through passion and obsessive jealousy into darkness.

Carmen has the least poetic language of our four operas and is the most successful drama. The dialogue is a flat prose, reflecting its naturalistic prose source. The most successful images are those born of pure action: the acacia flower Carmen throws at José, which comes to symbolize his passion for her; José's mother's kiss of forgiveness, and José's answering kiss; the mysterious ring Carmen flings at José, precipitating his final rage. These are images that appear once or twice, but are not developed dramatically or literally. It is abstractions or the specific qualities of characters, rather than specific objects, that are given musical motifs: Escamillo's elegance and bravery, José's ecstatic passion, Carmen's Fate, public celebration. This use of musical motif clearly places emphasis on the dominant characteristic of each character. These sub-arcs of *Carmen* are distinctly dramatic in nature, concerned with character qualities and the links of those qualities to action. *Carmen* is not so much poetic opera as pure music drama. *Carmen* is poetic in that its imagery and ideas are concerned with the creation and destruction of human love, but its essence is pure dramatic action, based in the dynamics of the soul.

Act 2: La fleur

THE PROTAGONIST'S STRUGGLE WITH PASSION AND HONOR

Musically and dramatically, José's *La fleur* aria is clearly the musical climax of Act 2. It is, in our terms, a lyric poem sung to soaring melody while enclosed in scintillating, exquisitely-orchestrated musical form—in short, an aria which offers us a glimpse into the inner life of a major character. This lyric exploration of personality allows us to empathize fully with the conflict of forces within him. The description of José's internal struggle in the aria is also a summary of the conflict that will propel the plot forward: his passion for Carmen versus his sense of duty.

Such conflict is typical for serious opera, which explores the themes of illicit love, its destructive effects on sentimental love, the condemnation of eros by society and/or Fate, and the inevitable appearance of square-toed death in passion's aftermath. What is extraordinary about *Carmen* and the character of José is the astute blending of literary, dramatic and musical elements that gives the plot of this opera and the internal world of these particular characters such enticing clarity, profound emotional effect, and depth of meaning.

Summary of Act 2

Act 2 occurs at night a month after Act 1. The setting is Lillas Pastia's inn outside Sevilla's city walls, somewhere between the sunny square in Sevilla and the mountain wilds of Act 3. Lillas Pastia is a smuggler and his inn is an open door to the underworld of crime. This act traces José's descent through that door. He will struggle hard with the forces tearing at him, and he will—momentarily—seem to win: he will find the strength to resist Carmen's charms. As with Oedipus, however, Fate has predetermined José's destiny; the forces—Carmen's nature and José's passion for her, Zuniga's interest in Carmen and José's resulting jealousy—swirling within and about him mix disastrously and hurtle him out of Lillas Pastia's inn into the mountains whose freedom *Carmen* so loves. This same freedom proves to be torture for a dishonored soldier with nothing left to lose but Carmen.

In Act 2, the plot provides Carmen and José with ample development. Carmen meets her match in the rising star of the bullfighting world, Escamillo of Granada, whose entrance aria we have briefly tasted in the *Prelude*. Escamillo is a stalwart figure and offers Carmen the final step up in her ladder of lovers. Yet she hesitates because of her debt to José. She also turns down a smuggling escapade to wait on José. (He was released two hours earlier.) "He's a good-looking guard and I like him," Carmen says. José's voice echoes off-stage and Carmen begins to consider the recruitment as well as the seduction of Don José.

After Carmen welcomes him, José's conflict over passion and honor soon begins. As Carmen's enticing dance rhythms are overpowered by the military trumpets, she tries to force José to choose between her charms and military duty. The crisis of choice elicits José's only aria, in which he describes his struggle and pours out his longing for Carmen. Challenged, the gypsy temptress forces his hand: Choose! José sadly chooses duty, but before he can depart, Zuniga forces the door of Fate open. In an act of jealous pride, José accosts his commanding officer and is forced to join the Gypsy smugglers. Already demoted and dishonored, he is now a criminal. With his mother and Micaela in the distance, he attempts to become Carmen's lover in the mountain wilds.

Four major musical numbers precede José's *La fleur* aria in Act 2. The first remarkable ensemble creates atmosphere and shows Carmen in her native habitat. The second is Escamillo's powerful and elegant entrance aria. The third is a comic quintet, emphasizing the theme of the power of feminine charm. And the fourth is Carmen's solo dance for José, the interruption of which by the trumpet of roll-call, presents Carmen with an unexpected challenge. All this precipitates José's outburst of soul in *La fleur*. This response to Carmen's scornful dismissal of his passion reveals his deepest longing and the conflict he feels between his passion for her and his sense of duty to the military—and, by extension, to his occupation, his place in society, Micaela, and his mother. At this point, he is still enough in control to act rationally. The forces of Fate will soon defeat this last vestige of control.

Act 2, Scenes 1, 2 and 3

Typical of French opera, the first scene of the act offers local color to set the scene and create atmosphere. We are swept into Act 2 by a *Romalis*, a Gypsy dance, full of swirling motion and feverish rhythms. The orchestra recreates the vibrant strumming of the guitar and the tambourines ring. Rings sparkle against dusky cheeks. This piece's ever-increasing rhythms sweep us up, hinting at the erotic fantasy that Carmen offers and José has dreamed of for a month from his prison cell. José is not on stage to see the dance, but it helps us understand his obsession with Carmen throughout the opera. Afterwards, Carmen and her friends refuse to accompany the soldiers to the theater—as they have so often done. Zuniga tells Carmen that José has been duly punished for letting her escape, and was released two hours ago. Before the soldiers leave, Zuniga says he will return in an hour. This he does, despite Carmen's discouragement.

Enter Escamillo, a man who immediately shares a toast with the military, for both men enjoy combat. In the *brindisi* that follows, Escamillo gives us a rich description of what we will hear off-stage in Act 4: the roar and blood of the bullfight. He describes the atmosphere of the arena as passionate, thus recreating the passions of the dance we have just experienced and attracting all who hear him, especially *la Carmencita*. Like Rodolfo, he speaks of the dark eyes watching him as he fights. Love is his reason to fight and his reward. Like Carmen, he lives with danger: *Toreador, en garde!* Sparks fly between the kindred spirits: Carmen is dangerous, and Escamillo lives for danger.

In fact, the entirety of *Carmen* is laced with danger from Carmen's *prends garde à toi* through this aria to Act 3's opening *Prend garde de faire*, the duel later in Act 3 (*Mettez vous en garde*) to Frasquita's *Prend garde* to Carmen before she exits the arena to meet José. Many operas occur in times of political danger or social upheaval, and many are situated at least in part in an underworld of crime. All four of our operas, for example, involve the demimonde. All involve prostitution, in that three of our heroines (Mimi, Carmen and Violetta) are prostitutes, while Tom Rakewell is seduced by one, Mother Goose, in *The Rake's Progress*.

After Escamillo exits, the Gypsies get down to business, but Carmen refuses to fulfill her usual role for the smugglers. She eagerly awaits José and even the flattery of the quintet cannot budge her. This quintet, while distinctly comic in effect, stresses a theme central to *Carmen*: woman's power to seduce. While the subject is fancifully addressed, it takes its place as part of the complex musical-dramatic tapestry of a remarkably well integrated and consistent dramatic structure. While the quintet can agree on the subject, Carmen will not budge from her refusal. Like José, she chooses love over "duty," at least in the moment.

Whimsically, Dancairo suggests that, if Carmen will not come alone, then she might as well draft her latest conquest, José, to their cause. After all, she has never let love get in the way of business before. Carmen decides to try. It begins as a mere whim, but quickly involves her pride; what began as a whim will have extraordinary consequences for both José and Carmen.

Scene 5—José, Carmen

José's entrance is heightened by his off-stage singing, which draws nearer as he sings a Basque song dedicated to fighting and loving. (Later in the act, the *retrait* trumpets are directed to approach in the same way, but they pass by the inn. Composers love off- and on-stage music, which is used to great effect in all four of our operas.) After José has voiced his passion for her, Carmen teases him with the mention of her dancing for Zuniga earlier. To calm his jealousy, she agrees to dance for him and she does so, to pure vocal melody while accompanying herself with castanets. José, like Rodolfo, openly admits to being jealous, a quality indicative of his lack of self-knowledge and control. Bizet now chooses to express José's conflict in purely musical terms. As Carmen performs her wordless song and dance, the military trumpets we first heard in Act 1 begin to sound in the distance. As they near the inn, they become more pronounced and overpower her, foreshadowing José's ability, at this point, to risk resisting her charms.

The scene builds effectively through a duet juxtaposing Carmen's mocking of José's sense of duty with his pleading for her to understand his conflict. Carmen admits bitterly that she was "almost in love," while José admits he had never known real passion before her. But Carmen cannot retreat from her jealous mockery of his values, until she has more emotional ammunition to get what she wants. For Carmen, José's aria is little more than information about José that she can use to control him, to gain the upper hand.

José's aria is the first of three scenes in *Carmen* crucial to his character and the drama as a whole. Though Jose's vocal part is quite demanding, this aria is José's only sustained solo vocal effort. It shares with the Act 3 and Act 4 Finales certain organic qualities—including quality of poetic expression, melodic contour and orchestral color—reflecting the dramatic values essential to great music drama: creative union of plot and character in the literary-dramatic-musical weave of elements in theme and musical form. These three musical numbers record the birth of love, passion's turn to hate, and finally love's death. In each musical scene, a growing conflict in José becomes more evident. Finally, his obsessive desire for Carmen gnaws away his guilty, obsessive soul until a raging specter of a man remains.

José's love for Carmen was from the beginning pure passion, erotic in nature, but it becomes sentimental and possessive. And Carmen never allows such passion the luxury of sentiment—until Escamillo. In contrast, José's duet with Micaela was about sentimental love of house and home. *La fleur* is, however, about passion and passion's transformation into love. Carmen has become a luminous image to José. When at the climax of the aria, José utters, *Carmen, je t'aime*, he has opened himself to betrayal, crossed into dangerous lands. He is vulnerable and Carmen knows just what to do: she continues her teasing, ever more sure of herself, until she drives Jose to distraction. No, she utters. You do not love me because you will not do what I ask: desert and become a smuggler. Later, in Act 4, José will finally offer to give in voluntarily and do whatever Carmen wants. But by then it is too late: Carmen no longer loves him enough to care what he does.

There are two crucial moments in Act 2: José's declaration of love is the first; it is an internal revelation shared with Carmen. The second is determined by external forces, by Fate: it is Zuniga's entrance, just as José attempts to leave Carmen to return to his duty as a soldier. The first is character-centered, the second a function of plot. Believable character action is usually determined by a balance of internal and external forces—forces of character and plot. Zuniga's appearance awakens José's jealousy and the resulting swordplay sends the former corporal on his crooked path into the mountains, then a month later back down toward the bullring in Sevilla.

After attacking Zuniga, José has, as he puts it—*Il le faut bien*—no other choice but to join the Gypsies. This flippant remark is perhaps meant to repay Carmen for her ridicule of the values and occupation earlier. She accepts his barb, ironically calling it *n'est pas gallant* (not very gallant). José has entered Carmen's verbal world, resorting to sarcasm, a medium we cannot imagine him employing earlier. Carmen, being contractually bound to Jose, is hoisted on her own petard here. Her own pride as a seductress is at stake and Carmen, even though scorned, is flexible enough at this point to accept José as lover and fellow smuggler... for a time.

José's Aria

José's aria is striking for its musical variety and in its portrayal of contrastive dramatic elements of hate and love with honesty and passionate strength. In both its lyric and dramatic qualities, it is outstanding. The aria represents the struggle between irreconcilable forces, and depicts the struggle beautifully through the organic use of literary, dramatic and musical elements. The aria's text is a lyric poem and as such also a study of imagery, real and remembered. Bizet bases the first of José's rhymed quatrains on the flower Carmen threw at José in Act 1. He kept the dried and faded flower on his chest during the lonely hours in prison and the scent of the flower came to represent Carmen's exotic beauty and fueled his passion for her.

After exposition in the first two quatrains, in the third verse José remembers his disgrace and demotion, and his passion comes close to hate as he bemoans his destiny. But the fourth quatrain contains the turning point of the internal argument: he accuses himself of blasphemy and, senses reeling, is overwhelmed by his memory of his one hope, one desire while in prison: simply to see Carmen again. His rapture is rhythmically delineated as he worshipfully recalls the first time her eyes captured his heart in the four lines of the last quatrain; and he quietly declares his love.

The poetic text of this aria consists of four sections—remembrance, conflict, resolution and declaration. Each has its own melodic power, and each leads logically to the next section after reaching its own climax, in a pattern of ever-increasing intensity that peaks quietly and decisively with the words, *Carmen je t'aime.* The first section is calm and descriptive, its melody broad and attractive. The beginning intervals of the melody are sometimes large and involving, as if José has trouble beginning to express his feelings, but the first melody quickly becomes smoothly shaped, almost wave-like as he begins his narrative until it climaxes with *je m'anivrais* on a high A-natural. Throughout the melodic development of the first section, notice the off-beat pulse of the accompaniment underlying the melody and creating a tension reflecting José's uneasiness at his heart overriding his conscience. This same rhythmic tension will return in the final duet of Act 4, as José pleads with Carmen to return to him, but the melodic design is quite different in the Act 4 duet.

The second section charts the growth of his resentment and then hatred in rising lines, and the third section transforms this tension into the realization of desire in gradually-ascending, non-melodic phrases. As the voice ascends, the orchestra grows more intense in support of the voice: the strings generate swelling patterns and woodwind and brass join in supporting chorus with a strong rhythmic pulse. As always in *Carmen*, the woodwind colors are striking. This realization peaks on a pronoun representing Carmen: *Te revoir, O Carmen*, and the rhapsodic fourth section begins. Three ecstatic phrases now descend, not reversing the earlier climactic transition from conflict to ecstasy, but tracing the lingering waves of pleasure following it.

Notice how three descending phrases are now followed by a contrastive, ascending one. As the third phrase fades away, a warm chord on the harp introduces the calm, ascending declaration of love that climaxes on a high B-flat. José's voice gathers the warm strength of the middle register before ascending to the upward extremity of his range to demonstrate passion. Contrast is one of the great structural principles of musical, as well as dramatic structures.

Each section of the aria contains a distinctive climax, which is signaled by a tone in the upper register of the tenor voice, and each climax increases in power until the final one takes the tenor to the extreme of his range. From the singer's perspective, this aria is lyric, yet the forceful vocal power it demands is expressive of José's blunt, needful character. It begins in an exposed vocal area, on F-natural, and the sudden jump to the A-natural at the climax of the first part is strenuous. The second and third parts are tiring to sing—the entire vocal part of José is strenuous—and the final phrases demand technical elegance to sing well. José's voice must be full and strong to answer the dramatic and vocal requirements, for the orchestration is quite full at climactic moments. Yet a controlled delicacy is required at several other crucial moments, including the final phrases of this great aria.

La fleur and the Luminous Image

This aria creates a luminous image of great power and beauty. It is José's internalized image of Carmen. This is the second luminous image José has created. The first was José's mother, in the Act 1 duet with Micaela. These two luminous images symbolize José's inner conflict: his mother represents sentimental love, occupation, social respectability, while Carmen represents erotic and illicit love, danger, and living outside social constraint. The image of the flower is also crucial and signals the death of sentimental love in José. As the flower wilts, so does his memory of his previous life, and the women in it, Micaela and his mother. But the fragrance of the acacia, representing illicit passion, lives on. If the flower represents all women, all wilt with the flower except Carmen, whose dark passion the flower's fragrance has come to represent for José.

The entire aria is a reminiscence, a frozen moment in which José collects his thoughts. It works to persuade Carmen of José's love and also to inform her of his vulnerability. Musical form reflects character in *La fleur*. A three-dimensional figure stands before Carmen and us at aria's end. This aria recounts internal growth, the blossoming of passionate love from shame and lust. The aria is also a confession of sorts, and the wrong one to give a secular priestess. José the actor takes a dried flower—a stage property and a poetic image of surprising power—from his uniform's tunic, then tells the story of his emotional journey to Carmen, the cause of that journey. He stands in uniform, the emblem of his occupation, in a dimly lit inn where we have just witnessed both the impassioned, whirling dance of the Gypsy crowd and a comic quintet as contrastive numbers.

He has, at *Carmen*'s insistence, removed his sword, belt and helmet. His gestures are few: he is describing a lonely journey of the soul. He must encircle and convince Carmen with his words, not his weapons. He must convince and persuade Carmen of his love and sincerity, as Alfredo will convince Violetta in Act 1 of *La Traviata*. The intricate emotional nature of José's struggle is also reflected in the cross rhythms in the accompaniment and alternating use of force and lyricism in the vocal lines. Most importantly, at every moment in the aria literary, dramatic and musical elements are united by musical form and dramatic purpose, which continually enhances character and advances the plot.

The aria is introduced by the plaintive statement of the "Carmen's Fate" motif. The melancholy rendition of the motif here seems to recreate José's lonely cell and embody the enticing pull of Carmen's eyes on him; just as the aria's final striking chord of the harp heralds his commitment to Carmen and the release of his tormented spirit into passionate longing. *La fleur* is a highly individual, finely cut musical gem, firmly set in *Carmen*'s musical-dramatic necklace. It contains enough common images and themes to place it firmly within the plot structure as literature, drama and music. It also has enough unique qualities to indicate the complexity and dynamic growth of the complex character that sings it. Poetically and musically, it represents the internal world of a major character in emotional crisis.

At the end of Act 2, José has no choice but to retreat to Carmen's mountains, which are no doubt as symbolically charged as Hemingway's white hills. José joins the chorus praising Carmen's *liberté*, but the damage to his character is done. Act 2's action continues the rising action begun with the *Seguidilla* at the end of Act 1, and the tensions will continue to rise through the Act 3 finale—the opera's dramatic climax and the *peripitae*—the turning point—of its protagonist, José. We are now firmly embedded in the rising action, the stress and strain of the wrestling of individual character destiny with the greater force of Fate—and of eros and thanatos, which Fate wields.

Act 3 Finale

THE HERO'S TURNING FROM EROS TO THANATOS

The plot's action continues to rise throughout Act 3 to its climax in the magnificent Finale. In this ensemble, all major characters and issues bring their force to bear on the protagonist, who is called on to make hard choices once and for all. José is here forced to his *peripitae*, Aristotle's term for the critical turning point of the plot based in character crisis. José fought the good fight in Act 2 and lost. Suddenly isolated from all he knows, José reluctantly chooses to join Carmen at the end of Act 2. For Carmen, José's choice is now of no concern, for her affections have moved from José to Escamillo. Sensing this, José struggles with the loss of the only thing he now desires to possess. José's need to love Carmen obsessively indicates his flaw, his inability to prevent his passions from overriding his sense of right and wrong. When he utters the haunting phrase to Micaela *Laissez moi, car je suis damné* (Leave me, for I am damned) in the Act 3 Finale, it is clear that on some level he recognizes that Carmen is only part of the larger mechanism of Fate pulling him down to—in his own terms—hell. Oedipus has similar insight into his personal destiny only at the very end of *Oedipus Rex*.

Would José qualify as an protagonist using Aristotle's criteria? In every way but one: José is not of noble birth. Yet we feel his fall as strongly as we feel Oedipus's. We are the products of Western Civilization's long process of democratization and belong to a culture where nobility is more a function of behavior than birth. José is a country lad and, as Romantic tradition has it, more inherently noble than a city dweller. In the end, we are citizens of a modern world: our emotional criteria for catharsis have changed. The origin of our heroes is not as important as it once was. If an American salesman can be a tragic hero, why not a corporal in the Spanish army?

Act 3 Finale

Act 3 opens with a dark, moody warning to all listeners: dark forces lie in wait for the unwary—among whom, we will soon find out, are all the major characters of *Carmen*. One slip, sings the chorus of smugglers, and all is over. It is the story of José's life. Yet he is making the best of it, singing along with Carmen and the others of courage and reward. All is not well with the lovers, however, and almost immediately we see that José and Carmen are at odds. The issue is freedom—hers. He attempts to "make peace" with her, but she wants personal autonomy. She loves him "less than before" and if this continues, she says, she will not love him at all. Their confrontation turns violent and she asks darkly, "You'll kill me?" She will soon read this in the cards. José then mutters, *Tu es le diable, Carmen?* We see right to the bottom of the pit. These lines will be repeated in slightly different form in the lovers' final confrontation in Act 4.

Now comes musical lightness in the form of the card trio, a musical number of great musical charm and complexity. It is also a most concise statement of the theme of Eros and Thanatos—*l'amour è la mort*. Passion and death are musically and dramatically tied together in this number with a power unique to opera. The three Gypsies turn and read Tarot cards to highly descriptive music. Frasquita and Mercedes offer two variations of the theme of a dominant woman's seductive power: one marries for love, the other for money; both fulfill their fantasies. Carmen, however, finds only violent death in the cards: first for herself, then José.

When these two distinct ideas—romantic fantasy and death—mix in the charged atmosphere of a musical-dramatic form, there is a distinct depth of effect that is only created in a fine opera ensemble: opposites combine in harmony. *Recondita armonia*. Amidst the excited chatter of her friends, Carmen clearly feels death's cold hand on her throat. Still, she is determined to live freely—she agrees to "pacify" the border guards with Frasquita and Mercedes. This will ensure safe passage for the smugglers, but Carmen enjoys expressing her pleasure at the prospect of making love to another man—with José's knowledge. She will blind him with pleasure, she brags, so that her friends may pass. This declaration of personal and sexual freedom is unique to Carmen in opera. This is the life she must have to live at all; she must have the freedom to express herself sexually exactly as she chooses. José has attempted to keep her on a leash in the mountains for a month. She has had enough and uses her "professional" responsibilities as the occasion for her declaration. Typically, it is short and blunt. Once again, José is reduced to an ineffectual bulk, able only to mutter her name passionately, ineffectively. She is clearly too clever and manipulative for José in her chosen environment. His rage grows and will break out in the Act 3 Finale.

In immediate contrast to Carmen's passion and superstition, we now experience Micaela's sentimental love and religious faith. Micaela enters and, in fear for her life (as well as in despair for her love), offers a beautiful prayer, orchestrated with some of the colors of the Act 1 duet she shared with José. Her prayer is interrupted by nagging doubts and despair, then resumes, so that the aria is in ABA form. An appeal for strength opens and closes this powerful aria. It begins with a nervous cello pattern set against French horns singing of certain faith. Clearly, the French horns tell us that Micaela is a character with strong faith and nobility of purpose. This enticing setting is interrupted by part B of the aria, an image of Carmen featuring jagged melodic patterns representing the dark dangers of illicit passion and danger. Michaela then recovers and returns to the original plea for courage to fulfill her mission in the wild mountains. This aria features remarkably beautiful accompaniment in the strings and resolute power from the brass. That Michaela's prayer is interrupted by her fears represents a psychological truth and does not diminish this character's stature. Yet she too will be swept away by the mechanisms of Fate.

Act 3 is a study of danger and conflict. Both increase until the Finale. José and Carmen are at each other. Micaela is torn by dismay and doubt and will soon be shocked by seeing her worst fears realized. After Micaela's aria, Escamillo enters, bringing word to José of Carmen's intent to move on to another man, Escamillo himself. Violence quickly breaks out between the rivals. José's violence rises to the surface and does not sink again. He tries his best to kill Escamillo, but fails. Just as Carmen saved José in Act 2 by interrupting his duel with Zuniga, she now saves her Escamillo from José. Both times, Carmen saves her future lovers, demonstrating her strength and control of immediate circumstances.

Escamillo taunts José and invites Carmen to his bullfight in Sevilla with these words: "Those who love me will come." He departs, his message clear. Scorned and defeated, José's fury bursts out and, fueled by Micaela's pleading, he threatens Carmen's life before everyone and condemns her in a jealous fury. Overcome by jealousy and injured pride, he cries that he himself is damned (*Car je suis condamné!*) and to Carmen snarls, "You are mine, daughter of Hell." Evoking the powers of Destiny and Fate, he swears never to leave her. As the chorus warns José *Prends garde*, Micaela offers her final sad bit of information to crush José: his mother lies dying and wishes to see him. José's mother, Carmen's dialectical opposite and the only remaining symbol of decency and goodness in José's consciousness, lies near death. It is important to remember that, when José enters in the next act, he comes from the grave of his mother and that he left a wiser Micaela there at the graveside.

José leaves with Micaela, but cannot depart without one final threat to Carmen. Escamillo has the last word, however, as a reprise of his entrance aria drifts like Act 1's sensuous smoking chorus over the ravines to Carmen, who smiles secretly in the knowledge of her power to shape the destinies of the men about her. But, as the strains of the smuggler's chorus which opened Act 3 softly close it, there is an uncertain, almost comic sliding of the melody's end downward toward chaos.

Character Development

As we review Act 3, we should briefly analyze *Carmen*'s four major characters and their relationships. Foils like Escamillo and Micaela serve to elucidate the main characters by contrasting with them in appearance, action, and values. The vital purposes of this subplot are to contrast with, give variety to, and causally vary the main plot. The main plot of *Carmen* is a study in passion: at first Carmen is—to use Marcello and Rodolfo's Act 1 metaphor in *La Bohème*—the fire and José the wood; later, the elements are reversed. The suspense and tragic irony that stalk these two from their chance meeting to their final argument never fails. We wait for what we have known from the beginning must happen in the paradoxical marriage of themes that constitutes poetic tragedy.

Carmen is both cunning and courageous; she is, above all, a survivor. She reacts provocatively to those around her, and usually gets her way with them. She knows just how to entice the naive José and manipulate him to let her escape. Yet she is not mean or ungrateful; she sticks to her bargain. When she meets a man who is her equal (Escamillo), she does not rush to impress or claim him. She is cool passion and sensuality to both José and Escamillo at first meeting.

The flute in the lower register expresses her sensuous nature, and the seductive rhythms of the cello pulse through her actions, suggesting the sensual nature of her depths. Notice how differently Bizet uses the cello to differentiate between Carmen and Micaela in arias crucial to character portrayal. Carmen's cello in Act 1 is all lithe sensuousness in the *Seguidilla*, while the restless architectonics of Micaela's Act 3 cello expresses her emotional unrest.

Freedom is Carmen's essence, but her need for love and control is also great. Perhaps deeper is a need to surrender, but to one who shares her need for freedom. She sees this man, her male counterpart, in Escamillo. Carmen usually sings in a closed verse form, i.e. a verse form carefully structured by rhyme and rhythm reflecting the need for order, as in Carmen's *Seguidilla*, but this form is expanded into a duet so as to give it the appearance of freedom. Contrast this with José's more free, organic verse form in *La fleur*, which, it might be argued, reflects faith in an inherent order. The verse forms thus indicate character values: Carmen is calculating and understands the need for absolute control when faced with the chaos of existence, while José acts spontaneously and with faith in Goodness (represented by Micaela and his mother) and order (the military). This patterning of poetic form constitutes a literary sub-arc and complements the musical dramatic arc of this greatest of all musical dramas.

Carmen's dialogue, songs, recitative and ensemble work all melt into the dramatic action, making her the central vocal component, as well as the length-iest dramatic role in the opera. Carmen's dance and her own accompaniment of her dance with castanets indicate her independence and sensual nature. She also uses silence and wordless sound in her total range of expression; she is remark-able for the variety of her gestures. Yet her flashy exterior and sensual attitudes attract us. She is outside the law and strong, a minority cosmopolitan seeking social station. She is both cunning and honest—unique in literature. In utter contrast to Carmen is the figure of José, who is, initially, more acted upon—by Carmen, his mother, Micaela, Zuniga, and, ultimately, Fate—than in control. It is not unusual for a mythic hero, from whom the Greek protagonists evolved, to remain passive for the first part of a story. José will, of course, become an instru-ment of action after he is threatened by the forces surrounding him. When, how-ever, José does take moral action, i.e. resists Carmen, he falls victim to the machi-nations of Fate in the form of Zuniga's bursting through Carmen's door in Act 2.

José does love passionately and deeply. For her part, Carmen cannot know the nature of this conservative Basque when she first approaches him, and she cannot foresee the circumstances that will drive his unique combination of despair and guilt into tragic action. She does, however, see her own and José's destinies in the cards in Act 3 and bravely faces the possibility that the cards do not lie. José is violent and moody. We know this from the music given him. There is an air of melancholy self-doubt reflected in the bassoon of the Act 2 interlude, which hints at José's Act 2 entrance aria, and the haunting *cor anglais* solo that introduces his great aria later in the act. Yet his personality is complex and dynamic, despite its moodiness and directness. He grows from the month in prison and emerges a man of awakened sensibilities. His duet with Carmen and the following aria in Act 2 demonstrate his heightened awareness. His aria has an organic quality expressive of naturalness, openness and maturity, with each section pulsing with its own rhythmic center and flowing effortlessly into the next. His self-knowledge will not protect him from Fate, however. Nor can it protect Carmen, who ultimately feels she can deal with whatever Fate sends her, even death.

Micaela is innocent and pure, but—like Anne Truelove in *The Rake's Progress*—also strong and determined. Her actions speak louder than her words, but the words of her Act 3 aria are quite strong. Her music, like José's, features strings; and, like Mimi, her stronger moments are supported by the French horn, instilling them with nobility. The numbers she sings have the effect of being predictable and sometimes religious in tone. She embodies the standard, sentimental and socially acceptable impulse. She, like Carmen, has courage, honesty and strength—otherwise they could not be more different. One clue to her character is her music, which must be sung by a strong, full lyric soprano. Her soaring melody lines reflect lyric honesty and a strong character.

Escamillo has the self-confidence of the professional athlete. His character is set and is reflected in the standard, regular forms of the songs and duets he sings. Brass accompanies him in his showy entrance aria, as it will in his parade to the bullring. Both numbers echo the ritual of the bullfight and Escamillo's role as social hero. Escamillo contrasts with José, who touches us more deeply. Despite his touch of bravado, José is youthful and vulnerable. Bizet treats José in a different way from the other principle characters. He is gradually defined musically, primarily in terms of his sensual awakening by Carmen. He is not given a formal entrance aria, as are Carmen and Escamillo. His music contrasts with the defined forms given others, and his development is marked by increasingly unconventional musical patterns, climaxing with the Act 3 Finale.

BIZET'S *Carmen*

Act 4 Finale

ASCENT AND DESCENT

In Act 4, we return to the city of Sevilla, where we began. We have journeyed with our characters out into the wilds of nature and now return to where the story of Carmen and José's passion began. In Act 3's Finale, we come to the *epitasis* of the plot; we are on top of the plot's inherent building tension. The violent resolution of this tension still lies before us, but first we will witness the contrastive, vibrant return to local color for which Carmen and French opera generally is so famous. You will remember this method of providing scenic closure for an opera from *La Bohème*. You will also see it in *La Traviata* and *The Rake's Progress*—though nothing in Stravinsky's great opera is quite what it appears at first glance.

Carmen's mode is straightforward realism. Any romantic elements are subdued and ultimately defeated. *Carmen* might in some ways be seen as operatic Naturalism, with its environmental determinism, gritty settings, and the ambivalence of Nature. As the denouement of *Carmen* begins, however, we are overwhelmed with brilliant orchestral music and pure operatic spectacle. As always with Bizet, there is purpose in such effect. In brilliant contrast to the gloomy setting and seething emotions of Act 3's Finale, we are immediately deluged at Act 4's beginning with visual and auditory splendor. Crowds swarm over the stage, creating the festival atmosphere that was predicted in the *Prelude* before Act 1 and described in Escamillo's Act 2 aria. It is the day of the bullfight, starring Escamillo of Granada. Remember the opening of *La Bohème*'s second act? Puccini learned a great deal from Bizet.

Three of our major characters are here, somewhere in the crowd. Escamillo and Carmen have ascended to the heights of passion and success, while José has descended to a personal hell: he has lost everything he ever wanted and is now clinging to the luminous image of Carmen in his inscape. Presumably, José's mother is now in her grave. Of Micaela we learn nothing more.

The *Cuadrilla* begins its procession—reminding us of the procession of the Paris Guard led by the *Tambourmajor* in *La Bohème*—with the brilliant march we heard in *Carmen*'s *Prelude*, before the Act 1 curtain. The urchins of Act 1 are also there, hailing another kind of public hero. As the march crests and Escamillo appears, cries of "the blade" remind us of the omnipresence of weapons in Carmen, and then strains of Escamillo's entrance aria ring out.

In a quiet moment, Escamillo and Carmen publicly express their passion. Escamillo wants to prove worthy of Carmen's love by the brilliance of his performance. Striking a deep tone of irony for the wary listener, Carmen swears that death may take her if she has ever loved a man more than Escamillo. The discordant brass interrupts these pleasantries, as the mayor enters. Frasquita has seen José in the crowd and warns Carmen. Carmen will not retreat and stays to face José as the crowd enters the arena. The orchestra warns us of the danger by alternating sliding motifs of cold fear with the retreating refrains of the march.

Rarely have public order and impending personal chaos been so successfully and simply juxtaposed as in the great final duet of this opera. One thinks of the final scene of *Aida*, the first and final scenes of *La Traviata*, the Auction Scene in *The Rake's Progress*, but nowhere is it so simply and clearly done as here. The duet, which begins with two simple statements, is a literary, dramatic and musical watershed. To Carmen's initial declaration of bravery and honesty, José says he does not want to threaten; he begs her to come away with him. In Spain, he is a wanted man, so he begs her to leave with him for a new land. Carmen refuses flatly, insisting that their affair is over. José does not seem to hear her and claims that she can save them both. Carmen answers fatalistically that she knows it is the hour of her death, but even so she will not yield to José. She will not give in. Then, the two repeat their statements again in duet: it is clear that neither hears the other clearly, so full is each of their own despair (José) and superstition (Carmen) with regard to the other.

For José, his duet contains the moment of realization that Carmen really does not love him any longer, to which Carmen, choosing to ignore the pain and despair in José's tone, bluntly answers, *Non, je ne t'aime plus* ("No, I don't love you"). Locked into her superstition, Carmen confronts the desperate José recklessly with the truth of her passion for Escamillo. Soon both are reduced to the violent gestures that can only lead to a tragic conclusion. As José's pleading intensifies, then slowly transmogrifies to denial then rage, the integrity of Bizet's understanding of the musical-dramatic formula becomes evident. The final duet pulls plot action, character and theme together as no other musical scene in opera. A great deal has to do with interlocking qualities of character and the musical portrayal of these qualities.

José's musical expression progresses, especially rhythmically, from a sensuous pleading (heightened by syncopation in the accompaniment) through passionate denial in melody—*Carmen, je t'aime, je t'adore!*—until, finally, a stunned realization is announced by the brass and echoed in José's declarative statement *Tu ne m'aime donc plus!* Finally, fury at the chaos his life has become without Carmen overwhelms him.

If José is a musical stream that becomes a torrent, Carmen is the rock he cannot move. She scornfully declares the death of her love for him. She even mocks him, calling his efforts "superfluous," meaningless. Her new love is as strong as her unshakable need for freedom. Her music glows in intensity, but varies little rhythmically. This expresses her determination, her—in her own words—inflexibility. Carmen is, she feels, in control and her music shows this by its steadiness of rhythm. Her language is also consistent: it grows in intensity, but until the very end reflects control and inner security. A part of this may be Carmen's attitude toward death, the thought of which she lives with every day; death is, in short, a part of her reality. (José is himself no stranger to death.) In the final stages of José's pleading, off-stage snatches of the infectious Procession of the *Cuadrilla* burst from the arena to thrill Carmen and drive José to jealous distraction. Bizet's musical design represents Fate at this point, and both

Carmen and José are caught in its orchestral web.

Underlying the scene, the Fate motif weaves its ever-insinuating and intrusive presence into the audience's sense of the destiny of these two lovers, until the tensions grow so great that musical order seems to break down altogether after the first choral intrusion into the lover's final quarrel. As the chorus climaxes, the stage directions call for Carmen to utter a cry of "pride and joy." As she attempts to run to the arena, José traps her physically. No longer free, Carmen becomes even more scornful, precipitating José's final furious acts. Now the two pawns of Fate can only scream at each other while caught in the musical whirlwind of chaos. Never has the chaos of human love gone wrong been more vividly created than when José and Carmen can only struggle violently and shout their basic needs at each other as the orchestra's machine-like writhing perfectly mirrors Fate's destructive mechanism: José: *Où vas-tu?* ("Where are you going?"). Carmen: *Laisse-moi* ("Let me go!") This is a most striking, almost surrealistic use of musical effect to capture the futility of human striving in Fate's hands.

We have not reached the emotional height and dramatic climax of the duet. This follows Carmen's forceful confession of her complete love for Escamillo, echoing her fatalistic acceptance of the cards. This seems to provokes José's extreme response to the situation: *Je l'aime, et devant la mort meme, / Je réperai que je l'aime.* ("Even in the face of death, I repeat that I love him.") José's abusive rage then bursts forth as the Fate motif dominates his musical expression, filling every gap between his utterances and overpowering the reappearance of the March motif from the off-stage crowd.

As the Fate motif musically overpowers the march, which at this point perhaps represents Carmen's unattainable goals, Carmen once again throws an object at José, this time a ring he gave her to represent their love. At this point, José comes to personify that cold force that Carmen has long expected: Death. And the orchestral brass sings out a resonant warning as José surrenders to the authorities. *La Bohème*'s final orchestral statements—also in the brass—concentrate on Mimi's final voyage and, indirectly, on the tragedy of her life; but *Carmen*'s final orchestral message is a warning primary to operatic territory: beware the effects of reckless passion on gentle souls. That so pregnant a symbol as the ring should be used so briefly and effectively in the final scene says a great deal about the economy and effectiveness of how literary, as well as dramatic and musical elements are employed in *Carmen*'s action.

Consider also the extraordinary use of all elements at the first point of character realization of this last duet when José asks, "in anguish," twice, *Tu ne m'aimes donc plus?* ("So you don't love me any more?") The first utterance is introduced by pulsing timpani and is in José's lower register, suggesting its emergence from his depths. He considers the possibility, but it is not real to him. The second utterance, however, reflects the full force of his conscious fear: it is in his upper register and accompanied convincingly by brass—the orchestral color of dramatic truth. The silence between the phrases also plays a part in the power of this passage, which lifts opera out of sentiment and melodrama into its rightful realm of heightened poetic expression. Silence is to music what punctuation is to language.

José's characterization and fall from the little glory his destiny held for him uses every element at the operatic composer's command. His descent is mapped with verbal clarity in poetry as he moves from eloquence in his great Act 2 aria to incoherent pleading and psychosis in the final duet. His emotional descent is clearly portrayed by music, beginning lyrically in Acts 1 and 2—sometimes with syncopated cross currents of uncertainty underneath—but progressing to ever-increasing forceful, finally violent outbursts in Acts 3 and 4. The plot moves this character from situations where his control fails him further and further along into situations where he becomes less aware that he had ever had control. José is a protagonist of great dramatic power. The crux of this tragedy is expressed in the final action in the final scene of the opera: from his lowest point, his social/ professional/personal nadir, José pulls Carmen down from her social and personal heights into his vertiginous descent into death.

BIZET'S *Carmen*

The Operatic Ensemble

The operatic ensemble is a point in the drama, one could argue, at which musical form with its simultaneous voices encroaches on dramatic logic, i.e. linear cause and effect. There are several factors to consider when approaching ensembles critically. Poetically and dramatically, they are on the surface difficult to immediately comprehend as literature, because many characters may be singing different lyrics simultaneously. The listener must prepare him- or herself before encountering an ensemble.

Great operatic ensembles unite musical form, dramatic logic, and psychological truth. Within musical-dramatic context, it also creates a defining dimension crucial to opera. Time stops, then expands as we hear many voices express diverse thoughts simultaneously. It is really quite extraordinary in that the linear aspects of literary and dramatic time are suspended, and musical form reigns supreme. We can begin to discuss music's contribution to opera in general terms now. The operatic ensemble is largely the creation of musical form, which treats soloists as a group of instruments playing simultaneously. Words disappear into musical complexity. This makes the words no less important, but it does make special demands on the audience: one must prepare for a performance to fully appreciate it.

Dramatic high points in Greek poetic tragedy inevitably involve the chorus and/or a number of characters other than the protagonist. The same is generally true for opera. The musical climax of *La Bohème*, it seems to me, is clearly the quartet that ends Act 3; of *Carmen*, the great Act 3 Finale; of *La Traviata*, the Finale of Act 2, scene 2; for *The Rake's Progress*, the Auction Scene (Act 3, scene 1). All of these scenes occupy the same position in the plot as the others, roughly three-fourths of the way through the plot. These scenes are the dramatic, visual and musical climaxes of their operas.

The Nature of the Ensemble

Ensembles are the result of music striving to fulfill its natural role in the evolution of music drama. Great art in all forms tends toward a balance of complexity and integrity (the number of elements functioning simultaneously in harmonious clarity). Vocal music can fulfill itself only in the ensemble, where several, sometimes many voices present diverse literary, dramatic and musical perspectives simultaneously.

Following the principles of musical harmony, ensembles make the (dramatic) present multi-dimensional. This presents us with a wonderful challenge that we can easily meet with minimal preparation, one that reflects the reality which surrounds us as sentient beings in every waking moment of our lives. Our senses limit us to one channel of perception at a time, but the operatic ensemble is, in a sense, asking us to expand our abilities. Opera is, in a sense, giving us an opportunity to recognize the beauty and complexity that envelop us every waking moment. That is one of art's purposes, generally speaking.

The primary reason that operatic plots often appear jaggedly episodic, i.e. broken into scenes separated by weeks or months, is in part because of the compression of real time demanded of plots involving musical forms that simultaneously freeze real time and expand human consciousness. The musical number does freeze time in that during an aria, we enter into the still inner world of character reflection and memory and experience their fantasies, dreams, visions. In contrast, duets such as Mimi and Rodolfo's Act 1 duet, or Micaela and José's, are exposition and they almost always advance the plot.

In great ensemble scenes—the kind Wagner hated—linear expression is transcended by music form in that several different characters can simultaneously express different thoughts. It is as if we could read and simultaneously comprehend the minds of several persons at once. As listeners, we must have already read what each character says in such an ensemble to begin to enjoy—in the sense of understanding—that ensemble. As you will see, *La Traviata*'s 2, 2 Finale is an extraordinary ensemble. Every character in the opera is present, plus the chorus, and each character speaks their individual thoughts in the striking patterns of repetition, development and contrast within the ensemble. Bizet's *Carmen* adheres to the new school that, following Wagner, wishes to delineate each line of dialogue, especially those vital to the plot. Even though no line of Act 3's opening chorus is vital to plot, the words are set to be understood. In contrast, the great chorus that opens Act 4 is not meant to be clearly understood, because it is pure local color and not essential to plot.

Every word of the Act 4's final duet, however, is vital and is treated like a precious jewel. The only time Carmen and José sing at the same time, they are repeating passages they have already sung, word for word. In this particular repetition, which occurs in the middle of the Act 4 duet, there is a profound psychological effect gotten by the combined repetition of verse in musical form, as if a distorted echo of thought is occurring, expressing a lack of clarity which must be resolved in what will follow the repetition.

As opera became more refined in terms of music composition—in the nineteenth century in the hands of Bellini, Verdi, Berlioz, and Wagner—ensembles become delineated to allow the text to be understood and the simultaneous-sounded voices are absorbed by the orchestral weave, which begins to emphasize motivic structures in imitation of poetic form. *Carmen*'s Act 3 Finale is perfectly delineated, with great attention to details of plot and character, with all literary and dramatic elements dovetailing beautifully in *La Bohème*'s Act 3 quartet, whose form was clearly dictated more by compositional considerations. It may appear that Bizet makes it easier on the interested listener. This is true and not true: it is true in that we can follow the word-based action better in *Carmen* than in *La Bohème*; but Bizet also wants to free us from complexities of form in order for us to become more involved in the psychological delicacies of the drama. In Bizet we find a composer who valued his text and wished for every word to be understood. Since we are beginning our study of opera with the text of operas, a simple reading of the layers of text to be sung in an ensemble will begin to give us the information we need to begin to fully appreciate what we will hear sung and see performed.

So ensembles are by their very nature the visual and auditory high points of operas. In some important ensembles, the chorus may be off-stage, as in Act 4 of *Carmen*, or the final scenes of *Aida* and *Faust*. (I am speaking of serious or tragic operas now. In comic opera, the chorus is often there at the opera's climax.) The choral ensemble may be a natural climax to an opera, as we have seen in *Carmen* and will see in *La Traviata* and *The Rake's Progress*, but a skillful composer will use the choral ensemble in diverse ways. This is the case in *La Bohème* where a reduced chorus, i.e. a vocal quartet, is substituted at its dramatic climax in Act 3's quartet.

Carmen's Final Ensemble

Let us glance again at *Carmen*'s final ensemble, considering some of the above ideas. The final duet/ensemble brings all the dramatic forces of the plot into focus. Carmen has perhaps found her man in Escamillo and a facile relationship that will offer her the personal liberty she desires. We can clearly sense the lovers' happiness in their short, harmonious duet in the previous scene. Desiring complete freedom in the present, Carmen must exorcise all demons from her past, including José, to fully love Escamillo. Her confrontation with Josè also results from stubborn pride, a basic element of her character. She must resolve this affair, which she instigated, then seek the social stratum and calm happiness that has always been denied her. Ironically, Escamillo appears in the final scene only after Fate has run its course; and then he can only stand mute while José confesses his crime and voices his undying passion for his Gypsy lover. Fate has finally hammered Carmen into submission.

In the first part of the duet, José pleads with Carmen to restore the past, the pulsing counterpoint in the strings evoking his original vision of her in *La fleur*. Time is compressed for José in this scene. The second section begins with his realization of Carmen's present attitude toward him. This evokes José's insistent pleading, heightened by despair. Finally, this despondence having been fully transmogrified into rage by Escamillo's victory within the bullring and the vision of Carmen's happy future with the matador, he does with his knife what he can no longer do otherwise.

Bizet's music, new ideas included, are woven into a solid motivic framework so firmly united with dramatic action that the musical and dramatic elements become one. This bonding typifies the greatest music drama. If the conclusion of *Carmen* seems somewhat perfunctory, it would be typical of great musical dramas, which often end without moralizing or sentiment of any kind. Bizet maintains the dramatic integrity of his masterpiece by letting the action speak for itself as psychological paradigm, and giving his protagonist a brief, heart-felt confession and request for punishment after his violent action has resolved the plot.

Carmen's Plot

Although each of *Carmen*'s four major characters are distinct and clearly defined, the forces of plot are primary. External forces appear to dictate the personal destiny of each character. Just as Mimi's disease was fatal, Carmen and José are trapped by a greater force than either can fight. Clearly, they are themselves forces of plot where the other is concerned, but neither is greater than their sum total, their Fate, which is described, exponentially intensified and enhanced by an orchestral dimension of luminous power.

At this point, we can say with some certainty that both *La Bohème* and *Carmen* are tragedies in Aristotle's sense of the term. Tragedy is "not a representation of men but a piece of action, of life, of happiness and unhappiness"; it is "the imitation of an action that is serious and complete in itself." The plot is the great arc of action of a drama that determines character development. Opera's themes may encompass such ideas as ecstatic passion (José, Rodolfo, Mimi), sentimental love (Micaela), or absolute personal liberty (Carmen, Musette, to a lesser degree Mimi and Anne), but forces of plot—Mimi's disease and mortality; Marcello, Rodolfo, or José's jealousy; Zuniga's power of office, society's moral code—will not allow the fulfillment of such extremes of human longing, nor sometimes even the smallest fantasy, such as Mimi's dream of bathing in Spring's first rays or smelling the real, fragrant roses in Paris.

Aristotle's logical recipe of tragic elements holds true for opera, even though in his *Poetics* he allocates the three elements—verse, music and spectacle—which create opera's most accessible beauty, to the lowest aesthetic value. *Carmen*, despite its three-dimensional characters, fine verse, extraordinary music and brilliant spectacle, is first and foremost a brilliant stream of action in which characters are swept along by forces of plot far beyond their control. As in all great drama, plot and character are in crucial moments hardly separable. In *Carmen*, sub-arcs of literature, music and visual elements support a great story. Literature contributes steady, tight verse forms, pungent dialogue and images of clarity and power. Literature's images are integrated into music in such a way that luminous images result and, in *Carmen*, not one but two opposing images appear in José: Carmen and José's mother. Drama makes its contribution through clear characters, a mesmerizing plot, and visual images like the flower and knife that come to represent aspects of character. Music's contribution to *Carmen* is profound, as it enhances literary, dramatic and visual elements, and defines emotional, aesthetic and even philosophical abstractions with remarkable clarity.

In addition to musical motifs, consider Bizet's use of visual motif, e.g. the repetition of a physical gesture. Although there is no mention of a flower in Act 4's dialogue, Carmen will throw another crucial object at José, a ring. The repetition of such acts constitutes a visual motif, elucidating character qualities. Carmen's throwing of objects is a kind of intense, even violent teasing, typical of her flirtatious nature. Mimi is more subtle, but is also clearly flirtatious. As operatic Fate would have it, both women choose jealous partners with short fuses.

If one wishes to force an exegetical interpretation on either of these first two operas—or on the next two for that matter—it is possible. For the interpreter who does not believe that "Fate" exists, then substitute "God's will" for Fate and you have tragic opera as moral document. Opera—both serious and comic—specializes in, in the final analysis, highly moral thematic material. With extreme rarity does evil or even bad behavior go unpunished in opera. Certainly Eros is punished by Thanatos in serious opera, it is tempered in comic opera by marriage. The word marriage is mentioned only once in *Carmen*, and is ridiculed throughout *La Bohème* and its source, *Scènes*. In both dramas, the main characters are obsessed with passion and death. In both, as in *La Traviata*, it is the female lead who dies on-stage.

José may be the figure who most fully engages us in *Carmen*. His moral disintegration is the chief product of *Carmen*'s plot. His emotional understanding that Carmen no longer loves him is the dramatic turn of the final duet (and begins to precipitate the duet's murderous final moments), just as his violent castigation and murder of Carmen is the dramatic climax of the opera. José is Orpheus, an artist who could move hell with his grief, but a lover who cannot control his own passions. Jose is also Oedipus, who could not control himself or his Fate. Compare him to the lesser figures we have seen in *La Bohème* and will see in *La Traviata* and *The Rake's Progress*. We cannot know the others as well as we know José. Their text, music and actions do not allow us to.

The great character of *La Traviata* is, however, a character named Violetta. Let us begin to look at her character's portrayal in the music of this great operatic score.

Part 4

VERDI'S *La Traviata*
AND MUSIC DRAMA

La Traviata and Music Drama

Verdi's *La Traviata* is among the handful of truly accessible operatic masterworks. It was, more than any other Verdi opera, most energized by the master's life experience. Verdi saw Dumas *fils'* play *La Dame aux Camélias* soon after the premier in Paris on February 2, 1852. He became fascinated with the subject Dumas explores. Dumas's novel of the same name was published in 1848, only a few months after the death of Marie Duplessis, the historical personage on which the fictional and dramatic character Marguerite Gautier is based. Verdi was also in Paris in 1848 and may have read *La Dame* in the first edition. (He had certainly read another book in similar vein that he was tempted to set, *Manon Lescaut*.) He may have known the historical figures on whose lives the story of *La Dame* is based.

During the period during which he saw *La Dame* on the stage, Verdi was living with the woman who was to become his second wife, Giuseppina Strepponi. Strepponi had been a very influential opera singer earlier in Italy and had played a crucial role in establishing Verdi's early career as a composer. Their relationship had become something of a scandal in Italy, and they had moved to Paris, in part, for Verdi's mistress's peace of mind. So Verdi was in a unique position to understand the character of Violetta, a woman hounded by and living outside of respectable society.

Verdi accepted and understood the character of this woman defamed by society, this character who had already been so carefully drawn by Dumas with a mixture of blood and acid. There was already a tradition in French literature of the portrayal of prostitution in prose fiction. There was the figure of Manon Lescaut, a literary character that becomes a prototype, internally, for the heroine of Dumas *fils'* novel, i.e. she keeps the novel at her bedside. Hugo and Balzac had both portrayed courtesans in literature previous to Dumas *fils*. Verdi and his librettists transformed the character of Dumas *fils'* novel—and the play—in specific ways, in order to make the character conform more to the expectations of the contemporary opera audience. Yet, they were innovative in their desire to make their heroine a figure of some nobility—and from this innovation they created perhaps the finest musical-dramatic portrait of a female character in opera. *La Traviata* was not the only opera Verdi worked on during this period. Immediately preceding it, Verdi created two remarkably varied operas in rapid succession: *Rigoletto* and *Il Trovatore*. Each of the three operas was a romantic masterwork with ill-fated, passionate love as its theme.

Verdi's Violetta—the Character

As with Puccini's adaptation of Mimi from *La Vie*, Verdi and his librettist purged their Violetta of some of the original character's practical and mercenary aspects. In *La Traviata*, this has the effect of making the character of Violetta somewhat more consistent with the character types opera viewers had come to expect in 1853. Even so, *La Traviata* created a scandal in its initial performances because it was seen as even more immoral than its source, because in Verdi's treatment of Dumas's bittersweet tale, the title character, a celebrated prostitute, emerges as a vulnerable, luminous image of great dramatic power. And this demimondaine, Violetta Valery, has lost none of her charm to this day. Her struggle for freedom is as memorable as Carmen's, but we know her so much better than we are ever allowed to know Carmen. Carmen holds us at a distance, but Violetta's struggle becomes ours.

Although *La Dame* was condemned by critics as being immoral in theme, its adaptation into operatic form—like most opera—is clearly moralizing in nature. Violetta is severely punished for her sins, as are Mimi and Carmen. The story of the passionately sincere ex-*grisette* who knows that society—represented in *La Traviata* by Germont, the father of her lover—will never allow her to forget her past is dramatically affecting, as has been amply demonstrated by successful 20th century productions of Dumas *fils'* play. In *La Traviata*, the emerging nobility and compassion of Violetta's character is traced in Verdi's fine musical shadings and overpowers any criticism of the story's romantic themes. Inspired by the subject matter, Verdi is also using *La Traviata* to reshape opera into a new and more flexible art form.

Our discussion in Part 4 will add opera's foremost element, music, to our recipe for music drama as literature. We now move back 22 years from *Carmen*'s premier into the prime of the greatest of three giants of operatic composition, Giuseppe Verdi. In Verdi's *La Traviata*, we encounter perhaps the most complex and complete heroine in operatic history. We have seen Mimi and Carmen reveal their inner worlds and values in arias; we have seen them react to fearful and abusive lovers with clinging and reckless courage. Once again, in four scenes, we will see a woman rise to the height of erotic ecstasy before she is crushed by a unique combination of internal and external forces, forces of character and plot, of society and Fate. Once again, eros—in this case, full-blown romantic passion—is punished with thanatos.

Verdi begins this stage of his refinement of Italian opera with a brief *Prelude*, which we will come to recognize as a musical portrait of Violetta, *La Traviata*. We will see that this opera is rife with splendid melodies, artfully used to emblemize emotion, idea and structure. The *Prelude* is a tone picture in adagio form, with strings dominating. Strings are clearly the glory of *La Traviata*, and in the Prelude the violins introduce an essential motif, a lovely descending melodic design worthy of Mozart. Verdi repeats this melody in the celli and lets the first violins dance in a gay-yet-wistful countermelody. In this music, our heroine has appeared: she emerges from the opening measures' haze of pain with the longing of the passionate woman, full of charm but, like Mimi, ill-fated.

The Essays on *La Traviata*

The first essay will discuss Act 1 in terms of its musical and literary elements and the way in which Verdi skillfully weaves dramatic power from vocal and orchestral weave. In Act 1, he lays the musical-dramatic groundwork for his heroine. This Verdi accomplishes by portraying musically the forces that shape Violetta. Most important, he paints her emotions, the internal forces which determine her actions and, equally important, her reactions to those most important to her, principally Alfredo and Germont. Father and son represent Romantic love and social respectability. Verdi gracefully portrays the dramatic conflict of these elements within a generous, but guilt-ridden heroine with consummate skill. How he accomplishes this feat with his use of orchestra, voice and musical form is the subject of Part 4 of our discussion of opera.

Never had the external and internal dramatic forces of an opera been more clearly and subtlety portrayed by the orchestral palate. The spare—natural, cosmic, religious—poetic imagery of this act objectifies aspects of Violetta's character. As with *La Bohème* and *Carmen*, all major imagery in *La Traviata* directly reveals an aspect of—or quickly becomes associated with—the opera's heroine. As with Mimi and Carmen, Violetta's actions will sometimes complement and augment imagery, enriching the dramatic tapestry of the story. All three, for example, speak about, then use flowers as objects. Such objects, because of the interplay of the literary value and dramatic meaning in opera, inevitably become symbols.

The second essay is dedicated to explication of *Sempre libera*, one of the great arias for soprano. Act 1 ends with this complex aria, splendid in its variety of character mood and depth. Verdi's genius here is not only to show us character inscape, as Puccini does so successfully with *Mi chiamano Mimi*, but to illustrate how character internalizes plot: Violetta considers on a deep emotional level what Alfredo earlier described in *Un di felice*. Alfredo's vision is not Rodolfo's "castle in the air;" he rather offers Violetta a proud, universal (*misterioso, altero*) vision of love, a luminous image of shared pain and ecstasy. This is a symbol of universal resonance, and it touches Violetta deeply. She repeats his words and their musical intonation verbatim: *croce e delizia al cor* (agony and delight of the heart). But even so, in the brilliant *Sempre libera*, the *coloratura/fiortura*—rapid, patterned movement of the voice—represents Violetta's emotional denial of true intimacy. And in its wounded honesty and false flight of imagined ecstasy, it heralds Violetta's imminent surrender to romantic love. The dream of love fulfilled is every romantic heroine's need. We see how deeply this heroine has been moved by Alfredo's vision, and we witness her struggle to surrender to that vision. It is most effective dramatically.

The third essay explores Act 2, scenes 1-8. The scene occurs in the countryside near Paris. Act 1 occurred in August—it is now January. An emotional duet between the heroine and her antagonist, Germont, constitutes the essence of this act; it is also the high point of the plot in that it contains the dramatic turn of the heroine. Her fateful decision to leave Alfredo—precipitated by Germont's emotional blackmail—seals Violetta's fate. The duet is framed by two arias, one each by the two men who have and will shape the remainder of Violetta's short life. Both arias are tuneful and both reveal the emotional honesty of the character that sings them. Neither honest, well-crafted aria touches us deeply, for neither is meant to. These arias are not essential exposition; i.e., they help explain Alfredo and Germont's motivations, but do not directly affect Violetta's internal struggle.

In Act 2, scene 1, our concentration centers on the psychological sub-tlety of Germont's clever and methodical manipulation of Violetta and her noble, if very human reaction to it. He ultimately drives her into a guilt-ridden corner of her soul where she can only draw strength from the knowledge that Alfredo will one day know of her sacrifice. She equates the death of her love for Alfredo with her own death.

The fourth essay analyzes Act 2, scene 2. Scenes 9-13 advance the action to its dramatic and musical high point: the magnificent finale, scenes 14-15. The *Largo del Finale II*, which begins with Germont's entrance, is a significant musi-cal climax. After each major character has had a solo passage characterized by intense, confessional utterance, the solo and choral voices combine in patterns that capture the emotional turmoil of Violetta and those close to her. The earlier choral/ballet number in this scene is entertaining in its own right and has been criticized for this very reason: it contributes little or nothing to advancing the plot. Yet, it serves a contrastive purpose, capturing the effete coterie of the demi-monde and sketching out the empty corruption that Violetta had momentarily escaped in the country. The finale then follows the ballet by only a few minutes. Like *Carmen*'s third act finale, the finale of *La Traviata*'s Act 2 is a crucial ensemble serving as the musical climax of the opera. It is a triumph of musical form, yet it is also consummate musical drama, full of character exposition, imagery and ideas.

The fifth essay discusses Act 3, which—like *Carmen*'s final act—reintro-duces musical material from the *Prelude* and Act 1 to begin our final musical journey through Violetta's inner world. This concluding act is as darkly brilliant as any act in opera. We know now that the first music we heard from the orches-tra, even before the curtain rose, is allowing us to experience the state of mind and the fading memories of a very sick young woman, one that in Act 3 we quickly see is on death's doorstep. As with *La Bohème* and *Carmen*, *La Traviata*'s final act will be a watershed of musical and literary elements. Nothing we have previously heard, however, can prepare us for the extraordinary power and grace of the means by which Verdi will accomplish the character transfor-mation that will lift this opera to its fulfillment of operatic form.

Music and Character

In *La Traviata*, choral elements are used very carefully and cleverly as elements of contrast. As Francis Toye notes in *Giuseppe Verdi: His Life and Works*, the contrast between the glitter of Violetta's wanton life and the pathos of her miserable death is vital to the opera's musical balance. Used to symbolize Violetta's *pompose feste* and the lifestyle that defined Violetta's existence before Alfredo, the choral numbers seem vital echoes of Violetta's former existence, an existence from which she attempted to flee. Some critics have criticized Verdi's use of chorus and ballet in Act 2, scene 2 and in Act 3, calling it intrusive. It is true that Verdi does not integrate Chorus of Gypsies and Matadors of Act 3 into the plot as he does the *brindisi* (toast) in Act 1, but we should consider that, musically, the Gypsy number—scenes 10 and 11—is the only number in Act 2 that exhibits orchestral energy on the level of the Act 3 finale. It also prepares for Alfredo's determined, unsettling entrance and declaration of "not knowing" where Violetta is. The chorus and dance numbers help make Act 3 the musical climax of *La Traviata*. Like the dance that opens *Carmen*'s second act and the parade that concludes *La Bohème*'s second act, this number might fall into the category of local color. In the French romantic movement, one great desire was *cultiver la couleur locale* (to cultivate local color). And *La Traviata* is, simply, a great romantic opera that happens to occur in Paris.

The final essay of Part 4 will continue the discussion of musical form. This musical drama was revolutionary in its form, as well as content. *La Traviata* was seen as a deliberate attack on the institution of marriage, a defense of free love, and a plea for easier divorce; but it also advances musical dramatic form with stretchy musical forms yielding musical-dramatic continuity. It is, in its own intimate and deeply intense way, an important step in the musical revolution in opera. Opera at mid-19th century was beginning to imitate the novel form by employing prose fiction's full complexity of elements to develop character. This required the expansion of existing musical forms as practiced by Mozart, Rossini, and Verdi (up to this point), and would precipitate the cultivation of new forms and tonality (Wagner, Strauss, Berg). The composer of *La Traviata* was an important innovator.

The music of *La Traviata* throws the dramatic evolution of human passion into striking relief. It is imbued with deep emotion and dramatic power. It is also decidedly intimate, approaching, at times, chamber music in scope. The orchestra had never before been empowered to so clearly illustrate the modes and motives of characters. *La Traviata*'s music is absolutely linked to the dramatic action. In terms of characterization, Violetta surpasses even the title character of *Rigoletto* (1851) in musical depth and subtlety. The revolution in orchestration and instrumentation signaled two years earlier in Verdi's *Rigoletto* is fulfilled in *La Traviata* and with less sensationalistic dramatic effect.

Music is a subjective art form with its own language and way of communicating. It is clear that music creates powerful visual associations when it is identified with visual images within a dramatic context. When we see pictures and hear music at the same time we invariable make a connection, if only on an unconscious level. In good opera, music maintains a close illustrative relationship with the action of the plot at all times. The story of the central characters is the focus, and music reveals the inner life of the character. Music must also illustrate the story conflict, as well as growth of character and character relationships.

Music often portrays the mental processes and emotional patterns of the character, the forces that motivate a stage figure like Violetta. Music may provide the whole emotional subtext of character. Music says things that cannot be said in dialogue or pure poetry; it creates the psychological shading of character thought and feeling and defines core relationships between characters in different situations. Verdi is especially adept at portraying internal conflict of character by musical means. Rich harmonic language is also useful in portraying dramatically charged situations because it, along with orchestration—the use of the orchestra to create a particular meaning with regard to the environment, character, or action of a character—creates a musical analog for distinct levels of emotion and thought. Music also provides the environmental factors not immediately visible and the emotional facts of character not found in dialogue, yet implicit in the causality, chronology and action of the narrative.

We saw in *La Bohème* and *Carmen* the interweaving and development of a number of themes initially identified with a particular character or situation. We want to keep a sense of the opera's larger form as we read and listen to *La Traviata* and *The Rake's Progress*. Since, thematically speaking, most great art concerns itself with passionate love in one of its forms, we might expect opera to concern itself with passionate love—of which there are two general literary/dramatic types. (1) Sentimental love is acquiescent to social propriety. (An example of this kind of love is not present in *La Bohème*, but in *Carmen* it is the love Micaela offers José. In *La Traviata* it is the love Violetta's guilty soul longs for—for such love would be tantamount to forgiveness and social acceptance. And in *The Rake's Progress*, we will see that Anne Truelove, like Micaela and as her name indicates, represents pure and sentimental love—true love.) (2) The second kind of love is the thematic mainstay of opera: eros—sexual passion—which violates conventional values, generates possessiveness and jealousy, and usually leads us through a sequence of events culminating in a tragic event: the death of one or more of the lovers. Romantic opera's dedication to the deadly struggle of passion and propriety reflects, it seems to me, one of the clear truths of human existence in a civilized state—we are torn between satisfying our instinctive passions and socially acceptable behavior. When Anne sings "The wild boar is vanquished" to Tom in the final scene of *The Rake's Progress*, she is emblemizing the defeat of lust, of eros. (Anne Truelove is Micaela's twentieth century reincarnation.) But we are getting ahead of ourselves.

Freud has taught us that both within our psyches and the dramas we make of our lives, there is a constant struggle between eros and thanatos, creation and destruction, love and death. *La Traviata* is about how a great character internalizes this conflict and rises above it. That is the meaning of Violetta's story and of *La Traviata*'s great interwoven arc of plot and character.

La Traviata and the Primacy of Music in Opera

La Traviata's first act combines melodic grace with rhythmic insistence to propel the three-dimensional character of Violetta to the surface of the Parisian demimonde as a graceful, pain-filled figure. We quickly see that, despite her bravura and teasing, she is as fragile as the exotic flower she wears. What better medium than music and what greater musical form than the aria could be found to express the innermost fantasies, dreams, joys and fears of a great character like Violetta?

Before beginning our analysis of Act 1, let's review the idea of the great arc—the flow of musical drama and its meaning—and the sub-arcs that support it. The plot is divided into units or divisions—acts, scenes, and musical numbers—and the interaction of character, environment and thought within this arrangement of action forms the complete plot. The musical, literary and visual sub-arcs all support this dramatic arc with recurring patterns of idea or image. A sub-arc creates patterns of meaning built on the principle of association. Part 2 of this book was concerned with literary sub-arcs, primarily patterns of poetic imagery and idea and the relationship of these patterns to environment and character. Part 3 explored the dramatic patterns formed by the forces of action, setting, character and visual symbol. Part 4 will explore the role of music in intensifying and augmenting these literary and dramatic sub-arcs. Part 4 will also trace through musical sub-arcs, primarily those based in repetition and variation of melodic material. Musical sub-arcs will support plot, character, and idea. Consider *La Bohème* in this regard.

Mimi has, we noted, her own musical realm, an orchestral dimension carefully developed by Puccini from her first entrance. Her great first act aria introduces the melodic motives which echo about her like dove wings in Acts 3 and 4. Music is the most repetitive of all art forms and thus has clearly defined sub-arcs. Puccini combines literary images and melodic motifs into especially clear sub-arcs that support arcs of both character and plot. Remember also that big form rhythm is concerned with the entirety of the musical-dramatic plot, while small form rhythms form the structure of the units of which that entirety consists. As we will see, the structure of these smaller units is in many cases miniatures of the larger form. In the terms of chaos theory, smaller units appear to be, structurally speaking, fractiles of the larger form. In every great work of narrative or dramatic art, there is always a big picture, and a number of smaller ones of which the larger one is composed. It is desirable to learn to see both at once. An additional factor to consider in appreciating the integrity of a great work of art is to keep in mind the sequence of parts: what comes before and after each unit as it is being experienced. By placing each event or fragment—act, scene, ensemble, finale, aria, recitative—within the context of the work of art as a whole, we gain insight into both the internal and external causal relations of the work. This approach involves detective work and idea play, and creates a deeper enjoyment of the opera.

On Musical Form

In its most general sense, musical form includes all the elements and relationships that distinguish music from any haphazard combinations of sounds. Even the simplest melody has relationships of pitch (interval) and time values (rhythm) and thus has form. All the basic elements of music—rhythm, melody, harmony, texture, etc.—contribute to musical coherence and are thus components of musical form. More specifically, form is the scheme of organization that determines the basic structure of a composition: it is comparable to an architectural plan. There are a considerable number of these schemes or plans that we may call musical forms. They fall into two groups: single and composite forms. Composite forms are those that consist of two or more movements, so we might consider an opera's great musical arc as an extended and remarkably varied composite form. Our primary interest is, however, in single forms, of which there are two general types: *sectional*, those involving patterns of repetition and variation denoted by the use of letters A, B, C, etc. to indicate repetitions; and *continuation*, which contains through-composed and imitative music. In *La Bohème*, Puccini uses unique combinations of continuation and sectional forms in his great arc, as he also employs complex motivic literary and musical sub-arcs. While Rodolfo's first act aria is through composed, Mimi's first act aria approximates a sectional form, the rounded binary form: [A BA].

Bizet's *Carmen* features much more sectional music, often falling into simple sectional form of verse and chorus, e.g., Carmen's entrance aria, echoing the Greek structure of strophe and anti-strophe. Carmen's final duet in Act 4 is a magnificent example of continuation, using elements of repetition (in off-stage music) sparely to heighten the dramatic dynamics inherent in the character confrontation. Opera's unique weave of musical and dramatic elements resists neat classification in terms of musical form in its entirety and even in its acts, though small units often consist of clearly recognizable sectional forms, some of which are most fully realized in operatic form, like the aria. We know by now that the aria is an elaborate musical number for the solo voice. It may include, as Violetta's Act 1 aria does, elements of complexity, even virtuosity. In Alfredo's Act 2 aria, the second, or melodic part of the aria is preceded by a short recitative that serves to further the story. Alfredo tells us in the recitative portion of his aria how Violetta has left her wild life in the Paris demimonde to be with him in the country, while the melodic section gives the character opportunity to express his feelings. In Essay 3 of this section, I'll discuss Violetta's great aria in its entirety. In the hands of masters like Verdi, such great arias constitute scenes in themselves. Far from being purely musical numbers, they are essential constituents of plot, character, and idea.

Prelude

La Traviata's first act is shaped more successfully and economically in terms of revealing and developing believable dramatic character than any other I know. The social milieu of the demimonde is captured in both its driving rhythms; frantic, splashy excesses of orchestral color and tone; and, later, in the more subtle, sneering tone of its (on stage) chamber music. In contrast to this is the somber elegance of Alfredo's *un di*, which cuts through the hollow frenzy to personal truth. The grace and beauty of the music of Act 1 are undeniable, as is the bright gaiety of Violetta's later coloratura vocal flights. Alfredo's noble ardor is musically portrayed in a melody very like that lovely descending melody of the *Prelude* that characterizes Violetta's movement and person. All of these diverse colors are contained, rainbow-like, in an over-all structure as smooth as Germont's silk tie and as logical as a treatise by Kant. Let us consider them.

As with *Carmen*, *La Traviata*'s *Prelude* offers the material of two vital sub-arcs, both of which are essential to an understanding of the plot and the title character. All of these elements are ingeniously contained in the brief *Prelude*, whose form might be designated as [A BB']; that is, a binary form with variations of the second theme. Seen from the dramatic perspective, the *Prelude* is in essence, however, a portrait of Violetta, featuring three distinct aspects of her character: first, the distended consciousness of the invalid; second, the grace of a beautiful woman, enhanced by longing (the dream of love fulfilled); and, third, the social allure and charm of the coquette. As in *Carmen*'s *Prelude*, we are offered here a vital musical sketch. Both these *Preludes* are subtle acrostic gatherings of melodic motif. Each *Prelude* begins with music that will begin the final act of the opera. The second theme of each *Prelude* emerges during a crucial moment in Act 2 of the opera. The third melodic element of each *Prelude* is largely symbolic in nature, representing a quality or idea essential to the title character rather than a motif that fits into a distinct dramatic context. These preludes are enticing puzzles more easily solved on second and third hearings of the operas, rather than through immediate comprehension.

The opening musical phrases of the *Prelude* feature Adagio strings and portray Violetta, the invalid. The diaphanous delicacy of the harmony and instrumentation hints at the delicacy of the title character. This vulnerability will become startlingly clear by the beginning of the final act. At first, Verdi's score exhibits few discernible melodic or rhythmic characteristics; its harmony impresses us as nebulous, frail in its extreme beauty, and characterized by a longing that borders on suffering.

Budden[i] points out that this scoring for divisi violins indicates frailty, the diminishing phrase length physical decline.

The second part of this melody has the effect of piercing sadness:

Note the similarities of this melody to the fragmented theme of the clarinet in 2,1 as Violetta writes her farewell to Alfredo. Verdi here repeats a melodic fragment in such a way that it is reduced to an essence, an essence that represents in this case Violetta's loving despair.

The second theme, introduced by the violins, is identified usually as one expressing Violetta's love for Alfredo, but it is also meant to represent a second aspect of Violetta's character: the grace, elegance and sensuous appeal of the beautiful courtesan. It will be employed by Alfredo in a slightly different form to win Violetta's heart with the words *Di quell'amor*.

This melody is repeated in the viols and woodwinds, with a counter-melody in the divisi violins, augmenting the melodic grace with an air of flirtatious charm.

After this delicate and brief introduction to the title character, we are abruptly engaged by the vivacious party music that propels us into the gathering underway at Violetta's apartments. *La Traviata*'s first act is the basis for this masterpiece's great arc of action. Let us now examine the first act's literary, dramatic and musical sub-arcs.

Act 1

As is true of *Carmen*'s opening, a rising series of chords accompanies the rising curtain. Then each character is introduced and must assertively sing against the bright, insistent party music of the full orchestra. Although the music is constant, the tunes vary, as they would at any party. Violetta both charms and teases the men gathered about her; both Gaston and Alfredo insist they "are not lying" to her, and before the act is over, she will agree with them. Indeed, by the end of the *brindisi*, it is clear to us that Alfredo and she are destined for each other. Verdi accomplishes this initially and most cleverly through his use of musical form, the *brindisi*—a musical toast.

The *brindisi* is the first musical number of the opera and a charming, dazzling composition that cannot fail to delight the listener, but it is important to us for two reasons. First, it demonstrates Verdi's genius at varying musical form to create great musical drama; and second, it introduces imagery that indicates qualities of character and plot. The *brindisi*, a toast or drinking song, is a gratuitous number in many Italian operas. In *La Traviata* and *Otello*, however, Verdi integrates it into the plot in such a way that it seems an integral part of the great arc of action. In *Otello*, Iago makes the toast an occasion to get Cassio drunk and begin to work out the ambitions of his unmotivated malignancy, while in *La Traviata*, the *brindisi* becomes a delicate icebreaker for Violetta.

The form of the number is basically verse with chorus. Alfredo sings the first verse celebrating love. The melody is to be sung *con grazia*, with grace and a certain delicacy. Like both Rodolfo and José, he mentions the eyes of his beloved. The second verse is Violetta's, and her answer is a distinct poetic and dramatic response to what Alfredo has sung. She states the pleasure-seeking philosophy of the demimonde: enjoy pleasure at a rapid pace, for love is a flower that blossoms then quickly fades. Notice the familiar image of the flower, with its connotations of renewal and Spring, and the casual omnipresence of death in the heroine's thoughts. As is usually the case in the sub-arcs of imagery, love (passion) and death are closely tied. This was also the case with both Mimi and Carmen, though not this early in their operas. This is literary, i.e. poetic theme, echoed in stage action. The literary element foreshadows through imagery and is something for a literary detective to consider in a fine libretto.

Following the second verse of the *brindisi*, Verdi interjects four solo lines of dialogue before the third verse. These four crucial lines allow Alfredo to forcibly make his point to Violetta: it is his destiny to be her true love. Then, for the remainder of the third verse, the voices of the two lovers rise above the chorus, which is relegated to instrumental figures of accompaniment. The third verse thus serves to unite the voices of the lovers in two different ways: first, in linear duet (conversation); and, second, in harmony. In terms of musical form, we surmise that the two young lovers are meant for each other—already united on an unconscious level. Dramatically, they are intimately involved; literarily, they have yet to accomplish this step. Words often follow feelings at some distance.

After the *brindisi*, orchestral music is transferred to a small ensemble on the stage, preparing a more intimate atmosphere for the lovers to initiate their relationship. The music, however, is not charming, but brilliant and witty. And as Violetta fights for breath after telling her friends she will rejoin them, the woodwinds and strings sneer at her struggle with teasing indifference.

This motif serves as background to Violetta's broken, consumptive phrasing of *O qual pallor* as she studies her image in the mirror. This is touching, but does not yet evoke pity. In some ways, this subtle, but startling moment illustrating the demimonde's supercilious lack of concern for individual destiny presages the loneliness of the heroine's final days in Act 3.

A clear mark of Verdi's greatness as a composer is his ability to use

counterpoint, not only as a purely musical phenomenon, but as a musical drama-
tist, i.e. to interface dramatic and musical elements. Consider the ironic tension
between what Violetta is feeling here—think of the first theme of the *Prelude*—
and what the gay, mechanistic on-stage music is saying. The most celebrated
courtesan of the demimonde is left gasping for breath while the world dances on
about her, unconcerned.

Now Alfredo appears and the on-stage ensemble accompanies the revealing
repartee of the couple, a continuance of the four-line debate buried in the *brindisi*. Violetta's fainting spell has made her more vulnerable, and she is impressed
by Alfredo's forceful sincerity. He cuts through her teasing with *Ridete?... e in
voi v'ha un cor?* (You laugh? Do you have a heart?) The dialogue here takes the
form of fluid *recitativo accompagnato*.

The intensity of the conversation builds until Alfredo begins his striking
arioso.

Un di felice describes Alfredo's vision of sublime love. It is a universal image, a
luminous image not grounded in the personality of the lover or beloved, but
rather in a romantic idealization of passion: *misterioso, altero, / Croce e delizia*
(mysterious, noble / full of both sacrifice and delight).

Rhythmically, this declaration is insistent as its melody is beautiful, and it
does touch Violetta, for she attempts to interrupt its graceful descending line

with a flirtatious scolding of Alfredo's seriousness:

But Alfredo overpowers her vocally, his voice crossing above hers.

Notice that Alfredo's vocal line is typified by *legato*—smoothness, without separation between notes—phrasing, reflecting certainty and strength, while
Violetta's feature irregular phrasing and *staccato*—short notes, emphatic in their

brevity)—gives the listener the impression of flightiness, irresoluteness, possible vulnerability. Then she is reduced to murmuring her lines *Non arduo troverete / Dimenticarmi allor* as Alfredo's voice crosses above hers, signaling his musical (emotional) conquest. In this manner the short, impassioned duet ends with the two drawing ever nearer in terms of dynamics and phrasing, until they emerge as near-equals at the end of the duet. Alfredo's voice is, however, still above Violetta's, making clear the victor in this battle of emotions.

Their intimacy is interrupted as Gaston bursts in on them, bringing with him the return of frivolous dance music. Infected again with a social mood, Violetta makes Alfredo promise to speak no more of love. Momentarily defeated, he wishes to leave quickly. She senses his unrest and makes a startling decision; she offers him a camellia from her breast, recalling her earlier phrase *un fior che nasce e muore*—Alfredo should return when the flower begins to wilt. Understanding, he is overjoyed.

Alfredo departs, his heart light, knowing only that he will be welcome the next day in Violetta's arms. The chorus exits boisterously with a *stretta*, which serves in immediate contrast to the extraordinary musical event to follow: the musical embodiment of ideal love. The dramatic ideal of *La Traviata* is abiding, passionate love, while the idea or theme is the defeat of that love by social convention and Fate. The ideal is represented by a musical theme we first hear sung in the phrases *Di quell'amor, ch'e palpito* Alfredo offers to Violetta in Act 1 the first time they are alone. This melodic unit/motif, with slight variation, recurs at least four times in the opera, creating a substantial sub-arc. With each appearance, the theme becomes richer in meaning because each time it appears, it does so in a different scenic and dramatic context—thus we are constantly comparing the same idea in different contexts. This motif structure allows us to trace the metamorphosis of a passionate love from its breathless inception to its tragic demise.

The first appearance of this descending melodic motif was in the lovely melodic line of the *Prelude*, so Alfredo's Act 1 description of love was subtlety foreshadowed there. Alfredo's *di quell amor, quell amor che palpito* introduces a lovely variation on the original descending melody of the *Prelude*. This variation is later quoted in Violetta's Act 1 aria, where the reflective calmness and beauty of the setting lets us know that Alfredo has touched her deeply: she has internalized his words, but more importantly she has internalized their meaning, the luminous image of love he offered her. Later in the same aria, Violetta hears Alfredo's voice phrasing this melody over and over. The second and most dramatic recurrence of the initial essential melody is in Act 2, scene 1, where with the words *Amami Alfredo*, Violetta tears herself from her beloved and runs to the waiting coach. This appearance of the melody is heard as we first heard it in the *Prelude*. The next appearance occurs in the solo violin at the beginning of Act 3, as Violetta reads Germont's letter yet again. This scene demonstrates Verdi's great lyric gift. After this brush with sentimentality, a contrastive utterance follows: Violetta utters "Too late!" in a "sepulchral voice." The motif will

VERDI'S *La Traviata*

eerily return in the closing moments of the opera as Violetta's tortured spirit negotiates its final freedom from the flesh.

This melodic sub-arc and its variations illustrate the evolution of Violetta's character. It is one of many things Verdi does to create, emotionally and intellectually, a great character. Each such pattern has its own rhythm, which complements and intensifies the flow of action and thought of the plot. This melody represents the essence of character and the ideal of *La Traviata*—the dream of love fulfilled, or perhaps the ultimate yearning for and impossibility of realizing that dream—and brings with it the memory of that love's promise. Ironically, its fifth and final reiteration occurs as Violetta rises from her deathbed to utter her final delirious phrases. Her final actions are a broken attempt to sing the word *gioire*, as she had in her Act 1 aria. Verdi uses motifs with such spare subtlety and effectiveness.

By reputation, Verdi drove his librettists mad with requests for revision. In the case of *La Traviata*, they had to give him the poetic structure and imagery to inspire the spare freedom of musical motif necessary to create the inscape of a great heroine. Because Violetta is tragically fated, the great arc of plot is hers and every sub-arc must support the development of her character. This is nowhere more obvious than in the remarkable aria that closes *La Traviata*'s first act. Here Verdi's melodic genius and mastery of musical form are the means by which poetic thought and form are complemented and augmented to reveal depth of character through inner conflict, complexity of plot, and intensity of thematic content.

VERDI'S *La Traviata*

È strano... sempre libera
DENYING THE DREAM OF LOVE FULFILLED

Always the master of dramatic contrasts in the musical-dramatic form, Verdi proves himself the Shakespeare of opera here: we are torn from the fortissimo of the exiting chorus to silence, from drunken philandering to metaphysical debate, from light to dark. Every expectation we bring to the aria form is fulfilled and elucidated here. Like every scene of *La Traviata*, this final scene of the first act is ripe with beautiful melodies. The variety of musical idea and varied dynamics keep our interest. Most important, this scene is dramatically revealing of character, and expresses a conflict within the title character that is inherently fascinating. This "scene and aria" is an occasion on which we gaze deeply into the depths of Violetta's character and see her greatest hopes and deepest fears. She reveals to the listener a luminous image that she has carried since girlhood and then, frightened of the idea of loving or of trusting any man completely, she withdraws into frantic denial, vowing to lose herself in the dissolute—unreflective, unquestioning—life of the demimonde.

This aria is important, not only for its powerful development of Violetta's character, but for the way it advances the plot by bringing the issues to a head within the title character herself. Verdi shows us that the title character has internalized the pleas and arguments of Alfredo. Not a word has been lost on her. The subject of the aria is the love he described in *un di*. After questions—"Can it be that I am finally to love?" and "Is he the one?"— she quotes his luminous exposition of passion, *Di quell'amo*. Then later, at the height of her resistance to surrender, she hears his voice echoing in her head: *croce e delizia al cor!* One of Piave and Verdi's great accomplishment here is to have a character summarize crucial elements of the plot of Act 1 in an aria of great power and beauty. We understand this character now with utter clarity: we know her deepest desires and fears. Psychologically, this aria takes us fully into Violetta, where we stay for much of the rest of the opera.

A note on classic aria form: Its basic structure is recitative-song-*stretta*. The *stretta* is an up-tempo, brilliant finale to the aria as the Italian masters of the late eighteenth and early nineteenth centuries had developed it. The basic structure of this musical form interposed itself on the dramatic unit of the scene. The child of this union is called *scene and aria*. Violetta's aria is referred to in the libretto as "Recitative and aria," but the complete orchestral score refers to it as "*Scena ed Aria Violetta*" or "Violetta's scene and aria."

The Question

This great aria begins in silence, in immediate and striking contrast to the exit music of the boisterous chorus, then continues with *È strano!... e strano!* uttered as *recitativo secco*. In Verdi's hands, the extended aria form impresses us as both organic and elastic. The aria begins quietly, with the honest admission that she has been touched to the quick by Alfredo's confessional vision of

125

passionate love. The opening passage of recitative exposes the issues before Violetta with lucid honesty. Its phrases are supported by a tension alternating between wonder and fear.

E strano!. . .-e strano! .. in core	Strange how his words
Scolpiti ho quegli accenti!	echo now in my heart!

This remark sets the tone of honesty we may now expect from this character. It also prepares us for the reprise of *Di quell'amor* within the aria's structure. She asks her troubled soul if she dare love seriously.

Saria per me sventura in serio amore?	To really fall in love?
Che resoli, o turbata anima mia?	Turbulent soul, dare you?

Never before has she allowed herself to love a man, but at the thought of surrender to Alfredo her voice ascends in excitement and melts at the thought of loving and being loved.

Null'uomo ancora t'accendeva...	No man has inspired me to
O gioia	such joy—
Ch'io non conobbi, essere amata	to surrender to love,
amando!...	to being loved

Still, she hesitates to accept his offer, even though she sees her life in this reflective moment as empty folly. Does she dare to love Alfredo, give him her love?

E sdegnarla poss'io	Can I disdain his passion
Per l'aride follie del viver mio?	for this folly I call life?

Now begins her melodic exploration of herself, hesitant and breathless,

featuring the interval of an octave with a *dolcissimo* (sweet) tone. *Is he the one, my soul?*

Alone amidst echoing tumult of habitual pleasures augmented by the false flashes of fashion, Violetta's internal debate goes on. Is he the one—the ideal and perfect lover for me?

Ah, fors'e lui che l'anima	Is he the one, my soul?
Solinga ne' tumulti	With tears and tumult,
Godea sovente pingere	You have pictured him
De'suoi colori occulti!...	in your deepest dream.

Do I risk the death of my dream, my dream of love fulfilled. This is the Romantic heroine's ultimate and final question. Her answer will determine her fate.

Internalizing the Luminous Image

Into this world of falseness she now must reckon with the sincerity of

Alfredo: *Imagine his modest vigil when I was feverish.* Now she says she feels a new fever—not one of sickness, but one of passion, *Lui che modesto e vigile* (his abiding concern for me):

All'egre soglie ascese,	when I lay in fever
E nuova fabbre accese,	Now I shiver anew
Destandomi all'amor,	pulsing with love

and her vocal line builds to her restatement of Alfredo's declaration of love.

You will remember how Puccini and Bizet use the French horns to ennoble Mimi in *Mi chiamano Mimi* and Micaela in her prayer? They learned this technique in part from Verdi. True to orchestral form, it is the French horns that prominently accompany Violetta in this reprise.

A quell'amor ch'è palpito	Ah, love's pulse
Dell'universo intero,	fills the universe—
Misterioso, altero,	mysterious, proud,
Croce e delizia al cor.	these painful delights of the heart.

Now comes a verse rarely performed because, I assume, of its esoteric content. It is, however, one of the clearest descriptions of a luminous image, curiously and uniquely combining the idea of the sacred longing with secular passion:

A me fanciulla, un candido	When just a girl
E trepido desire	a timid and pure desire
Quest'effigio dolcissimo	sweetly marked a figure
Signor dell'avvenire,	as master of my heart.
Quando ne'ciel il raggio	When at prayer he appeared
Di sua beltà vedea,	in rays of light,
E tutta me pascea	I adored him as if divine—
Di quel divino error.	an illusion of grace.

Truncating the text immediately above in favor of neater musical form does damage to the psychological depth of Violetta's attempted rejection of Alfredo's love in the passages that follow, in which she returns to Alfredo's words. As she again sings *Croce*, she tries to bring herself out of what she associates on an unconscious level with a girlhood religious fantasy. It is the connection she makes between her childish, quasi-religious idealization of men and the image of the cross that shocks her out of her romantic reverie.

She is no longer that foolish girl! She must avoid such delirious follies. *Follie!... follie!... delirio vano è questo!...* (Insanity! I'm delirious!) And now we see into her deepest fears.

Povera donna, sola,	Poor woman, alone,
Abbandonata in questo	abandoned in Paris,
Popoloso deserto	this sterile mirage
Che appellano Parigi,	for the lustful blind.
Che spero or più?... Che far degg'io?...	
Gioire,	Hope is torture. No!
Di voluttà nei vortici perire.	I'll abandon myself to joy!

And Violetta resolves to dedicate herself to forgetting the possibility of love by drowning herself in pleasures of the demimonde.

Her voice explores the extreme of her vocal range in feverish excitement, as she lists the pleasures she will experience.

Sempre libera degg'io	I want freedom forever,
Folleggiar di gioia,	joy following joy,
Vo' che scorra il viver mio	with no end of pleasures,
Pei sentieri del piacer.	No more tears or sighs,
Nasca il giorno, o il giorno muoia,	only endless laughter.
Sempre lieta ne' ritrovi	I will sing every song,
A diletti sempre nuovi	always seek the latest delights—
Dee volare il mio pensier.	only freedom in my heart.

She denies the very thing she has most longed for since childhood, substituting will and freedom for love and intimacy.

But Alfredo's voice now echoes through her being, repeating *Di quell'amor ch'e palpito*: and Violetta murmurs, *Alfredo!* as he voices the phrases that are both a demand and a warning: *Misterioso, altero / Croce e delizia al cor.*

Stretta

Then, in florid musical denial, Violetta repeats her longing for freedom and her desire to lose herself not in another, but in the excesses for which the demimonde is famous.

Coloratura, the use of rapid scales, arpeggios, trills, and similar musical designs of a virtuoso character, is used in opera to express various extremes of mood and emotion. Nowhere is it used more successfully than here, where it is used to capture the unique combination of feverish resistance—to emotional surrender—and deep fear in a great character.

So Act 1 ends with the same furious energy it began with, but we are now focused not on the demimonde, but on a singular character. The heroine's dream (of love fulfilled) seems safely buried under the veneer of a numbing, pleasure-filled lifestyle in the underworld of Paris. But Alfredo has awakened Violetta with the appeal of a sincere and fulfilling passion. Alfredo's evocation of the luminous image of Romantic passion creates in Violetta a deep desire for the luminous image—her ideal man—awakened in her during childhood. Yet she panics at the thought of surrendering her independence to the whim of an idealized passion, a girlhood dream. For a cool moment at the end of the first act, she looks coldly at the world she knows to be unkind and sees there the emptiness of her existence. Then, frightened at her momentary weakness and vulnerability, she resolves to drown herself in pleasure and new temptations.

Like every great protagonist, Violetta has a weakness amounting to a flaw. This weakness will bring her down, but it will also raise her into the ranks of the immortal characters of music drama.

VERDI'S *La Traviata*

Act 2, Scene 1

THE HEROINE'S FLAW

The Greek word *hero* is the title given to a man of outstanding courage and nobility. Aristotle does not consider in his *Poetics* whether a female protagonist should have the same characteristics as the male, but logic requires it. Certainly Euripides, the youngest of the three great Attic tragedians, assumed it. Violetta is clearly the protagonist of *La Traviata*, and Germont the antagonist. Violetta's *hamartae* (tragic flaw) will play a crucial role in her downfall. This heroine's fall is precipitated by a member of respectable society who confronts her and to force a sacrifice from her. It is through her response to this desired sacrifice that Violetta earns the title of heroine; and it is through her story and actions that *La Traviata* joins the ranks of the very great works of Western art in terms of its balance of structure and meaning. The great theme of this opera is the growth from passion to compassion in the character of Violetta. This growth is triggered in Violetta not by *hubris* (pride) or terror, but guilt. Ultimately, she does not believe she deserves Alfredo, or the happiness his love brings. Before her guilty, striving soul is finally freed in Act 3, Violetta will suffer greatly at the hands of those who love her. The two great scenes of Act 2 contain the steadily rising action of Violetta's dynamic story. Scenes 5-6 of Act 2 (2,1) raise dialogue (recitative and duet) in Italian music drama to greatness, and scenes 9-14 (2,2) are ennobled by one of the greatest Finales in all of opera.

Alfredo's Aria

Arias open and close Act 2, scene 1. We have already experienced Violetta's complex aria, which closes Act 1. In contrast, Alfredo's aria is constructed in a simpler, more standard fashion: the recitative, a strenuous mixture of secco and accompanied recitative, is followed by the aria proper, a carefully structured musical form featuring a short lyric poem, a notable melody and supporting orchestral accompaniment. The recitative of Alfredo's aria, *Lunge da lei*, has the great virtue, dramatically speaking, of informing us of what has happened in the two months between Acts 1 and 2. Despite her initial resistance, Violetta has left her rich life in Paris and has utterly surrendered to life in a country house near Paris. Note the sparse, heavily accented accompaniment, which in some ways approximates the chording patterns of the keyboard instruments so artfully used to accompany recitative in the eighteenth century. The second and melodic portion of the aria, *De' miei bollenti spiriti*, immediately following the recitative expresses urgency in the unique vocal dynamics, with alternating fortes in the upper register and pianissimo in the middle register. The accompaniment is also restless in its variety of bowed and plucked strings. The aria climaxes with the words "almost in heaven." Alfredo and Violetta's country home is almost heaven, according to the Romantic doctrine, which views civilization—represented by the city, in this case Paris—as an agent corrupting man's nobler instincts.

In the brief second scene, Alfredo learns from Violetta's servant, Annina, that Violetta has been selling her possessions to support them. Shamed, he rushes off to Paris after singing the stretta to his aria, which constitutes scene 3 and is rarely done because its grand qualities and military rhythms detract from the essential intimacy of the opera—especially in this setting. So our Adam leaves abruptly for Paris and our Eve enters, soon to be followed by the Snake.

Confrontation and Duet

Scene 5 begins as Joseph ushers in a gentleman Violetta assumes to be her lawyer, the man arranging the sale of her possessions in Paris. She is shocked to be confronted by a stern and commanding stranger, Germont, who immediately accuses her of trying to ruin his son. Violetta responds that he should withdraw before he continues in this unpleasant tone. Germont is taken aback, but proceeds to probe: How can they afford to live in luxury? Violetta immediately produces documents proving that she is selling all her possessions to finance this retreat. Germont is impressed by the document, more so by Violetta's person; still, he has a mission and presses onward, probing with an air of moral superiority. He is here to protect his daughter's—Alfredo's sister's—future happiness, as well as the respectability of the family.

Soon he senses a weakness—Violetta's guilt—to exploit. Germont begins subtly and insistently to probe until he hits the numbing nerve. Finding the opening he wants, he mocks her for selling the possessions she has acquired in the demimonde: "Ah, does past shame accuse you?" Is this a form of penance, he asks, for your sinful life? Violetta now answers, "My past no longer exists, because I love Alfredo and God has answered my penitence with forgiveness." Germont is now on firm territory and praises her: "These are noble sentiments indeed!" Violetta takes him at his word and thanks him for his "sweet words." Germont now senses his window of opportunity. Rising from where he seated himself in judgment, Germont begins to make his demands and he does it directly, using the vocabulary and imagery of religion which Violetta herself has introduced. He senses her new dependence on religious belief in her life—absent from both the novel and play on which the libretto is based—reminding us that in the final analysis opera is, generally, a conservative and moral medium—and demands that she "sacrifice" her feelings. Not only must she repent, but she must transcend her past sins by making the necessary sacrifice on the altar of social propriety. With this psychological masterstroke, Germont has exercised his social and moral advantage on a "sinner"—*La Traviata*.

Germont is here a father figure in every sense, not only of Alfredo but, by extension of society and of the church, even of Violetta. He has sensed in Violetta's admission—"I foresaw it, I knew it,... I was far too happy"—of guilt. In Germont's stern, fatherly presence, she senses judgment and begins to see herself as unworthy of happiness. To some degree, Germont now assumes the role of priestly father for Violetta. If she confesses and agrees to sacrifice herself, he—and society and the church—will forgive her sins. Later in the scene, after confessing her terrible twin fears—losing Alfredo and dying—she asks to be embraced "as his daughter." She wishes to become the faithful daughter of a socially respectable man, one who will hear the confessions of her deepest fears and longings and will forgive her for them. Germont evokes a lengthy confession from her, but blinded by biases is unable to appreciate her pleading as anything other than hysteria. She, who mocked men two months ago, becomes now completely vulnerable to this representative of bourgeois respectability. Germont is now ready to play his trump card. He reveals that his daughter's future happiness lies in Violetta's hands. In giving up Alfredo, Violetta can save her beloved's sister from misery. The duet now begins as Germont describes his daughter as 'an angel' whose well-being Alfredo and Violetta's indiscretion now endangers.

Alfredo's tryst with Violetta has endangered the "Rose" of his sister's love, a proposed marriage.

Now a frantic Violetta begins to understand Germont's drift and to plead with him. "Perhaps I could leave him for a short time." "No," Germont insists, "I want more." And Violetta herself states what he wants. He senses he can demand this, because he has tapped fully into her terrible guilt. Violetta must give up Alfredo forever. In her desperation, accused of destroying the happiness of an "angel," Violetta now confesses her greatest fear to Alfredo's father, her death. As we saw at the crucial point of her aria, she, like Mimi, fears being alone, *sola*. She now has no one but Alfredo, she insists, in the world and has staked everything on him. To be alone—without her beloved—is now like being dead. The music is frantic and sincere.

In the second stanza, she asks him directly, "Do you know that I am dying?" She must dedicate the little time she has left to Alfredo. If she cannot do this, she would prefer to die now instead of in the near future. From this point on, it will become clear to us that Violetta associates her love for Alfredo with life itself—even with that love's ability to heal her deadly illness.

Germont is both embarrassed by the profusion of emotion his request has elicited and, knowing nothing of Violetta's illness, presses on, finding ways to overcome her appealing arguments. "The sacrifice is bitter," he admits, but Violetta is young and beautiful. She can have many more lovers.

Violetta interrupts him, "No, I could love no other."

Germont's persuasion enters now its most cruel stage and he says, "But my dear, men are so fickle!" The distraught Violetta can only murmur, "Oh, God," as Germont proceeds to draw a verbal picture of her and Alfredo's love grown old, for, he adds with casual malice, "Your union will never be blessed by heaven." Violetta is struck to her soul and murmurs, *E vero!* In the following remarkable duet, Violetta first bitterly confesses to Germont and then accedes to his commands. Note that throughout their recitative and duet, both characters use the vocabulary of Catholic worship and prayer.

Now two remarkable dramatic events occur. First, at the height of his pleading with a penitent Violetta, Germont first asks Violetta to have pity on him and become an angel capable of blessing his daughter's marriage. Then he addresses Violetta as "daughter" and claims that he is inspired by God himself: *E Dio che inspira, o giovine, / Tai detti a un genitor.* (God himself inspires me, daughter. / He speaks through me.) From this point to the end of the opera, Violetta will begin to refer to herself as his daughter and as an angel who blesses others. She has assumed a metaphysical cloak of the righteous victim.

Second, in broken phrases, Violetta bitterly confesses to Germont: "God may forgive me, but man has no pity in his heart." She implicitly castigates men as a sex and mankind as a society, then assumes the duties of an angel of mercy. How different from *La Bohème*, where religion is mentioned only in passing by Mimi and under terrible stress by Musetta, and *Carmen*, where superstition has assumed the role of religious fervor for the title figure. She then sings, in transparent tones,

"Tell your sweet girl that an unfortunate victim made a sacrifice for her and she died." Near the conclusion of Act 3, Violetta will say something similar to Alfredo with music similar in tone to the music here. "Tell the woman you marry that someone among the angels prays for her and you." She is both confessing to a father and bowing to his request that she become a sacrificial figure. The orchestration, in the passage in 2,1 and later in Act 3, has the simplicity of Mozart, while the vocal writing is sublime. Their voices unite as Verdi builds this powerful duet into a dialogue that yields a certain understanding between them. When it is over, Violetta simply says, after a profound silence, "Command me," but the details of the arrangement prove difficult. Violetta says, prophetically, that no matter what she does or where she goes, Alfredo will follow her. And this he does.

There remains a powerful end to the duet, which reintroduces the idea with which Violetta has become and will continue to be obsessed—her death. "I will die," she says, but do not let him curse me. One day tell him of my sacrifice and that I loved him until my death. As Germont insists that she should live to accept the rewards such a generous sacrifice will yield her, Violetta dismisses Germont, who leaves to skulk in the garden until Violetta has left for Paris.

Amami Alfredo
Violetta now writes two brief notes, one to Flora accepting her invitation for that very evening, the second to Alfredo. As she writes to Alfredo, the clarinet plays a plaintive melody, full of longing.

Alfredo enters, worried that his father may visit them. Violetta must now perform the most difficult task of her life. She rallies her emotions, explaining away her paleness, her trembling as a nervous condition, and uses the anticipated arrival of Germont as an excuse to leave Alfredo and make her escape to Paris. She puts an actress's mask on her despair, pretending to encourage Alfredo about meeting his father. She asks Alfredo if he loves her. He answers as he did before his Act 1 exit: *Oh, quanto...* but with an entirely different music. Then she promises to be just outside, in the garden with the flowers, ... always.

Caught now in what she forsees as the last moments of natural ardor she will be allowed with her beloved, she sings with all the strength remaining her, "Love me, Alfredo"—

Her plea, the most evocative use of the motif first heard in the *Prelude* and then varied by Alfredo in Act 1 (*De quell'amor che palipito*) is sung here with power and delicacy. It is in terms of dramatic eloquence and musical expression an aesthetic high point of the opera.

We will hear this melody twice more, hauntingly, in Act 4, but its appearances will be shadow-like. Although Alfredo introduces this theme of great and passionate love, Violetta lives it. When we hear it again, it, like Violetta, will be a shadow of itself. Like Mimi, Violetta dreams of flowers and the season of their glory, but does not live to enjoy them. The religious and flower imagery of the act end here. They will be renewed in Act 3, as Violetta prays alone, then greets her beloved's return.

The Return to Paris
Alfredo is overcome by Violetta's outburst and confused by the arrival of

his father. Joseph, a servant, enters with word that Violetta has left for Paris. As Germont approaches, the gardener brings a letter from Violetta informing Alfredo of her return to the demimonde. Alfredo falls into his father's arms, who immediately attempts to persuade him to return home to Provence with a sentimental aria, with which he hopes to evoke a sense of place and family loyalty in his only son. Alfredo responds to his father's sentiment with a biblical reference of his own: "A thousand serpents devour me." And no pleading by his father can hold the young man bound on vengeance from pursuing his lover into the depths of Paris.

Violetta, a more pristinely romantic figure than her models in Dumas's novel and play, sought her salvation in the country with Alfredo. When she returns to the city, it is to her destruction and death. She makes this clear in the words she speaks to Germont, but he is too obsessed with his mission to comprehend them until several months later, in Act 3. Alfredo's concern for Violetta's well-being dissolves in fury when he believes she wishes to return to her old life. This we will clearly see in the next scene.

The poetry that surrounds Violetta—from the first verses—is rich with images of mortality and death, as well as desire and pleasure. In Act 1, love is a flower that blooms, withers and dies (the *brindisi*). In her great aria, she sees herself as alone and friendless. In 2,1, we have seen how her pleading with Germont immediately brings her expectation/fear of death to the surface as her love is threatened. "Don't you know," she asks Germont, "that I am deathly ill?"

Later, we will see that she clings to Alfredo with the hope that somehow his love will ease, perhaps even defeat her impending death. The religious imagery in 2,1 is not prepared for in Act 1 and may seem farfetched to our smug contemporary skepticism, but if we take Violetta at her word that she has indeed confessed and been absolved of her sin within the Catholic faith, she has started a new life. If this is true, the nature of her sacrifice becomes even more touching and Germont's request more callous. As her terrible guilt emerges in the scene with Germont, we can imagine the confession of her life of sin in Paris must have been as difficult as its forgiveness was precious. To have it then thrown in her face by Germont is, we have seen, difficult for her ... and terrible in that she senses that even if God forgives her, society—*L'uomo implacabile*—will not.

Now, Alfredo and his father will follow her into the city, where corruption rules and Violetta will face her fate. She flees from happiness to what will be for her the lonely misery of the demimonde. It is in this world of her former glory that her great passion will become compassion and the true nature of her character will be forged, tested and raised to incontestable greatness.

VERDI'S *La Traviata*

Act 2, Scene 2

PUNISHING ILLICIT LOVE

As we read the refined, pristine analyses of skilled music theoreticians, like Julian Budden and Denis Arnold, we admire them for their ability to find an understated world of dramatic meaning in Verdi's score. Since music is the aesthetic glue of the remarkable complex of elements of which opera is comprised, we owe them an enormous debt of gratitude. There is, however, a huge world below the musical tip of the aesthetic iceberg. Sometimes the justification for aesthetic acts that are not explainable in terms of one art form can be more completely evaluated by considering the interaction of music with the three remaining disciplines that make a essential contributions to operatic form. In addition to the literary, dramatic, musical and visual arts aspects, which will be discussed in the fifth section of this study, there is the element of performance art.

Verdi insisted on being intensely involved with the development and refinement of each of these elements in the early productions of his works, especially in the early and middle stages of his career. At first, of course, the apprentice was familiarizing himself with each discipline and exploring its possibilities within the realm of opera. Later, the master was making sure that his vision was realized upon the stage. That he reshaped and refined the vocal, orchestral, dramatic, and to some degree literary aspects of Italian opera is clear. That his remarkably successful formulas for music drama have inspired the visual arts to newer heights is to be expected.

Act 2, Scene 2

Scenes 9 through 15 of Act 2 constitute, it seems to me, a separate act and are generally treated as such in production. The musical structure of this group of scenes seems most logical if they are considered a musical-dramatic unit. Scene 9 begins much as Act 1 did, with engaging, energetic music in a social setting:

Instead of Violetta's, however, we are at her friend Flora's.

The first scene introduces the character of the doctor, who will play a larger role in Act 3. He is surprised to hear that "Violetta has left Alfredo forever." Scene 10 features a brief spat between Flora and the Marquis, which functions dramatically as a comic adumbration for the deeply serious scene between Violetta and Alfredo which will shortly follow.

The intensity of the environment heightens in scene 11 with a massive and entertaining chorus number and dance. Structurally, this number and the magnificent finale dwarf the dramatic intimacy of scenes 12 and 13, in which Alfredo confronts Violetta. Seen as the second half of Act 2, scenes 9 - 15 may appear at first glance as musically unwieldy—intrusive upon the basic intimacy of the largely "domestic" drama, which mood has been carefully developed in smaller domestic scenes of unsurpassed quality. Taken as a unit unto itself, however, scenes 9-15 prove a balanced unit both in dramatic and musical terms. The two striking ensembles, which raise the emotional content of the act ever higher, function to represent various aspects of a society that, in its schism of moral values, both produced Violetta in the empty frivolity of its demimonde and will crush her with the high moral dictates of its public domain.

The larger musical-dramatic picture makes it clear that these two ensembles represent the social forces that created and will destroy Violetta. It is not unreasonable to suggest that this aspect of Verdi's handling of large-form musical elements will receive its ultimate expression in *Aida*, which offers an even more acute contrast of domestic intimacy (individual/eros) and magnificent choral ensembles (society/death). *Aida* also features sublime orchestral, choral and solo vocal music—as well as epic visual effects—in every scene, from its most vast to its most intimate.

The tendency is to see scene 11 of *La Traviata* and much of *Aida* as pure entertainment, but *La Traviata*'s obligatory chorus and ballet number is justified, it seems to me, in terms of large-form aesthetic balance. *Aida*'s great ensembles emblemize the monolithic power of the Egyptian theism that will inexorably crush Aida and Rhadames, while scene 11 of *La Traviata* illustrates clearly the appeal and excesses of the demimonde which once so entranced Violetta. It is so easy, critically, to demand homogeneity and pristine balance of musical form, while forgetting about the necessity and dramatic power of contrasting elements, of which Shakespeare makes us so constantly aware. *La Traviata*'s 2, 2 is wonderfully engaging, with the Finale demonstrating once again a unique glory of opera—the ensemble in which a great variety of issues and characters are combined in large musical form to freeze, then expand crucial moments. If there is a problem of balance between the intimate and grand scenes in 2,2, it may be simply the extraordinary success of the former that makes the latter seem somehow intrusive. Perhaps Verdi is simply trying to accomplish more than operatic form will allow; in aiming so high, he invites criticism for this risky flight into near-perfection. Certainly the Finale of 2,2 is that, but we are not so far along in our analysis.

After the ballet and chorus, the atmosphere is charged for Alfredo's entrance. He enters with a musical flourish and publicly dismisses Violetta. "Bravo," answers the demimonde. With Alfredo's entrance, however, comes a new unease with a quavering figure in a minor key, which may be meant to suggest, on a literal level, the shuffling of cards. There is a restless striving in this music, a searching of lover for beloved.

Gambling and love are the complementary topics at hand, and Alfredo will later note sardonically that he has become the well-known cliché.

Violetta enters, her state hinted at in the stage directions: "leaning on the Baron's arm." Upon learning that Alfredo is present, Violetta utters *Ciel!* The Baron warns her to absolutely ignore Alfredo. This she cannot do. Sensing a confrontation, Violetta sings, "Why did I risk this?" in a lyrical, arching phrase full of tension with the accompaniment.

This phrase hints at the significant melody on which the Verdi builds his final ensemble of 2,2.

Verdi the melodist is in supreme form here, describing emotional states with melodic contour.

As Alfredo wins at cards, he implies that his luck was earned by misfortune in love, though he insists that he will take his winnings and live in the country with the woman he loves. The Baron uses Alfredo's lucky streak as an excuse to goad him into reckless betting, and Flora and Violetta withdraw. Alfredo continues to win, the impulsive actions of the gamblers driven on by the restless, quavering motif established earlier.

As in Act 1, dinner is now served and Violetta uses this opportunity to beg Alfredo to cease his jealous raging. He will leave only if she accompanies him. On her refusal, he—in a jealous rage—forces her to lie to sustain the truth of her promise to Germont. He then drags Violetta before the company and in a jealous rage throws his winnings in her face. The reaction of the chorus is immediate and powerful.

And thus begins scene 15 and one of the great finales in all of opera.

The River

Imagine now, if you will, that you are on a river. For some time, you have been a part of this singular river's mood and movement. You entered into the river, became a part of its irresistible drive and flux, in a series of almost-still pools where the current's rhythms were barely discernible. Yet there was subtle motion that moved you slowly on until the current began to draw you from the unclear lull downstream with sweeping, graceful movements.

Then you burst suddenly into the brilliant sunshine of dancing waves and tossing, gay sounds. The rush and outbursts of bright energy do not frighten you. You do not ever feel yourself separate from or endangered by them or by any of the elements enclosing you in your voyage down river, for you are a part of everything happening to you and the elements enclosing you. You are both observer of and participant in everything happening around you.

After a time, you become accustomed to the alternating calms and outbursts of energy that shape the geography of the river's progress toward the vast sea, *il mare profonda ed infinita*, at its end. In the stretches where the calming river broadens, you recover your introspective powers, yet feel clearly that this apparent calm of the surface hides deep and powerful currents that never rest. Then, after one such ambivalent section, you enter a broad and powerful section in which all of nature appears to combine in a pleasant, involving way.

Then suddenly the river contracts and the current becomes powerful in its narrow thrust, and the power propels you through rising stone sides until you think it impossible that you remain one with the elements about you. Then, in a cataclysm of wild motion, both unexpected and inevitable, you see immediately before you the blue of sky and feel the final thrust of current that will send you soaring off the top of a great waterfall.

At the still point at which you top the crest of the water's flow before it begins its crashing downward motion, you find yourself frozen in time for a long crystalline moment, utterly aware of the forces which brought you to this suspension of time and space. You are able now to consider the broad array of forces that brought you here and at the same time to study the great arc of cascading energy before you. It falls endlessly in vibrant patterns into an eddying, mist-filled series of broad mirrors below, and far beyond them a rippling silken ribbon of water joins the vast sea on the horizon.

In this manner we approach not only the Finale of 2, 2 of *La Traviata*, but also the Act 3 quartet of *La Bohème*, and the Act 3 Finale of *Carmen*. These are the great turnings of plot where characters writhe in fiery union, then separate—or recombine for a short time, only to part later—and hurtle toward their tragic destinies. At this point in the structures of these three operas, the entire cadre of interdisciplinary forces combine to create the extraordinary power of the operatic ensemble, which both freezes time and space and expands the consciousness of the listener. Puccini uses four voices, continuing to cultivate the essential intimacy he has so carefully crafted for his bohemian lovers since Mimi's entrance in Act 1. Bizet uses carefully delineated character development and exposition to build his great finale to the penultimate outbreak of José's rage in public. Verdi freezes us atop a music waterfall after two flooding acts of emotional development.

The Finale

To begin the finale, Germont's solo voice angrily denounces Alfredo's behavior. (This was preceded by Alfredo's abusive outburst and the fortissimo reaction of outrage from the chorus.) Now action moves into slow motion as each character reflects on the forces now loose in their personal universe. Within the powerful musical form, Verdi now simultaneously explores the inscapes of his diverse characters. Germont scolds his son severely for his outrageous public behavior, while Alfredo retreats into bitter self-recrimination. This evokes Violetta's forgiving Alfredo. She knows that they are both victims of a situation they can no longer control. The deep emotional currents he feels are justified by his passion for her. Only Violetta can fully grasp all the elements of the situation. It must remain so until Alfredo's unnamed sister is married.

After the chorus has berated Alfredo, it sympathizes with Violetta, then draws back—as a Greek chorus might—to become a distanced observer proclaiming friendship and sympathy. This distancing is accomplished musically by Verdi, as the chorus is drawn—as so often in Verdi choral ensembles (remember the *brindisi*)—into the mode of orchestral accompaniment. This creates the effect of a completely integrated musical-dramatic fabric, rather than the choral numbers that open each of *Carmen*'s acts and serve primarily to help establish the setting and environment—mood—of the act.

The words to the Finale describe the situation rather than advance the action. This is typical of the contemplative nature of operatic ensemble: time freezes, as dramatic context expands internally into character inscape. Both Violetta and Alfredo are victims here and do suffer. As so often happens in life and art, dramatic tension is created by what one character does not know. This is the case with Alfredo. What he does not know leads to greater suffering.

Verdi builds his great finale on a melody of architectonic power and elegance:

It is supported by a significant musical design.

Germont's outrage is based, because of his knowledge of a situation he himself has created, on old-fashioned values concerned with propriety. He is also genuinely shocked, I believe, by Alfredo's wild reactions to his machinations. Alfredo is genuinely in agony, as his broken phrases show. Violetta's faint but passionate response introduces the characteristic for which we most clearly remember her character and which will be developed greatly in Act 3, compassion.

It is this great character's movement from passion to compassion in Act 3 that raises this work of art above many compositions of near-excellent technical qualities.

Certainly then, we must look to this great character for the moving force of not only the plot but of this musical number. After Germont and Alfredo's solo utterances, it is Violetta's melody that the structural essence of the ensemble appears, when, having been joined by the chorus and soloists and accompanied by the haunting oboe, she sings the words "May God comfort you in your remorse." (Note her use of religious vocabulary.) Alfredo then takes up the melody with the words "I wanted to flee but, blinded by anger, could not," and his voice is joined by Violetta as it approaches the melody's peak. Then the violins and woodwinds voice the theme in its full splendor and the ensemble begins to build its elegant waves toward its climax.

Note the short alternating pianissimo and fortissimo phrases as the number draws to a close, signaling the unrelieved tension of the situation. Remember we have been exploring individual and collective inscape, a world replete with emotion and intention in this ensemble. All the pent-up tension will be manifested in the Baron's final visual gesture: he challenges Alfredo to a duel. (The duel occurs offstage between Acts 2 and 3 and, like much violent action in opera, the result of the duel will be mentioned *en passant* in the spattering of exposition that occurs within the first several minutes of the next act.)

Let me repeat that this great Finale is the musical climax and character turn of the opera. Damaged personally and publicly beyond repair, Violetta is helped from the scene. The next music we will hear will tell us everything we need to know about Violetta's future.

Act 3—Musical Form and Dramatic Content

THE HEROINE'S ASCENT FROM PASSION TO COMPASSION

The opening and closing acts of both *La Bohème* and *Carmen* occur in the same setting—scene or area—giving visual closure while at the same time allowing multi-dimensional contrasts for the good detective. Each opening act depicts the birth of love, while each final act depicts its death. In the final scenes of each of these three works of art, musical ideas and imagery are also repeated in patterns that recall the initial meeting of the lovers whose affair is the basis for the plot. The motivic return of material in each final scene also has the ironic effect of fading memory: there is no return to an idealized past; Death intervenes.

In *La Traviata*, the music and lighting of Act 3 create an immediate environmental contrast with what we experienced in Act 1. Everything about Act 1 of *La Traviata* is bright, vivacious, imbued with life; never has plot exposition been more engaging. In stark contrast, Act 3 is shrouded in dark hopelessness as death hovers about Violetta. We know from the first moments of this act that Violetta's guilty, striving soul has intuited that her death is near.

Literary image and theme, dramatic characterization and plot, and (above all) musical form will now join in one singular musical-dramatic entity to portray Violetta's emotions as she faces the last short chapter of her life. The character of Violetta dominates this opera as no operatic character, previous to 1853, had and as few have since. The imagery used to describe and enhance aspects of Violetta's character will now culminate in her recitative, aria and final ensemble. The familiar theme of the romantic countryside (2,1) will reappear briefly in duet form. Images of eros and thanatos flit everywhere as the act progresses toward its final musical form, the death march—marked by what Budden calls "those fatal tattoos on the full orchestra"—that begins after Germont has entered.

Notably, the religious imagery which has begun to ennoble Violetta since 2,1 will be enhanced through repetition and development in Act 3, as well as find major complements in stage action. For example, upon seeing Alfredo, Violetta's first impulse is to go to church and pray in gratitude. This impulse is complemented by Verdi's luminous music, whose haunting ascending passages begin early in the act to hint as the ascent of Violetta's *turbata anima* (troubled soul). The mechanics of plot, to which Aristotle ascribed such importance, bring all major characters together now. But the essential accomplishment of this act— and of all great opera—is in the unique union of character development and musical-literary integrity in the final acts as the unique tension between character and plot resolves itself.

Verdi's music also makes singular symbolic statements, which seek to describe the deepest and most ambivalent aspects of human experience, aspects ranging from terror to ecstasy, which only music can paint with its aural brush. Act 2, scene 2 has closed with its clamor and dumb show, and we now enter into the troubled mind, distended emotions and emaciated body of Violetta. We now discover the real meaning of Verdi's *Prelude*. The diaphanous strings again sketch the frailest of harmonies to serve as background and descriptive mode for the mortally sick Violetta. We discover her and hear her first waking utterances as the strings end this variation of the Prelude's opening section, sighing off the beat.

The imagery of this scene is economic and straightforward. Violetta longs for "a little light" and says she has taken great comfort in having received the last rights from a priest the evening before. She gives her last money to the poor as penance, remarking that she will have enough to last her. Religious imagery now fills her thoughts. Both her solo passages in this act will be addressed to God, prayer-like.

Violetta now reads a letter—for perhaps the one-hundredth time—from Germont, as a solo violin restates the melody representing her love for Alfredo. She despairs of him coming and repeats the visual motif of studying herself—*o qual pallor!* from Act 1—in the mirror, but now she looks deeper into the mirror and in an elegant conversation with her soul—represented by the oboe's plaintive echo of her vocal phrases—she begs God to smile on her now that her life is over. Budden mentions that this lovely aria is a "valedictory counterpoise" to a *forse lui*, but I feel that its great power derives not only from its place in the musical design. There is also the union of its images of fading dreams and roses with the ascending ends of phrases that seem to signal Violetta's escape from earthly longings and dreams into more eternal concerns and visions.

The off-stage chorus now intrudes upon the essential intimacy of *La Traviata*'s story for the last time, boisterously reminding us with its bacchanalian imagery that sacrifice is always needed for society's celebrations—now an ox must be sacrificed, now a high-minded prostitute who tries to climb above her station to a normal life. *Carmen*'s immediate juxtaposition of another beast of sacrifice with a victim of masculine passion in Act 4 is more directly accessible, literarily and dramatically, than this rhythmic echo of ancient times. My point here is that from a poetic point of view—based in the text's imagery—this distant yet intrusive chorus makes its literary contribution to the plot's logic. It is also the final, faint reminder of Violetta's former social vivacity, now reduced to two off-stage verses.

After the rhythm of the music doubles then quadruples, Alfredo enters and the lovers relive memories of happier days in the country. "Neither man nor devil shall part us, my angel," she says to Alfredo, unconsciously continuing her religious imagery. All the music which accompanies Violetta in the next sequence describes her frailty, feigned gaiety,then her terrifying realization that she does not have the strength to rise and go to church with Alfredo,... that she cannot survive now, even with his presence and love. Her panic and terror become clear in the jagged phrases and insistent rhythms of the cabaletta, "Dear God, to die so young." Her denial and panic over, Violetta greets Germont, who huffs in only to realize that every mention of death Violetta had uttered in the country house had been meant literally. He now addresses her as "daughter" as she had requested of him at the end of their duet in Act 2, scene 1.

Violetta's character now reveals its most precious recesses and begins to dedicate itself to insuring the peace of those she will leave behind. As the death knell begins in the orchestra, she calls Alfredo to her side, takes out a locket, and in heavenly tones instructs him to marry. In a stroke of poetic as well as musical genius, Verdi has Violetta repeat the phrase with telling dramatic effect—so that that which Violetta had most wanted in life, she now wills another in death. She asks that Alfredo describe her as an angel to his wife-to-be. And as the solo violin again voices her declaration of love for Alfredo, she experiences a final delusion of well-being, and collapses.

Verdi's musical form and instrumentation have made the same point time and time again as this act has progressed: the heroine's death approaches inexorably. This is important, not because it might be conceived as morbidly deterministic, but because it emphasizes fully the bravery and strength of Violetta in overcoming terror in the face of death. Violetta's character is the essence of *La Traviata*. The ability of Violetta to transform passion into compassion raises *La Traviata* very high in the pantheon of Western art. The deepest secrets of this character are first hinted at musically, then defined in musical-dramatic context, the means of which is so lean and economic that it is sometimes difficult to believe the power, even more so the elegance, with which Verdi has offered us Violetta's transformation within the painful chrysalis of Paris's demimonde.

NOTES:

[i] After examining the essays introducing the ENO libretto, you will find two informative discussions of Verdi's *La Traviata* very useful: (1) Julian Budden's discussion in *Verdi* (New York, 1987) on pages 226-31, and (2) Charles Osborne's in *The Complete Operas of Verdi* (New York, 1969), 263-76. Both these books are fine additions to the aficionado's library.

Part 5

STRAVINSKY'S *The Rake's Progress*
AND THE VISUAL ARTS IN OPERA

The Rake's Progress and The Visual Arts

It is rewarding to consider the stage picture as a three-dimensional painting. The proscenium arch is its frame, characters its living figures. All materials that fill the frame of the painting are carefully coordinated in terms of color and texture and are mediated by filtered light to create a singular, multiple-surfaced "stagescape." This part of our discussion emphasizes the visual aspects of *The Rake's Progress* and of opera generally.

When music is added to this setting, environment—the feeling created in the viewer by the setting—is enhanced. Consider the frigid outskirts of Paris in Act 3 of *La Bohème*, the lazy warmth of Sevilla at mid-day in Act 1 of *Carmen*, the brilliant midnight soiree of Act 1 of *La Traviata*, or the lonely depths of a London street in Act 2 of *The Rake's Progress*. Each element of each scene is carefully measured, cut, stretched, painted; shaped or plastered. The elements are then assembled and lit to create a specific visual effect and mood that complements character, action and music. So important is this aspect of opera that excellent sets may draw spontaneous applause quite independent of character action—though rarely independent of music.

The Rake's Progress consists of nine scenes, two settings of which are used more than once. Each setting begins with the set designer's consideration of this bare stage space,

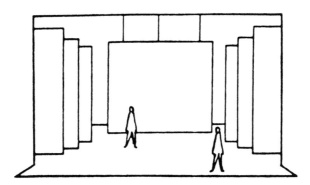

and ends as a living painting in which physical, verbal and musical gesture interact to create meaning. Text, plot, character and music interact with the visual in the opera's time-space continuum. It is vital to remember that in a staged, televised or filmed performance, the visual should, generally speaking, almost always be servant to the aural. The setting should be functional to the poet and musical-dramatist's art.

This opera is such a curious amalgam of literary and musical styles that a full appreciation of it in performance may be greatly heightened by investigation of the literary and musical elements from which it was forged. Both Auden and Stravinsky were unerringly intellectual and witty creators; both were fond of complex forms and game playing. There is much more to *The Rake's Progress* than meets the eye, yet what does meet the eye seems to me inherently fascinating and vital to an understanding of this twentieth century masterpiece. But those who approach it purely for the beauty and variety of its music will not be disappointed, for, as Vera Stravinsky remarked, this opera contains the most beautiful music her husband, the last great composer, ever created.

The first essay below explores some aspects of how the stage area serves as a visual base for operatic experience. The role of perception and visual aesthetics in the big picture of opera cannot be overestimated, whether one attends a staged version or views a taped/filmed one.

The second essay of this section traces aspects of the transfer of scenes, plot and characters from the famous oil paintings that were so popular in 1735 that William Hogarth created a set of eight copyrighted engravings of the oils. (It was the sale of these engravings that brought him a measure of prosperity.) Stravinsky greatly admired these paintings at a Chicago exhibition and approached the English poet Wystan Hugh Auden, a practiced librettist and playwright, about creating a libretto along plot lines carefully sketched out in Hogarth's visual scenarios. So this opera's initial inspiration was based on relatively pure visual impressions. For his part, Hogarth had consciously aimed at dramatic continuity and content in the narrative portrayed in his visual sequences.

The third essay is an intensive, text-based discussion of the final scene of *The Rake* as summary and conclusion. This substantial essay sketches out my analytic approach to opera in the general sense and will offer, I hope, some insight into this—or any other—opera's literary, dramatic, musical, and, often, visual subtlety. Auden's poetry is of such high quality, quite apart from Kallman's contribution to plot and character, that it cannot be too greatly appreciated. It is signal in the history of opera. Stravinsky's music needs no defense. That history united these two geniuses in this work is something of a miracle.

The final essay is a brief summary of this book's ideas. It offers a kind of map, but only a map. The real cosmos of opera, the heart and essence of each opera, must be discovered by the individual. Only the individual listener can bring opera to life.

STRAVINSKY'S *The Rake's Progress*

Aspects of Visualizing

I am constantly struck by the enormous richness of opera as an aesthetic phenomenon. Opera is theater and as such includes the ancient elements of verse, painting, and mime-dance. The curious blending of ancient (mythic plots and values) and modern (electric lighting) give opera pleasing timelessness, a dream-like quality in performance. This is even true of nightmare operas, like *Wozzeck* or *Lulu*. Opera is one of the most successful of artistic media for recreating human consciousness, especially its emotional aspects.

In its attempt to recreate the ancient Attic performers' chanted sound and accompaniment, early Italian opera made music (*melos*) rather than literature (*lexis*) its chief and determinant constituent. Spectacle (*opsis*) has become an indispensable element of most opera, just as it was to Attic tragedy. Costumes and make-up indicate the characters' external characteristics and, sometimes, point to internal values, while hand properties allow actors to externalize their thoughts by extending thought through stage action. The painted flat and three-dimensional set pieces are arranged in such a way as to represent, when viewed from the audience's perspective, an actual environment within the stage space. For these elements to become absolutely clear to the viewer one can view the back stage area before or after a performance, come to a working rehearsal, or—better yet—work backstage on a production.

The opera audience is bombarded with visual and auditory impressions in an operatic performance. When the audience has been prepared in advance of the performance—through reading and listening the work to be seen—and when the production itself is a successful blending of musical, theatrical, literary, and visual elements, a luminous image of the opera may emerge for the listener-viewer. This luminous image is likely to be associated with a character such as Mimi, Carmen, José, or Tom. This character will, in turn, usually be associated with a singular idea or ideal, e.g. romantic passion, personal freedom, obsessions such a jealousy or greed, or political or philosophical ideals. Almost always introduced in Act 1's exposition, this principle idea of an opera grows in richness as the audience gathers impressions from plot development. In theater, this line of development consists of verbal and physical gestures, and eventually acquires an emotional contour with which the audience empathizes. Opera employs both of these gestures to musical form, so that the music's ability to evoke an immediate emotional response charges a character's thought or action with a special power and poignancy essential to that character's definition and development. In the greatest operas, character and music are on some levels synonymous.

Music

Music is most effective in a dramatic structure when it is firmly grounded in a verbal-visual stage matrix, an environment replete with three-dimensional characters and dramatized human issues, both of which elements music can crystallize with symbolic power. We have seen this process occur in each of our operas: in the calm ecstasy of the flute trill climaxing Mimi's Act 1 aria; in the melancholy yearning of the *cor anglais* reiteration of *Carmen*'s fate theme at the introduction to *La fleur*; in the anguished clarinet solo (2,2) of *La Traviata*; and in the lonely coronet that will accompany Anne into London (2,2). In each of these moments, when firmly grounded in dramatic context, music lifts itself to new expressive freedom—*frei aber froh* (free only in discipline)—within the drama and makes a unique contribution to opera.

Here music expresses the inexpressible, that which can only be sensed in fleeting moments recollected in tranquility. T.S. Eliot speaks of this property of music as a fringe of indefinite extent, of feeling we can only detect, so to speak, out of the corner of the eye and on which we can never completely focus; of feeling of which we are only aware in a kind of temporary detachment from action.... This particular range of sensibility can be expressed by dramatic poetry at its moments of greatest intensity. At such moments, we touch the border of those feelings which only music can express.

Music performance is a science, but its effect is quite abstract in nature. For this abstractness to complement and augment the effects of word and action in opera, the composer must have a certain understanding of the greater dramatic purpose of the opera. Only occasionally is music permitted to speak in the context of musical drama with that "greatest intensity" alluded to by Eliot above. In such occasions reside opera's greatest gift to us, however, and we should listen for them carefully.

Listening

When we listen to a recorded opera, we discover that we are able to create human figures, action, and even settings and costumes in our mind's eye and to let them live in the theater of our mind. Opera's lyric poetry evokes special images and ideas. The combination of poetry and music in opera offers an immediate uniqueness and charm.

Words trigger visual images that give rise to concepts when combined in a mental process involving association. These verbal-visual concepts then fit into a dramatic environment already prepared for them by music or are emotionally charged with music as they are sung. The power of the word may lessen when the actual stage setting appears, simply because the mind fills with the immediate visual image. The fragile internal image is overcome by the external one. For this reason opera viewers have a distinct advantage when they have read the text and listened to the words within a musical setting before viewing the performance. Then, when the viewer does add the visual environment, they can compare their vision of the opera with Zeffirelli's, Rosa's or Hockney's in the filmed versions, or with that of a stage production.

Concrete or language-based imagery plays a primary role in most conscious activity, yet clearly thought without image per se exists, thought which we might describe in terms of intuition or a flux of sensory impression. Purely musical or visual images elicit this type of mental activity. It is difficult to "image" music except in abstract visual impressions, sometimes perhaps in the vaguest of gestures, in colors, or geometric shapes. We are moved by music, perhaps feel we understand it emotionally, and still have great difficulty describing it and its meaning, in "imaging" it in concrete terms. Images created in us by pure music often fall into this wordless, dreamy category of mental impressions. It has been argued that opera is inherently irrational because of the dominant role of music in the aesthetic hierarchy of opera. But the unique combination of operatic elements allows us to assign more concrete meaning to relatively pure emotional values through the musical gestures that rise out of the musical-dramatic tapestry like golden birds. These flights enhance the meaning of the text, but also augment it emotionally as only music can.

Music emphasizes the impressionistic aspects of words, setting and action; it may also aggravate the already considerable tension between the literal physical nature of an object and the image of it the stage designer gives us in the production he creates. Hockney's modernistic stage settings for *The Rake's Progress* emphasize this tension, rather than minimize it. Zeffirell's cinematic *La Traviata* and especially Rosa's naturalistic cinematic treatment of *Carmen* take other paths. Indeed, they belong to another genre, the filmed opera, as opposed to the filmed stage production. I chose to divide the recommended visual recordings between the two treatments of opera visual recording: *La Bohème* and *The Rake's Progress* are taped stage productions, while *Carmen* and *La Traviata* are filmed operas. The former are important because they keep our feet in the theater, where opera was born and developed. The latter are important because they adapt opera successfully to a new medium, film, and help us discover opera's flexibility and aesthetic viability in the age of television and cinema.

The Visual

We can describe abstract thought, e.g. the musical experience, in terms of "a skeleton of essential dynamic features" (Arnheim), none of which is a tangible part of an actual object. Music's power in opera is to project these "essential dynamic features" on the dramatic process, emphasizing the internal world of character and the environment where characters act. These images can be powerful within dramatic context. In art, the character of a human figure is reduced to the simple economy of an expressive gesture, as in the illustration on the following page, the sixth of eight engravings from Hogarth's series *The Rake's Progress*.

Here, in despair and frustration, our hero rages at heaven having lost all he owned. His fallen wig symbolizes the disorder in his mind. He raises his fist to the heavens, cursing Fate. Although his figure is central to the engraving's composition, study the frozen gestures and attitudes of the figures enclosing him. They will tell you much about the hero and the forces at work on him. Here—as in each of the eight plates we will later analyze in relation to character and plot—objects and acts of a purely symbolic nature complement the character's mood as well as the atmosphere representing the forces that destroy him.

It can be useful to approach a stage picture in this way, by discussing physical image and gesture in detail, especially since Hogarth's plates approximate the shape of the stage space within the proscenium stage opening. Opera is an art form that employs images in ways comprehensible to our perceptual and conceptual processes: images function as part of a complex visual environment in stage setting, as symbolic gestures in performance, and as signs through text. The fusion of all these aspects of image occurs in us naturally as listeners/viewers.

The Rake's Progress' Stage Setting

Earlier we described the contribution of lyric poetry to the aria, a musical form that plays a major role in developing character. Now we want to explore the role of the stage picture in indicating the external life of a character, the atmosphere of the operatic environment, and to a lesser extent the action of the play. Characters in *The Rake's Progress* are two-dimensional at best; they prefer to talk about rather than do things. And the stage settings are not as important in a literal sense here as in *La Bohème*, *Carmen* or *La Traviata*, where from the beginning the stage setting was regarded by the composers and librettists as an essential part of the opera's content. The settings of *The Rake's Progress* are largely dictated by musical form, it seems to me. Stravinsky's music is so unique and his—and Auden's—interpretation of Hogarth's dramatic content so colored by modern irony. Composing is not so much expression to Stravinsky as metaphysical construction and color. The scenic complement to his music may well be spare and essential to accommodate the formal linear qualities of his unique amalgam of musical styles, the striking colors of his orchestration, and dominating rhythmic drive.

These latter two aspects would seem to demand straightforward and predictable characters and plot interpretations, but scenic furnishings of a startling variety have typified productions of *The Rake*. They have ranged from period perfection to extraordinary abstractness. David Hockney's setting matches Stravinsky's musical irony with a storybook simplicity of form dominated by heavy geometric forms and vertical lines. Perhaps these bar-like patterns symbolize the determinism of Tom's narrative. Stravinsky's music is inherently satiric of the standard operatic repertoire, yet it has its own formal integrity and awesome abstract power. This opera is a unique hybrid.

The setting of *The Rake's Progress* is located largely in the orchestra pit. This may be one reason why the characters never develop beyond the two dimensions typical for a complex allegory. These two great creators deliberately chose a non-realistic form in which to explore the themes that fascinated them. Theirs is the intellectual world of satire and irony. They were supreme masters in their media and their set text generally dominates the visual elements, reducing visual effects to necessities or showy pantomime and giving us the opportunity to clearly appreciate the basic, complementary function of technical theater in opera. Every element is stylized to an extreme. The actors describe what they are doing to do rather than act it out. The music ventures into the depths of character only rarely and then only in melancholy situations. All this makes the visual aspect of *The Rake* a fascinating variable from production to production.

Reduced in this way to highly variable basics, the scenic elements of *The Rake* should become apparent, especially when we study which scenes and characters Auden and Stravinsky chose to maintain and develop from Hogarth's extremely dense visual tableaux. The stage setting's greatest contributions to an operatic performance are to create an environment for the action of the plot, an atmosphere to reflect character emotion and development, and—with stage lighting's aid—to complement the orchestral colors in creating mood. Before we begin to examine the visual source of *The Rake's Progress*, let us discuss the relationship between visual aspects and the literary, dramatic, and musical elements we have established so far.

The big picture we see on the stage within the frame of the proscenium joins the musical, dramatic and literary elements to affect us and create a total sensory impression. The effect of visual elements will depend primarily on each viewer's experience, taste and perceptual abilities. The more we know about what we see, the better can we appreciate the skill with which it was created. Here are a few ideas concerning color.

In terms of intensity, quality and texture, some colors will affect us more for objective reasons (bright, saturated colors please—dull, mixed ones do not), for physiological reasons (colors seem stimulating or warm, do not dazzle or disturb), or for associative reasons (colors remind us of a certain person, event, place or quality). We may characterize colors—they seem jovial or energetic, rather than treacherous or aggressive. These apperceptive types are the outcome of perceived properties of the colors. Doubtless each individual's perceptions are also colored by cultural orientation and the resulting values. All of these elements play a role in our reaction to the function of color in the stage setting of an opera, and color is only one aspect of the setting's aesthetic dynamic.

Texture and brightness are subtler aspects of color. The apparent weight of a color varies inversely with its brightness, darker colors appear heavier than lighter colors. The tone of a cello is darker and heavier than that of a violin, or the vocal tone of the bass darker than that of the soprano's. The following mood-tone and corresponding colors tend to be related: exciting (red, yellow or black), secure (blue, brown and green), distressed (orange, black), tender (blue, green), protective (red or brown), despondent (black, brown), calm (blue, green), dignified (purple, black), cheerful (red, yellow), defiant (red, orange, black), powerful (black, red). The feelings described by colors might be described as happiness (depending on lightness), showiness (saturation), forcefulness (color darkness), warmth (hue, especially redness), elegance (saturation and hue, especially blueness), and calmness (darkness, blueness).

In general, the setting, lighting and costume designers consider all these matters in their design and choice of material. They know that the other aesthetic qualities of the big stage picture such as emotional expression, atmospheric effect and religious feeling will be tremendously affected by the use of color and light. There is first a general dimension of aesthetic quality—the big picture—represented by form and emotional expression. Then there is a secondary dimension of representational accuracy meant to be contrasted with atmospheric effect and symbolic expression. This is true of pure poetry, music, and painting, as well as the mixture of these disciplines in opera. We begin with a big picture, then gradually settle down to the study of details, which immediately begin to interact with each other and create tensions through their contrastive aspects. Ultimately, we pick out visual-aural images that take on special meaning for us in terms of our personalities and expertise in the media, and we construe most of the other elements in light of those images or series of images, once they are crystallized in our minds.

In his attempt to transcend time and space, the artist overcomes the limits imposed on the separate arts by these dimensions by combining them. Thus the partially time-bound arts of poetry and music are fused with the spatial and scenic forms on the stage. Consider the importance of these elements in characterization, plot rhythm, atmosphere, and image value. The most original works create a new sense of space through the integration of all visual and aural elements into the design's big waves. Perhaps this explains why scenic designers and stage directors feel so free to vary the settings for an enormously original work like *The Rake*.

It is in combining contrastive elements that the most striking effects are achieved. Dissonance in music has its visual counterpart. Consider the opening scene of Act 3 of *La Traviata*. When those striking, skeletal harmonies and muted tone colors appear, a dark stage enclosure is discovered, perhaps hung with tones of blue, black or green and an area full of great, vague forms of veiled splendor. Against this gloomy tapestry a frail figure (image) in white reclines on a bed. At this point in the great arc of the plot, the whiteness and paleness of Violetta's costume and makeup provide a visual counterpoint—of desolation, loneliness and emptiness which is augmented by the delicacy and other-worldliness of the music and Violetta's condition—to the dark environment enclosing her. Then the human voice emerges from Violetta and we are shocked at the extraordinary weight of its symbolic power, its aesthetic reality.

Stravinsky's extraordinary music, rich in playfulness and artful burlesque of classical musical style and form, makes fewer emotional demands than does the music of Puccini, Bizet and Verdi. Both verse and music are unerringly intellectual and aesthetically playful, rather than melodramatically or realistically demanding. That this work walks the fine line between satire and originality makes it one of the miracles of twentieth-century opera.

In the filmed version I recommend, David Hockney, the contemporary British painter, has chosen to complement the unique modernist-Baroque richness of the Auden/Stravinsky amalgam with a kind of minimalist abstract surrealism. I find it highly successful in that it does not make realistic demands on a work highly symbolic and fanciful in nature. With its dramatic playfulness, Hockney's settings soften Hogarth's original dark satiric thrust somewhat, and we are irresistibly drawn, hopes intact, toward an unexpectedly tragic ending.

The Extraordinary Source
FROM ENGRAVINGS TO LIBRETTO

Libretti are drawn almost exclusively from dramatic or literary sources, and opera text legitimately inherits its tendency to create copious verbal and visual images. The operatic image is especially complex, however, because it is charged with multi-level symbolism arising from both the literary and musical elements in combination, even when not also charged with additional visual significance. *La Bohème* offers, as we have seen, several examples of such highly charged images. We not only see Mimi's *cuffietta rosa*, but we hear it sung about three times and so become aware of its significance for both Rodolfo and Mimi. A second image is Mimi's hands, which are seen and spoken of more often than the bonnet. Mimi's hands are in fact a *nexus* image, one in which a number of important ideas meet: cold, poverty, illness, loneliness, intimacy, vulnerability, a personal contract, beauty and love.

Mimi is an engaging character, but for those going on in Puccini's operas, *Madame Butterfly*'s Cio-Cio-San is a more complete musical-dramatic portrait. She is given more opportunities to react honestly to stressful situations, to blossom from them, to regress to her former life before our eyes, and to assume the mantle of a tragic protagonist. Mimi is given much less opportunity to develop as a three-dimensional character, yet because of her arias and the musical and visual images the audience associates with her, she lives on in our minds long after the curtain falls. She is herself a striking multi-dimensional image.

Imagery, Plot, Character

The most effective images in opera—in literature in general—are those whose meaning seems to emanate from the emotions and acts of the characters themselves, such as Mimi's hands, José's *fleur*, or Tom's Queen of Hearts. These images acquire symbolic value in relation to a particular character and often a particular situation. Together with their musical counterparts, they form striking synesthetic entities. Such images are both dynamic and transformational. José's acacia flower dries in prison, but his love blossoms. Mimi's love, like nature's flowers, blooms for only a short time—and in Winter—before dying with her. Tom finally comes to understand his "living pictures" of 2,1 in the graveyard (3,2), but it is too late. For these images to have maximum effect, they must be used with economy. Auden was aware of this principle when he wrote *The Rake*'s libretto, as Hogarth had been 200 years before him. Illica and Puccini were not so economic, or effective, in their use of imagery, but it was a different age, an age in which imagery was being (over)used in innovative ways in prose narrative, drama and poetry.

The story of Hogarth's Rake is simpler than Tom's story in the opera. The scenarios of the two great works are similar, however, and some of the engravings have been painstakingly reproduced as dramatic tableaus in the opera, especially plates 4 and 8. Stravinsky has fewer major characters, while minor characters swarm about Hogarth's Rake: lawyers, thieves, bill collectors, whores, a wife figure, a jailer, a keeper of the madhouse. But there is no Nick Shadow, no true antagonist, to corrupt Tom and rob him of his sanity; there is no Baba the Turk to clutter his life, and no Sellum to auction off his goods. In Hogarth, the antagonist is Tom—Everyman—himself.

In Hogarth's plates, human society preys on a corrupt Tom. Only his faithful Anne cares enough to follow him on his road to rack and ruin. Our final sight of her is in Bedlam, where she is attempting to comfort her hopelessly insane Tom. The characters added by Auden and Kallman to Hogarth's scenario are of extreme importance to plot, theme and style in *The Rake's Progress*. All the evil of London's macrocosmic environment and of mankind in general as portrayed in Hogarth's engravings is focused and crystallized in the character of Nick Shadow, who acts upon Tom's trusting nature with devastating effect.

Other newly-drawn characters appear to represent the opera's moral values. Truelove replaces Anne's mother as elder overseer of youth. Like well-meaning members of the older generation generally in opera, he is ineffective in combating the forces of corruption. Tom's wife in Plate 5 becomes the oddball, loquacious Baba, who may in an interesting way represent not only uniqueness in life, but Chance itself. She is, ultimately, an ally of Anne (Goodness) and a character of admirable sentiments. Both Baba and Sellum personify show business personalities; they are portrayed as cult figures of their time. Two of the new forces personify corruption: Nick and Mother Goose. Nick and Baba are very interesting and powerful characters; together, they almost wholly determine the plot's action. Being both humorous and grotesque, they are the focus of attention whenever they are on stage.

Hogarth's plates portray one-sided love (Anne's) lost to a callous human frailty (Tom's) and, ultimately, to the corrupting influence of society. Hogarth's Anne, too, has been corrupted by Tom, but survives, presumably through her "strength of purpose" (1,3). As Hogarth's series begins, Anne is pregnant by Hogarth's Rake and holds a betrothal ring in her right hand. Anne's mother clinches her fist in rage, while Tom's written promises of love fall from her apron. He offers her and her mother money, as he is being fitted for the clothing required by his new life in London, whence the whorehouses and gaming rooms call.

How different from the Anne we meet in 1,1 of *The Rake's Progress*! How different the leave-taking from the Truelove country home. Hogarth's Anne is raised in moral stature by Auden and Stravinsky. She has been elevated to a symbol of social propriety. We might in some ways compare her to Micaela. Yet Auden's Anne is, in her own way, liberated. Like Micaela, she knows when she is no longer needed. "Tom, my vow holds ever, but it is no longer I you need."

More importantly, what a different Rake is portrayed in the opera. Hogarth's Rake is shallow, as well as irresponsible, but Auden's Tom will hesitate before each step in his self-destructive path away from Anne and the love we gradually come to see he truly feels in 1,2. Auden's Tom is much more clever and sensitive than Hogarth's appears to be; Auden's Tom must have a perfidious

Nick to push him along the path to hell. Hogarth's Rake manages to cut his own throat quite well alone.

In fact, the Hogarth Rake's initial act in the first plate is far more indicative of inherent weakness of character than any act Auden's Tom commits. Since the operatic Tom is inherently more sensitive and refined than his predecessor, new plot devices must be created to explain his fall. Nick's presence is the chief plot addition. In it, Auden has also added a Faustian overlay to Hogarth's plot. Tom's soul is at stake, not just his Anne-centered love. In true economic mythic fashion, the two male figures become inseparably tied as twins or doubles, and it is only Anne's prodigious sentimental love that rescues Tom's romantic soul from the clutches of hell. Anne is Tom's Margaret, although Tom is only a poor, country nephew of Doctor Faustus.

Two Scenarios

The scenarios of Hogarth's engravings and the Auden libretto offer an interesting comparison. Before we make a more detailed examination of the engravings for details of character, plot, scene, visual image and environment, let's see what Auden took directly from Hogarth. In a way, we can recreate the creative processes of Auden and Stravinsky. The most drastic changes should result from considerations of character. Few of the ways by which we judge character are observable in purely visual art: costume, emotional state as reflected in body language and facial expression, and the appearance of gestures frozen in a limited dramatic context. Hogarth's scenario is on the left, Auden's on the right.

1. Tom's father's office	1. Truelove's Garden, afternoon in Spring
2. Tom's London House	2. Mother Goose's Brothel
3. A Brothel	3. Same as 1, night

4. The Arrest, street
5. The Cynical Alliance
6. The Gambler (White's)
7. Debtor's Prison
8. The Madhouse (Bedlam)

4. Tom's London House, interior, night
5. Tom's London House, exterior, dusk
6. Same as 4, but cluttered
7. Same as 4, but dusty
8. A Churchyard: "Starless Night"
9. Bedlam: Tom's Dream of Spring

Both scenarios share the Tom and Anne figures and several key locales. Tom's decline is traced from the country through a brothel to the interior of his house in London through marriage and scandal to madness in Bedlam. Needless to say, the practical considerations of staging an opera led the librettists to reduce the number of settings from nine to six.

It is natural of course that every character gain in stature in the opera, but, even speaking relative to the mediums, Anne grows most in dramatic stature. She has an entire scene (1,3) to herself and this scene, echoing the structure of *La Traviata*'s first act, is clearly the climax of Act 1. Further, both Anne and Violetta are lyric sopranos, the typical vocal type for young women. Anne has Micaela-like qualities of bravery and strength in suffering. In 2,2, she no longer stands behind the Bailiff as in Hogarth's tableau, but approaches Tom alone in London's evening.

The Bailiff has been replaced in this scene by Baba, and her delightful presence alone causes the next three scenes to be set in Tom's house, rather than in the gambling den or debtor's prison. Nick persuades Tom to gamble on the Stock Market rather than at White's gaming tables, and then lures him to a graveyard rather than Debtor's Prison. In the opera, not only Anne, but Anne's father—subtly conservative and proper in his deep bass tones—follows the "shuttle-headed lad," Tom, to his sad end in Bedlam. Neither she nor her father recognizes or effectively opposes evil. Helplessness in the face of evil is a theme common to both the engravings and the opera.

The growth in Tom's character and the introduction of Baba and Nick are the two major new innovative dramaturgical forces that re-shape and expand Hogarth's plot. As this re-shaping takes place, new action, scenes and images are introduced. The character of Nick facilitates the opera's plot, and Tom and Anne become only pawns in a much larger, endless war between Heaven and Hell. As Hell's representative, Nick is responsible for many symbols, principal among them the "marvelous machine," which leads Tom—and, through him, many sober investors—to a final folly. His counterpart is Anne.

Let's follow the "Progress of a Rake" through Hogarth's plates and illustrate which elements Auden and Stravinsky kept and what these elements contribute to the opera.

Plates 1 and 2—Character, Setting, Image

In tracing the Rake's progress from country to city, we are introduced to his character's weaknesses and the universally corrupt urban environment in which his naiveté will prove to be the trigger for a deadly environmental trap. For Hogarth, a Rococo artist, the country is no better than the city, morally. (In the late 19th century, Rousseau's romantic doctrine will pronounce the superiority of nature to Western civilization. Remember *La Traviata*'s 2,1?) The country lawyer in Plate 1 and the urban assassin in Plate 2 are equally opportunistic. Hogarth's Tom is less honest than Auden's, for Hogarth's Rake has written love letters promising marriage. They spill from the apron of Anne's mother.

These plates establish their own systems of image as symbol, adumbration and motif. To the left in Plate 1 lies a father's broken Bible, a sign of practical morality. It seems that Hogarth's Rake comes by his weakness of character legitimately. In Plate 2, the framed paintings of the fighting cocks prefigure Tom's gambling in Plate 6, as the verse beneath ("Prosperity, with harlot's smiles") prefigures Plate 3. The motif of Anne's vulnerability and helplessness is introduced in Plate 1 and seems to make a statement of the pathetic vulnerability of poor, female members of society.

In both Hogarth's Plate 2 and Auden's second scene, Tom is curiously child-like. He is surrounded and manipulated by the figures who crowd into his London house in Plate 2, while in Mother Goose's brothel he recites like a schoolboy, after which he then, utterly disarmed by Nick's ability to manipulate time and space, falls drunken into the arms of corruption. After this, Tom is swept into London's demimonde and satisfies one curiosity after another, until boredom sets in. In this condition, we find him as Act 2 opens.

The Tom we find as the Act 2 curtain opens is very different from the sleepy Adonis who greets us at the beginning of Act 1. The first scene of *The Rake's Progress* is set in the "Garden of Truelove's house in the country, Afternoon in Spring." The brass heralds our attention to the dramatic ceremony to follow. The curtain opens on a rustic scene in which orchestral birds and beasts play, keeping, in Anne's words, a "festival of May." Auden has instilled this scene and his verse with mythic elements and a strong ritualistic quality. It is Spring—as Tom will sing again, ironically, in the opera's final scene—and the annual return of Adonis from the underworld will soon be celebrated.

Our lovers prepare to re-enact the story of Venus and Adonis. The imagery and intended ritual of this scene will be interrupted by Nick here, only to be futilely re-enacted in the final scene of the opera. Anne (Venus) and Tom (Adonis) will never consummate their love except by a kiss (and two duets). Adonis will return to the underworld leaving only sterility and pain behind him. Remember that Auden's Tom unwillingly left a chaste Anne, who is both true lover and virgin queen, for the brothels, fairs and stock exchange of London. Hogarth's Anne has been Tom's dupe, he her cynical beau.

If you listen carefully to Stravinsky's magical contribution to scene 1, you will find that when Anne and Tom's voices join, their lines do not fit easily into the harmonies and rhythms in the orchestration supporting them. And once Truelove's doubting text joins the lovers' duet, the rhythmic complexity of the initial ensemble also reflects the unsettling quality of their relationship, perhaps even hints at a dire future. Underneath this trio the orchestral figures dance, swirl joyfully and laugh, admitting beauty but only at a cost. On the second listening to Anne and Tom's shared phrases "How sweet, how sweet," the listener will notice the dissonance created by the two solo lines, with a harmonic meaning far different from the etymological sense of the word "sweet." Then with Truelove's commentary comes an uneasy, stinging pattern of accompaniment in the strings. This Eden is not pristine.

So, underneath the visual gloss of the setting, the pastoral poetic description of the young lovers, and the pontificating of Truelove, the orchestra is hinting at the imperfect state of the world that awaits the lovers outside their unique vision of their Garden of Eden. Perhaps the orchestra is already indicating that "a year and a day hence," it will again be Spring and this Venus, Anne, will come to her earthly bridegroom, Adonis/Tom, in his new kingdom, Bedlam. But she will not stay with him there and we will have, to borrow from Joseph Kernan, an eighteenth-century story with a twentieth-century moral. Perhaps Stravinsky wishes for the orchestra to indicate this tension in the first scene and thus has the orchestra subtly indicate the tensions beneath the surface in its ironic, swirling laughter as the youthful lovers frolic in utopian idealism. Compare this to the sneering orchestra that haunts Violetta in Act 1 of *La Traviata*.

Plate 3: Creating Complexity of Character
Auden moves Tom quickly to the brothel's corruption, though he invests the scene with a complexity and integrity of character and plot that we cannot

expect of Hogarth's third engraving. Visual art can only portray character in poses, in frozen moments, in silent arias. As if to salute Hogarth's skill, Auden has the action of 1,2 freeze ominously at one point: Nick says, "See, time is yours. The hours obey your pleasure. / Fear not. Enjoy. You may repent at leisure." In that moment Tom is lost, forever.

Notice that in Plate 3, Tom's pocket is being picked of a watch by two prostitutes. This depiction of stolen time is a major motif in the opera: all of Tom's time will soon be stolen. Hogarth is beginning to work with the repetition of visual images. Notice the pregnant woman standing beside the door in the right of the plate: her position is similar to Anne's in Plate 1. As in Plate 2, musicians seem to accompany the action of the scene. In actuality, in this plate they are to accompany the woman undressing in the right forefront for a performance.

Nick will count the seconds again in 3,2. Perhaps the Rake's watch in this plate inspired Auden's play with time—the creation of that protracted suspended moment in which virtue and truth are lost forever. In another sense, however, Auden and Stravinsky may simply be playing an aesthetic game by taking a unique characteristic of operatic ensemble—freezing action while character inscape is explored and making it a part of the plot.

The mindless rudeness, destruction, debauchery, and thievery pictured in Hogarth's Plate 3 are figuratively described in the Act 1, scene 2 opera chorus' lyrics in the opening and closing choral numbers. Raucous alarm and noise are created by Stravinsky's bustling, bristling orchestration. The bawdiness pictured in Hogarth's plates is augmented in Auden's blatant verses and the raw musical settings chosen by Stravinsky to complement them.

In contrast to Hogarth's Rake, Auden's poor, drunken Tom displays an unforeseen depth of conscience in his romantic aria "Love, too frequently betrayed" before losing his virginity to Mother Goose and, concomitantly, his soul to Nick. With that fine intuition of the innocent damned, Tom senses the right way before he is swept by Fate into chaos. In this momentous aria, he calls on the Goddess of Love, Venus (Anne) to save him from this fate. In 3,2, he will call out for her again, but it will be too late—not to save his soul, but that human possession most praised in eighteenth century philosophy—his mind. The question then becomes, what is the soul without the mind? Is the text here hinting at another twentieth-century moral?

Does this seem too serious a question for opera? *La Bohème* asks, "What is the nature of love?" and "Why can some people not love without being destructive?" *Carmen* asks, "When will woman be allowed social freedom?' and "What is the nature of obsession?" *La Traviata* offers us a profound study of sacrifice and compassion in dying. It also asks, "Why do we judge a person in terms of appearance or things beyond their control?" All of these great works ask other incisive questions concerning haunting human problems: human insensitivity, obsession, social inequality, and poverty. Other operas ask important questions and give strong answers, not only about society but about the law, philosophy, religion, social problems (including the treatment of women and minorities), slavery, the suppression of minorities, spirituality and even the nature of life after death. We make a great mistake when we reduce opera to its melodic content, or its shimmering score. Opera is, it seems to me, worthy of being taken as a whole, complex entity—and on its own interdisciplinary terms.

Tom's aria in 1,2 contains the first reiteration of a major metaphor in the opera—Anne as luminous Venus, Goddess of Love—and marks the beginning of a major sub-arc of imagery. This literary sub-arc climaxes in 3,3 in Bedlam where the mad Tom hails Anne as Venus, a role that she proceeds to play convincingly in the earthly hell of Bedlam. Note that in the intimacy of the aria form we enter Tom's internal world and glimpse his conscience and longing for good—for Anne. This goodness is, for Tom, only found in Anne; in 2,1 he asks, "Who's honest, chaste or kind? / One, only one." But Nick's dark, gyring force is too strong for Tom, and neither Nature—"Green, unnatural mother"—nor the corrupting city, nor the force of goodness itself can save him. Tom is weak; Nick is strong; Anne is ineffectual. Were the characters three-dimensional instead of allegorical puppets, these factors could justify a truly tragic plot. *The Rake's Progress* is, however, a contemporary fable, and Auden and Stravinsky are geniuses whose twentieth century sensibilities drove them to embrace the ambiguity of tragicomic form.

It would be wrong not to mention the integrity of Stravinsky's work in Anne's Act 1 aria. This scene markedly augments Anne's character. There is a strong unity between scenic environment and Stravinsky's orchestration. The initial orchestral figures and instrumentation of this scene repeat patterns similar to those in the opening phrases of 1,1, but at a slower tempo and in darker tones: the bird songs now reflect sadness, worry and Anne's reflective mood, rather than her love for Tom. (Later, in 2,2, Tom will sing, "And on the frozen ground, / The birds lie dead.") The arbor of 1,1 is gone and will never return.

Note that much of the accompaniment of the first half of the aria is constructed of motifs from the first scene. Note also how reminiscent of Micaela is the accompaniment to Anne's prayer and its resolution into the splendid *cabaletta*: "O God, protect dear Tom, Support my father, and strengthen my resolve." She is supported here by Mimi and Micaela's noble French horns, and her back straightens to a similar purpose. Instead of facing *Carmen*'s wild mountains of Spain, however, she enters the human jungle of Mimi and Violetta's city. "London, alone, seems all that it can say." Remember Mimi's *sola*?

Plates 4 and 5: Anne's Integrity—Baba, a New Character

Plate 4 shows Tom's arrest, with Anne struggling to save him through her hard-earned seamstress wages. Tom is surrounded by riffraff again, this time by the street urchins who mock the adults they study in the streets. One Artful Dodger-type picks Tom's pocket. Baby clothes and various utensils fall from Anne's seamstress kit, informing us of her occupation and that her child by Tom has arrived. Tom has gone through his fortune, and his shock at being apprehended is registered in the lightning bolt in the sky. Note the similarity of theme and composition between this plate (4) and the final plate (8). A triangle of characters forms a balanced arrangement in relation to the centerpiece of the plate's composition, Tom. Anne, who is interfered with by a middle figure, struggles to reach Tom.

This basic triangle is also the unit of the stage picture framed by the proscenium. Anne is quite impressive in Plates 4 and 8. These two plates may serve as the basis for the effective stage figure Auden and Stravinsky constructed.

Auden makes this plate's visual elements the basis for 2,2, where Anne arrives in London and confronts Tom on the street in front of his apartment.

It is the subject matter of Plate 5, however, that greets Anne in the scene inspired in Plate 5, and not Tom's penury or lack of repentance. Hogarth's marriage concerns money, not sport. In a decaying, out-of-the-way chapel, Tom now offers the ring Anne held in Plate 1 to an aging dowager. The ever present and persistent Anne, her infant in arm, and her mother fight for entrance into the chapel. Tom eyes the widow's chamber maid with sanctimonious lechery, as the dowager eyes the priest. All affection seems relative but Anne's; corruption is everywhere.

In *The Rake*, this dowager is replaced by Auden with the fantastic Baba, and this ceremony occurs between scenes 1 and 2 of Act 2. Moreover, Tom's penury is delayed by Auden until the Stock Market Crash of 3,1; and the motivation for Tom's marriage is wanton folly or, at best, the desire for notoriety. This foolhardiness is generated by boredom and the need for attention; Tom wants to be the man "Whom neither Passion may compel / Nor reason can restrain." Soon enough he will realize his extravagance and folly, but by then it will be too late. Nick sees to that.

Stravinsky's orchestration in 2,2 is noteworthy for its use of pulsing strings in the lower register, alternating with thick fortissimo chords to introduce the lovely, simple coronet figure representing Anne's loneliness and the emptiness of a huge city when one has no home there.

As in the final ensemble of *La Traviata*, a rhythmic device serves as the basis for the accompaniment. Stravinsky's rhythmic device here denotes the necessity and uncertainty of physical action. "No step in fear" sings Anne, but the accompaniment implies another thing entirely, as a timid, irregular march figure steps, then hesitates, steps and hesitates. A study of Stravinsky's prodigious skill in portraying the emotional states of characters through such subtle rhythmic devices and metric variations would yield riches.

Stravinsky's glory is his rhythmic power and subtlety. Puccini's strongest element is clearly his melody, though, as we saw in *La Bohème*, he built his score around a rhythmic motif which would not be so terribly out of place in Stravinsky's less melody-oriented musical style. Remember how important rhythm has been to all our composers: to Bizet in the opening to Act 2, in the subtle variations of the Toreador Song used in Act 4, and in the striking variations of the *Carmen*'s Fate motif in Act 4's final scene; for Verdi in the final ensemble in Act 3, as well as in the Act 2 Finale. The use of rhythmic unit as structural device is enormously important in providing very subtle aesthetic glue to the complex music dramas we have discussed.

The Middle Scenes of *The Rake's Progress*—A Study in Augmentation

Plate 2, the setting of the interior of Tom's London house, is used for three domestic scenes in *The Rake's Progress*—2,1; 2,3; and 3,1. Each scene's action features another phase of Nick's manipulation of Tom and each setting features the consequences of the previous manipulation. The three settings can be seen as a sequence and each successive episode is an augmentation of the former in terms of the number of technical elements, the length of the scene, and the number of characters present—despite Tom's physical absence from 3,1.

Scenes 2,1, 2,3 and 3,1 present a pattern of plot, character and theme augmentation. 2,1 and 2,3 contain two of Tom's four wishes. In 2,1, Tom is alone, then Nick enters with Baba's poster. After Tom sighs out his second wish, "I wish I were happy," Nick overwhelms Tom with sophistic cant. Next, in 2,3, an ill-tempered Tom "buries" his chatterbox wife before he is again duped by his omnipresent servant into believing in a "wonderful machine." 3,1 features the awakening of Baba and is the musical climax of the opera because of Anne's "turning," i.e. her realization that Tom still loves her, in an oddly engaging ensemble. This ensemble approximates, in terms of the plot's arc, Puccini's Act 3 quartet in *La Bohème*, Verdi's great Finale to 2,2 of *La Traviata*, and *Carmen*'s Act 3 Finale.

Nick's trickery plays an entertaining role in 2,1, 2,3 and 3,1. And as Tom's naiveté is increasingly in evidence, every shred of available musical and theatrical trickery is needed to keep these three highly literate scenes moving forward. The two major characters are predictably static. Through use of the following elements, however, Auden and Stravinsky keep the three scenes from becoming dull. (1) The augmentation of number of characters, amount of action and even number of stage properties are all crucial. One such property turns out to be Baba herself. 2,1 features only a poster, 2,3 the crucial wig, the machine and Baba's possessions. 3,1 features the entirety of Tom and Baba's possessions.

(2) Sound effects are used in the second scene (breaking dishes, the machine's sound) and third (the bidding, the auctioneer's gavel, the crowd's shouts and reactions) scenes to great effect. (3) The fabulous Baba is engaging in 2,3, and both she and Sellum shine in 3,1. Baba breaks and smashes things, and Sellem's customers are most lively. Sellem himself is a wonderfully pretentious and lively character. Only Baba could dampen him, and she does.

(4) Tom becomes increasingly insensitive to others, as Nick's control over him grows. (5) Nick becomes increasingly powerful, addressing the audience directly in 2,3. The "snake" has greatest control in 3,1, when he is not even present. (6) Anne appears between the first two of these scenes, but appears commandingly in the third. (7) The chorus appears in 3,1 as a complex entity, not only to inform us of the stock market crash but also to comment on the stage action: "Don't interrupt or rail; / A scene like this is better than a sale."

(8) Stravinsky's music becomes increasingly more complex in form to match the growing number of characters, just as increased complexity of plot climaxes with the auction and extraordinary ensembles following it. 2,1 and 2,3 both end with a duet. (9) Off stage voices are used in 3,1. (10) In each scene, the plot heightens; the stakes become higher for every character—2,3 features boredom and its solution in a singular marriage; 2,3 features marital strife and a solution to world hunger; finally, there is the stock market fiasco, the auction, and Anne's determination to prevent Tom's final corruption by Nick.

(11) Musical ideas are repeated prominently with different scenic and musical settings: at the climax of the ensemble in 3,1, for example Anne's "I go to him" returns from 1,3 to begin the "Striate-finale." (12) 3,1 is a very complex scene, with many dovetailing elements. For a small example, notice that, like Anne, Baba also exits. She goes "'back to grace the stage, / where manner rules and wealth attends'" [*with an all-inclusive gesture*]".

Plates 6, 7 and 8—Tom's Final Plight

Plate 5 on the following page shows the Rake bare-headed, his fallen wig representing raging disorder, the chaos of a life gone out of control. Some of the same sycophantic and wretched characters that surrounded Tom in earlier plates are also here, especially noticeable is the figure seated to the right (Tom's left), studying Tom. Could that be Nick? There are few gambling scenes in opera and Auden did well to omit this one. Verdi's 2,2 is a tough act to follow.

Neither is there much reason to recreate Tom in the debtor's prison on stage, the venue of preaching, harping, disorder and despair. His wife screams at Tom, much less pleasantly than Baba in 2,3, while Anne faints in utter disorder, and her daughter rages. Tom himself sits seemingly in deep distraction, possibly depression, making the subtlest of gestures in response to the chaos around him. Obviously, it has all become too much for him. Notice the contrast between

Tom's gesture in Plate 6 and that in Plate 7. There are many details in these engravings that are rewarding to study, not least of which is the verse below each plate. The reader will forgive me for not undertaking their explication.

Auden combines the Hogarth Rake's rage, regret and despair into one scene, the graveyard, where Tom gambles—successfully, this time—for his life and where his despair and atonement are transmogrified into insanity in the instant of Nick's curse: "To reason blind shall be your mind. / Henceforth, be you insane!"

Our modern masters have done everything in their power to recreate Hogarth's final plate with exactitude, except in one important detail: Hogarth's Anne has obviously come to comfort and possibly fetch Tom. After her constancy to him during his entire slide toward hell, I find it difficult to imagine Anne leaving him now in Bedlam. Auden and Stravinsky, however, could. Even after death, the angel of Margaret returns to intercede for Faust; and Elisabeth goes past the evening star into heaven to atone for Tannhäuser's sins. Since World War I, however, we live in a different world, one in which glib pessimism and ironic game playing have been raised to the level of religion. To doubt this new "realism" makes one appear naïve or Romantic.

Faced with the moral chaos implied by this new moral paradigm, let us glance at the final plate with analytic eyes. It is a paradigm of pessimism. It illustrates no saving grace save Anne's compassion. She is now the only aspect of this society that is not corrupt or sick unto death. The "progress" of the Rake has begun, progressed and now ends here—in contemporary hell, Bedlam, the madhouse where, as the chorus tells us, night "never ends."

Mythological, religious and political elements play a role in the madness seen in Plates 3 & 4 and in the insanity played by the musicians as background for the corruption and frenzy at hand. Amidst the maddening din the faithful Anne finally wins over her faithless Rake.

Contemporary Anne's Growth

Anne's desertion of Tom in the final scene of *The Rake's Progress* and the resulting moral of Auden's fable is somewhat eased by the fact that Anne seems to know that Tom is about to die and therefore leaves to be spared that last trag-ic event: "Every weary body must / Late or soon return to dust." She tiredly acquiesces to her father's request that she "come home." Yet Tom's madness seems to have cleared during their final duet, signaling the healing power of love. Earlier, Anne has sung "O should I see my love in need / It shall not matter what he may be." Now she sings, "It is no longer I you need." She leaves him to God, or worse, when her father bids her to do so. Should we regard their vocal union in the duet as a sign that all spirits meet equally in the madness of love? We are not spared the joy and agony of Tom's "ravishing penitence," which is some of the most magnificent vocal music ever set by a great master. Anne answers with a lullaby.

When I hold my little son in my arms and we listen to Anne's lullaby together, I am able to rise above my own nagging fears and doubts about his future as the atomic age hurtles onward into the twenty-first century. It occurs to me, as we listen, that the vow of which Anne speaks in this scene is the essence of art: man's ultimate need communicate with his fellow man. "Tom, my vow holds ever." So my son's shudder of pleasure at the chorus' response to Anne's verses need not be explained, for I know that it is caused by the oboe's striving upward in gentle surges against the texture of the chorus. And I know that this paradox heralds relaxation and peaceful sleep for him. Perhaps children will teach us most about appreciating art, or, more importantly, about realizing the healing power of art's enchantment.

Hogarth's plates constitute a rarity: a single, complete, non-literary—though the moralistic verses beneath the plates are instructional—source. Auden's libretto is a miracle of invention and augmentation based on the visual elements of the original engravings. The resulting fable's characters are barely two-dimensional, but the depth of the poetic and musical integrity moves us deeply when we give them our close attention.

The great arc of the plot is clearly derived from Hogarth. The source of evil and destruction in Hogarth's world is man and his environment, but what corrupts the operatic Tom is a time-honored character, who happens to be one of the most popular figures of literature, stage, screen and, of course, opera. Once the decision was made to use Nick Shadow as the operative force of *The Rake's Progress*, Baba and Sellem had to be created to balance terror with humor.

Act 3, Scene 3 of *The Rake's Progress*

AN INTERPRETATION

The nineteenth century opera composer's striving for continuity through musical forms resulted in crucial development for opera. This growth was initiated primarily by Mozart's compositional and dramatic emphases in his da Ponte operas, and nurtured through the continuity established by both Haydn and Mozart in the symphonic form during the Classical Period. Mozart was concerned with this continuity of musical-dramatic form from his first operatic works. His later works developed certain characteristics encouraging continuity, from which such diverse works as *La Traviata*, *Carmen*, *La Bohème* and *The Rake's Progress* all benefited: subtlety of characterization, extension of the complexity and integrity of the orchestra's role in opera, subtlety in recitative, and general ennoblement of the *opera buffa* form.

Each of these four operas has a distinct great arc of action, usually with a quickly rising dramatic tension that ties the acts together. This arc of action reflects classical values, with an emotional turn occurring within the character of the protagonist about three-quarters of the way through the plot. This feature reflects primary concentration on character in opera. (A climax of stage action usually occurs closer to the end of the opera.) The musical climax of an opera usually occurs along with the emotional climax, e.g. *Carmen*'s Act 3 Finale, or *La Traviata*'s Act 2 Finale. This coincidence of character and musical form is a logical consequence of the music's primary role in opera and its special power in portraying the emotional lives of the characters.

Musical, literary and visual sub-arcs consisting of repeated musical ideas (or melodies and spoken or visual images) tie the scenes and acts together. These sub-arcs are an extension of character in that they may reflect a persona's moods, dreams, desires, and needs, but especially their fantasies and memories. The recurring musical motif is especially important since, when used to represent memory of a particular character, it allows the listener to experience the inner world of that character.

Musical sub-arcs may also represent ideas or concepts of a more abstract nature, such as the "Fate" motif of *Carmen*. Alternately, some sub-arcs may be primarily structural in nature, as is the opening motif of *La Bohème*. (Needless to say, this motif and many similar structural ones contribute to the musical atmosphere of the opera. Structure and function are intertwining, inseparable concepts.) Musically knowledgeable listeners will find the use of such sub-arcs elegant and will regard them as the essence of structural integrity.

Within the structure of an operatic act, the divisions of the actions into musical units—recitative, aria, ensemble and chorus scene—were further subdivided by the composer into smaller, more plastic units sharing interrelated features and thus overlapping easily. This development was, in part, facilitated by the growing rhythmic and harmonic freedom embraced by composers of the nineteenth century. In this regard, Act 1 of *La Traviata* provides a stunning example of continuity, on which example Puccini's *La Bohème* builds. Curious milestones appear as we enter modern times. Wagner had by mid-19th century set as his goal "unending melody" as the musical-dramatic ideal. A full century later, Stravinsky's modern intellectualism and wit finds its form in broad stylistic parody of Wagner's ideas, as well as of Baroque and Classical opera forms in *The Rake's Progress.*

The orchestra's role also grew and diversified in operatic performance, thanks primarily to the influence of Mozart, Beethoven and Wagner. Each of these masters to some degree served as the musical model for his successor. An individual instrument's qualities came to represent specific moods and emotional values and thus acquired implicit dramatic content. Musical elements such as dynamic antithesis were used to complement theatrical effects, providing new means of subtle emphasis in developing character and creating logical dramatic sequences by clarifying rising tensions.

There was a move to embrace and imitate literary form. This tendency has always been evident in opera's relation to the literature of its time. The opera composer generally takes his inspiration from a literary work of fiction or a drama, then begins his own unique creative process with a poetic reduction of this work, a short play in verse that must be fleshed with music. The tendency to complement literary form is thus natural, as is the struggle between word and music in the musical-dramatic environment.

The treatment of character and plot became more realistic in opera as a result of two influences: the subtleties of character motivation demanded by romanticism (a reaction against the formalities of eighteenth century Classicism) and the down-to-earth plots evoked by naturalism (a reaction against the excesses of romanticism). Both of these influences gave Realism, the essential aesthetic mode of all ages, new emotional and environmental integrity. This integrity carried over from literary into dramatic and musical-dramatic forms, and has the effect of engendering believable characters like Carmen and José, both of whom carry the power of archetypes within them.

Yet it is unquestionably the musical element of Bizet's *Carmen* that defines and ennobles these two embattled peasants captured by the writer-historian Mérimée in his novella in 1845 and lifts them into operatic immortality. It is in the elegance and subtlety of the motivic weave representing aspects of character and plot that Bizet's music—culminating in the watershed final duet—lifts tragedy to the level of Attic inevitability without a whisper of the determinism which will soon dominate literary and philosophical circles in Europe. In the greatest operas, music inevitably asserts its claim as opera's primary element.

Romantic and Ideal Love in Opera

Siegmund:
Du bist das Bild das in mir barg.

Sieglinde: (den Blick schnell abwenden)
O still! Lass mich der Stimme lauschen—

Mich dunkt, ihren Klang hort' ich als Kind.

Die Walküre, Act 1, scene 3

Tom and Anne:
Rejoice, beloved: in these fields of Elysium
Space cannot alter, nor Time our love abate;
Here has no words for absence or estrangement
Nor Now a notion of Almost or Too Late.

The Rake's Progress, Act 3, scene 3

These two passages are singular apices of profane and sentimental love in opera. The first passage was written in the mid-nineteenth century and the music composed some years later. The second verse was written 100 years later. Each is extreme in its tone and form, and in the role it plays in opera history. *Die Walküre* is in some respects the height of romantic expression, while *The Rake's Progress* is a twentieth century hybrid—and the result of remarkable poetic and musical integrity.

Wagner's lovers are brother and sister; their love is fated by power beyond themselves, a power that manifests itself in the lovers' anguish-bound passion. Auden's lovers are, by contrast, pristine. In Act 3, scene 3, of *The Rake's Progress*, they are united by a philosophical love that transcends the madness into which one partner has descended. Time and space have no power in this realm of absolute love, in this quasi-religious ritual of confession and forgiveness. Wagner's lovers flee from the beginnings of human civilization into a Spring night where their emotions break forth in imitation of nature's inherent chaos. Auden's lovers could not be further from the nature they idealized in the pristine wilderness of their past; they sit on a straw pallet, an unworthy altar on which a mad hero will expire at play's end. They are in Bedlam, London's subterranean asylum, and are fated to enact the tragic ritual of priest and sacrificial victim.

Wagner's lovers are capable of union with nature, and their passion is grounded in earth and flesh; they are creatures of blood and passion. Tom and Anne's passion is of air and fire, as fragile as the ideal of love, or of any similar philosophical dictum; for example, Hegel's notion that we mortals must always wear the spectacles of time and space when we think rationally. Anne will, of course, think rationally in *The Rake*'s final scene, and will desert her beloved—something Sieglinda is not empowered to do.

From a purely literary standpoint, a careful examination of the two texts and the dramatic context will show Wagner's blank verse phrases are a product of the doctrines of primitive mysticism, and draw upon the darkest hue of Romanticism for their power. A chthonic mythic force dominates the entire *Ring*, hinting at man's deepest psychic roots. Auden's refined stanzas reflect layers of sophisticated philosophical thought and classical values, representing far more space and time than the one hundred years separating the two librettists imply.

Both aesthetically and philosophically, far more than one hundred years separates these two works, whose climactic moments reflect the formal values of

173

the artists who created them. These compositional criteria manifest themselves in Romantic and Neoclassic forms, respectively. Auden and Stravinsky's opera is a masterpiece of poetic, dramatic and musical design. The final scene is a remarkable summary of the opera's plot. Consideration of the setting, verse and music as they define and affect character and shape the action—among the complex of lesser units of which operatic form consists—within the great arc of plot's resolution will demonstrate the musical-dramatic integrity of the scene.

The Final Scene as Summary and Conclusion

The final scene is both a conclusion of the opera's story, containing the climax of the stage action and a summary of all the opera's individual constituent elements, gathering those elements together in a familiar tapestry. This latter phenomenon is subtly accomplished by Stravinsky through the reiteration of previous motifs now vastly augmented by rich, new material, and by the repetition of image and idea by the librettist Auden.

When such repetition occurs, we are initially more affected by the feeling of *déjà vu* than by conscious recognition of musical or poetic/mythic ideas. With repeated listening and viewings, however, the integrity of such careful structuring of the literary and musical sub-arc yields multi-faceted and -leveled meanings. Such subtlety of poetic and musical patterning is unusual—though not rare in great opera, as we have seen in this book—and both Auden and Stravinsky prove themselves masters of it.

The final scene is a summary of the opera in several senses. First, the characters now act out the allegorical roles they previously alluded to in the opening scene. In this bittersweet distortion of a Romantic vision—the "future state / Ever happy, ever fair"—Tom, now insane, believes he is Adonis. In compassionate response, Anne pretends to be Venus. The literary irony is especially apparent in a contemporary setting. It accents the opera's underpinnings of despair and pain. Purely literary allusions in the first scene now become the histrionic basis of a disturbing play-within-a-play in the final scene.

Second, musical ideas from earlier in the opera are used, bringing with them an emotional charge recreating the former mood or the previous emotional state of a character in the listener's memory. Tom's confession to Anne, for example, begins with orchestral figures in the strings similar to those that introduced 2,2, where the instrumental accompaniment expresses Anne's loneliness and anxiety in London: Anne's loneliness is now Tom's, musically speaking.

Tom's vocal line in the confession is, however, fervent, and builds on the orchestra's coloring somewhat autonomously, rather than being restrained by it. There is an uneasy quality to the accompaniment, which atmosphere creates an effective interplay of tension between voice and orchestra reflecting the disparity between what we know to be real and what Tom is experiencing in his demented state.

Finally, the instruments that captured the "birds and beasts at play" in the natural environment of the opening scene of *The Rake* appear again, but this time either curiously subdued as in Tom's music, or else striving (sometimes shrilly) upward to break from the cage of Bedlam's madness, as in the chorus's response to Anne's lullaby. Stravinsky's use of woodwinds, especially oboe, English horn, and piccolo is, as always, noteworthy.

Immediately before 3,3, we have seen the power of good and evil amply demonstrated. Anne's love has saved Tom's soul, but Nick has used his remaining power—or, conversely, Tom's remaining vulnerability—to curse him: "To reason blind shall be your mind. / Henceforth be you insane!" The strength of Anne's love was futile to prevent this curse, and Nick's great power was echoed in the driving rhythms and heavy brass of his fiery exit aria.

The tremendous contrast between Nick's final powerful vocal efforts and Tom's child-like verses that immediately follow couldn't be more extreme in terms of dramatic or musical content. In Tom's nursery rhyme, Auden and Stravinsky have prepared the most pessimistic implication of the opera:

With roses Crowned, I sit on ground
Adonis is my name,
The only dear of Venus fair:
Methinks it is no shame.

The music that immediately precedes and follows these phrases is the music of the duet that will join Tom and Anne for the last time, later in 3,3. The occurrence in this passage would forestall any idea that the duet might represent a return to order (sanity) or be of lasting comfort for Tom. This music is carefully defining madness in terms we ordinarily ascribe to beauty, i.e. aesthetic order. Tom is from this point purely mad and no sense is to be made of it. If we attempt to make sense of it, Stravinsky seems to be saying, we are as mad as Tom.

Anne's act of compassion in 3,3 is found in her willingness to descend to meet Tom on the only level possible for him, the level of symbolism somehow common both to normality and the hopelessly insane, long enough to say good-bye to her "beloved." That this level is typified by music of the highest classical purity—Gluck at his finest—is a puzzling stylistic statement on the composer's part. Perhaps the ecstasy of great joy and the utter irrationality of insanity share certain formal characteristics that may be expressed, in Stravinsky's view, only in highly structured forms. Is he implicitly condemning Classical form by implying its relation to insanity? Or is he simply creating music to typify the mythic level of consciousness, no matter in whom it occurs? Or is he asking us to completely separate form and content at this point in the opera?

With such tensions established within the foregoing passing scene, 3,3 opens with the stately poetry and elegant music with which Stravinsky wishes to define the symbolic state on which Tom now exists in Bedlam.

The Stage Setting

The last visual impression of 3,2 shows Tom sitting on the grave of his sanity: (The dawn comes up. It is Spring. The open grave is now covered with a green mound upon which Tom sits smiling, putting grass on his head and singing to himself in a child-like voice.) This raised mound becomes a raised eminence, a raised pallet in the following and final scene. On this makeshift altar, Tom will expire, the victim of his own weakness and failure of will. 3,3 returns us to the pure impulse of Greek theater with its altar in the middle of the circular orchestra area. The Greek orchestra was originally probably centered by a sacrificial altar, where victims were brought to propitiate the Gods of planting and harvest. Tom is clearly the victim here, but to whom is he being sacrificed?

The most striking aspect of the stage setting in the final scene is the enormous contrast its melancholic, dark mood and closed Baroque musical forms with the surroundings of the first scene and its bright, hopeful colors, dancing orchestral figures, and playful, open musical forms. Romantic love blooms for Tom and Anne in the country. In horrifying contrast, the final scene's dreadful and disorienting environment signals the death of Romance in a way singularly contemporary and pessimistic.

The comparison of the opening and closing scenes of the opera is unavoidable and enormously important if one wishes to get at the dark beauty at the opera's center. Tom and Anne express their love for each other only in these two scenes. Anne and Tom are never absolutely alone, so perhaps they are deprived of the necessary intimacy to develop their love. The final scene is their intimate reunion and their ultimate parting. In the preceding scenes, love has failed to save Tom's sanity from Nick's vile grasp, and Anne must now surrender to circumstances beyond her control. She does this by accepting Tom's confession and by singing her swain to sleep with a heavenly lullaby, the verses of which contain the extraordinary patterns of imagery that range from Greek mythology ("islands of the blessed") to the Peaceable Kingdom so heralded in art and literature of the eighteenth century.

Most importantly, the first and last scenes of this opera are similar in action. The lovers meet to enact a seasonal ritual of love—Adonis has risen from the cold earth to be warmed in the arms of his Venus—but the final scene's atmosphere is as close to hell as the creators could devise. "Poor Tom's a-cold" as he attempts to instruct his court of madmen in the initial lines of 3,3.

> Tom: *Prepare yourselves, heroic shades. Wash you and make you clean. Anoint your limbs with oil, put on your wedding garments and crown your heads with flowers. Let music strike. Venus, queen of love, will visit her unworthy Adonis.*
>
> Chorus: *Madmen's words are all untrue; / she will never come to you.*

Great power of contrast is found in the tension created between the music given to each of these statements, as well as the contrast between the dark, hellish estrangement enforced by Bedlam's stone walls and iron gate, and the "fragrant odors and... notes of cheer" (1,1) of the opera's opening scene. Tom and Anne never regain the tenuous union with nature briefly established in the opera's first scene. In the first scene, Tom leaves Anne (at her request); in the final scene, Anne deserts Tom.

Tom has called Nature his "green unnatural Mother" in 2,1. After Tom enters the dread city, his contact with Nature is distorted. Anne, the virgin queen herself, is seemingly helpless in the face of the city's corrupting influence, although we might have sensed this possibility in the sylvan opening scene when she looks evil itself—in the figure of Nick Shadow—in the face and does not comprehend the tear that will dim Tom's and her dream of "joyous design." The closing scene shows the full consequence of each character's blindness to the possibilities of evil in the world.

The Characters

There are three major characters in the opera's final scene: Tom, Anne, and the chorus. Here the opera chorus functions as its counterpart in a Greek poetic tragedy, serving—even in its collective madness—as a source of indirect enlightened comment and order. Most touching, the chorus serves as a true middle-ground between Tom and Anne, for its members respond honestly to both the lovers. The classic chorus functions as narrator, commenting on the action and interpreting it in light of civilized values. The chorus is used as an element of dark distortion after Anne's exit and projects its restless unease onto the protagonist; its insistence that "No one has been here" is the final blow for Tom. His "heart breaks" and he "falls back on his pallet."

Ultimately, it is for the chorus and not Tom or even Nick, to indicate the ambiguous nature of Fate in *The Rake's Progress*. The chorus cruelly punishes Tom in his madness, and only after the little light of Anne's lullaby and the event of Tom's demise, can it be moved to "mourn for Adonis," thus fulfilling its ritual function of purifying the emotions of fear and pity so expertly aroused in this scene. The chorus also has an expository function. Its first solo action is to dance before Tom with mocking gestures while singing a "Chorus-minuet." The chorus Minuet is framed in driving rhythms where stinging brass accents the blind fury of madness and the oboe cries out for release. As the chorus prophecies, this study in chiaroscuro and distorted perspective will indeed be a deterministic "night that never ends."

The chorus functions here in classical elegance, rationally and to inform. But between this passage, with its ominous, descriptive elegance, and the final bereavement, the chorus also functions as the hopelessly insane, lacerating Tom and responding ecstatically only to the simple beauty of Anne's lullaby. With one exception, they hound Tom like the Furies until his death. The imagery here is of the darkness, strangeness and sameness of existence in the society in Hell. They are a vital force of truth in the scene and we cannot help but be reminded of Aristotle's insistence on the chorus's central importance as character in ascertaining tragic effect.

The contrast between Anne and Tom in the final scene is exceptionally strong. In portraying Tom's state of insanity, Auden and Stravinsky drew inspiration from Hogarth's secondary characters in Plate 8 of the series: one madman believes he is a king, another believes he is the Pope. Rather than portray Tom as a jabbering idiot, he is made to believe he is Adonis, the mythical character he prefigured in the opening scene; and he is made to act accordingly. A much sadder, wiser Anne agrees to assume momentarily the role she had earlier dreamed of playing in the bright sweetness of nature and not here in the frightful underworld—the role of Venus.

Stravinsky initially chose to depict Tom musically with a formal Baroque arioso, noticeably free of discord. His vocal line is ornamented and secure in its riding phrases. The melody's approach to the upper register, the rising of which could reflect hysteria, is instead gentle and well prepared, reflecting inner peace and certitude. But it is the peace of illusion and sanity lost. The world of madness is a world of Baroque musical order, of concord. In this world, reality is discordant. The oboe, bassoon and clarinet's reedy melancholy seem to debate and search hesitatingly within Tom's fragmented soul, yet all is ordered by Stravinsky's cool aesthetic in the Baroque structure.

Tom's arioso is accompanied by strings, with the piccolo and flute joining the orchestral palate only on the word "love." These two instruments also accompany Anne's lullaby. The flute is expressive of feminine images, and the emotions and ideas of female characters. Anne has become here a female Orpheus, descending to Hell to reclaim her mate. All Tom's lyric moments in the opera have been accompanied primarily by the string choir, with occasional woodwind colorations.

The arioso, music and word, is a vision inspired by madness, having its own order. The chorus cruelly responds and Tom can only murmur, "Come quickly, Venus, or I die." She does come, but cannot save Tom; thus Tom's notion that Anne could save him is relegated to the status of the madness enclosing him in Bedlam. The orchestra's agitated, teasing figures and the uneasy harmonies of the choral writing in the dialogue following Tom's arioso highlight the effect of this spiritual and physical tension on Tom: after his contrasting section, he falls back in despair, prefiguring his fall into death.

Anne, who at this juncture represents compassionate reason, enters but is helpless to correct the evil loose in this hell-generated nightmare and tries only to bring comfort where possible. She hears Tom's confession—although she does not forgive him: "How should I forgive?" she asks—and as priestess/goddess brings "solace to tormented brains" in Bedlam. With Tom and Anne's duet, a confession and absolution of sin, the main action of the scene is accomplished, and the audience attains its catharsis. The lovers are together again and Tom/Adonis declares his love for Anne anew. The music is lovely—as the Alfredo-Violetta duet in *La Traviata*'s Act 1 is lovely—but this romance is no longer possible.

The bitter twist of Anne's liberated exit and Tom's subsequent lonely death are more a projection of modern existential emptiness than a matter of dramatic verisimilitude. Tom's madness is dramatically problematic in that it offers the audience no real release of tension, except for that which may be gotten from Stravinsky's divine music or from the Epilogue. We are left with the problem of death: no clear relief for Tom from his terrible loneliness, or release for us from our fear through empathetic identification that such a restive fate might await any of us. The only satisfaction must be intellectual or literary; thus, the necessity for a moralistic Epilogue, ala *Don Giovanni.*

The final scene of *The Rake* presents the themes, characters, and situation of the opera's opening scene. It is in effect a dream re-enactment of the first scene's action and content in a hellish setting. We see this scene through Tom's eyes, from his point of view. It is the tormented chorus that tears us back again and again to the reality of the scene. Anne's acquiescence to Tom's distorted vision of reality augments involvement on the listener's part.

Anne: (softly) *Adonis.*
Tom: (raising his head and springing to his feet) *Venus, my queen, my bride. At last. I have waited for thee so long, till I almost believed these madmen who blasphemed against thy honor. They are rebuked.*

With Anne, we also want to believe that "this dream, too, this noble vision" will not prove "as empty as the rest;" but the chorus is the cruel instrument of reality and never lets us or Tom forget that the real world pounds on, regardless of what we want to believe.

Confession, Duet and Promise of Release

So much do we empathize with Tom that we believe his earlier contention that he will die if Venus does not come, and because she does indeed come we must pinch ourselves later, when he does die. The chorus has warned us throughout this last scene that "Madmen's words are all untrue," but we are like Anne: our first response is to say, "Adonis" and to pretend with her to enter Tom's sylvan vision. Auden's words and Stravinsky's music make it easy for us. After Tom's disordered existence within the reality of Acts 1 and 2, the ordered beauty of the music assigned to him in Bedlam makes a deeply ironic statement about the nature of the reality "in the city overhead." It seems Tom has retreated into "the beauty of insanity."

The gentle rhythms of Tom's second arioso "I have waited" contain such longing and sweetness that in our hearts we cannot help but applaud Tom's "They are rebuked." We do not want the chorus to be correct about the idyllic world in which Tom now exalts. Then the horns and woodwinds accompany Tom's invitation to Venus to mount her throne and hear his confession. These horns are the same ceremonial instruments that accompanied Anne on her crusade to save her beloved in 1,3. Like Micaela's horns in the wild mountains of Spain, their rich tone is the voice of religious fervency. Breaking Romantic music-dramatic tradition, they are utterly ineffectual here in Bedlam, which defines its own, highly formal musical beauty.

In the next duet, the worlds of madness and love mix in a religious and musical ecstasy. Anne has become Tom's luminous image.

Tom: (he kneels at her feet)

O merciful goddess, hear the confession of my sins.
In a foolish dream, in a gloomy labyrinth
I hunted shadows, disdaining thy true love;
Forgive thy servant, who repents his madness,
Forgive Adonis and he shall faithful prove.

Tom's voice intertwines with a dolce English horn and flute while the string choir pulses underneath in familiar patterns. His vocal ecstasy is that of the true believer. Stravinsky's delicate instrumentation complements Auden's words. The melancholy English horn now chimes in with Tom's words "Gloomy labyrinth," while his "foolish dream" is shadowed by Anne's sweet flute. These three voices—sincere Tom, the melancholy English horn, the sensuous flute—murmur confession and ask for forgiveness: "Forgive Adonis and he shall faithful prove."

Echoing Tom's newfound faithfulness, the English horn then phrases the question plaintively in a rising, inclusive pattern after Tom's voice quiets, seeming also to ask, "Will you forgive?" If we follow our hearts here, the music would lead us to believe that Tom's madness has not reduced him to senselessness, but rather has freed him from the world's disorder. Such is not the case, however.

With an increasingly strong pulse in the lower strings, Anne's ecstatic absolution is supported by both Tom's strings and the woodwinds, including Anne's faithful flute. The two lovers are finally united musically.

Anne: (rising and raising him by the hand):
What should I forgive? Thy ravishing penitence
Blesses me, dear heart, and brightens all the past.
Kiss me, Adonis: the wild boar is vanquished.

The flute and English horn join in harmony as Tom and Anne kiss. Because "the wild boar [lust] is vanquished," Tom and Anne can now sing sweetly in thirds, "Rejoice, beloved" to celebrate their bittersweet final reunion.

(Rakewell suddenly staggers. Anne helps him gently to lie down on the pallet.)
Tom and Anne:
Rejoice, beloved: in these fields of Elysium
Space cannot alter, nor Time our love abate;
Here has no words for absence or estrangement
Nor Now a notion of Almost or Too Late.

With the words, "Too late" the strings fall away in gentle patterns, even as Tom's consciousness fades. Tom then asks to be taken to Anne/Venus's breast and to be serenaded. He is secure in his absolution, his calm joy, his assurance that "the heavens are merciful, and all is well."

Anne's Lullaby and the Chorus's Longing

The ecstasy of the following verses provides *The Rake's Progress* with its only real emotional turn, a dramatic fact accomplished by the most tasteful poetic and economic musical means. Anne's words paint the Peaceable Kingdom in pure lyrics, and the chorus responds with couplets of great longing and beauty. They are given merciful respite through Anne's compassion. Like Tom, they are weary unto death.

> Anne:
> *Gently, little boat*
> *Across the ocean float,*
> *The crystal waves dividing:*
> *The sun in the west*
> *Is going to rest:*
> *Glide, glide, glide*
> *Toward the Islands of the Blest.*

> Chorus: (off in their cells)
> *What voice is this? What heavenly strains*
> *Bring solace to tormented brains?*

The accompaniment of these antiphonal responses contains the throbbing strings of Anne and Tom's duet, but now in cross-rhythms with the chorus's straightforward pulse. Combined with the strings is the striving oboe, always rising questioningly, perhaps begging at the end of each verse, asking for more and more peace and forgiveness.

The flute in the lower register and the piccolo accompany Anne's verses adding quaintness and a crystalline quality to the visual harmony she describes. Anne's clear lyric soprano voice and the simple, mounting melodic lines, joined by the flute and piccolo, create the "sacred music of the spheres," the musical absolution and evidence of harmony for which the inhabitants of Bedlam long.

Duettino: The Stalwart Desertion of Tom.

While the chorus reaches an emotional release in the lullaby, Anne gathers the strength to obey her father and leave Bedlam and Tom. She then addresses Tom, but more importantly, the audience with the verse below, *tranquillo ma resoluto* (peacefully but with resolution).

> *Tom, my vow*
> *Holds ever, but it is no longer I*
> *You need. Sleep well, my dearest dear. Good-bye*

Then, as her father joins her with a supporting melody, she bids Tom farewell:

> *Every wearied body must*
> *Late or soon return to dust,*
> *Set the frantic spirit free.*
> *In this earthly city we*
> *Shall not meet again, love, yet*
> *Never think that I forget.*

These words, which imply her understanding that Tom is close to death, the only possible release for him, are accompanied by a resolute march rhythm in the low strings. It is a final farewell and a stalwart desertion of unfortunate Tom by Anne. The marching basses indicate her resolution to go. The vocal line is set firmly in the rich middle register of her voice, reflecting the firmness of decision and emotional control.

In contrast to the great bulk of Stravinsky's score, Anne and her father sing in rhythmic union with the orchestra, creating the idea that her decision is, in terms of musical form, both resolute and universally acceptable. There is, however, syncopation in the bass line. Anne has saved Tom's soul in the grave-yard, but the scorpion's tale of fate has claimed him in Bedlam. Only death can release Tom.

Finale: Tom's Release into Empty Ecstasy

Tom: (wakes, starts to his feet and looks wildly around)
*Where art thou, Venus? Venus, where art thou? The flowers open to the
sun. The birds renew their song. It is Spring. The bridal couch is prepared.
Come quickly, beloved, and we will celebrate the holy rites of love.*

Tom's tortured spirit might perhaps be released in the ecstasy of the vision he shares with us, but he has slept for a moment and Venus has disappeared. The mad chorus crushes his fragile vision, without intent or purpose: "Madman! No one has been here."

Tom responds with despair, presaging death in his imagery and idea:
*My heart breaks. I feel the chill of death's approaching wing. Orpheus,
strike from thy lyre a swan-like music, and weep, ye nymphs and
shepherds of these Stygian fields, weep for Adonis the beautiful, the
young; weep for Adonis whom Venus loved.*

Tom's passage ends in mythic truth: "[I am] Adonis whom Venus loved."

Anne—Venus, the Virgin Queen—is the real source and emblem of sentimental love in the opera. For whatever reason, no matter how richly and lyrically accompanied by regretful strings or romantically-appealing the woodwinds, Tom's nature is weaker than his music and incapable of returning Anne's love except in the mock reality of madness. Although we know not to expect realistic qualities from an allegorical character like Tom, the extraordinary moral strength of Anne and the pity we feel for Tom lead us to expect more of a conclusion than this scene gives us:

*Mourn for Adonis, ever young, Venus' dear,
Weep, tread softly round his bier.*

Conclusion

The power of Stravinsky's music in this scene cannot be overestimated. Here is found some of the most beautiful music of this century, music that ranks with the best of Mozart, Haydn and Schubert. In Tom's final passage, the voices of the woodwinds fall away one by one: Tom's English horn fades last of all to leave him alone with the heart of the orchestra, the string choir. Finally, they, too, are silent. There follows the chorus's dirge with plunging bass, ceremonial brass, mournful English horn, and a final, lonely trumpet fading as the ritual ends.

Aristotle's ideal complex plot requires that a deed be perpetrated in ignorance and a tragic discovery be made afterwards. This is the pattern found in *Oedipus Tyrannus*. Tom commits no heinous crime of his own volition. He is the victim of supernatural forces, personified by Nick Shadow. Tom is merely a naive, flawed young man. Or perhaps Nick is simply the destructive machine, and Tom merely another victim of irrational fancy. Yet we are moved profoundly by Tom's plight, due primarily to the exquisite power of the music the last great composer has given us to describe in detail not only Tom's moods but the wrestling within his guilty soul throughout this late masterpiece.

It is to Auden's and especially Stravinsky's credit that we can become so much involved in Tom's plight. In maintaining the necessary balance between external (visual-dramatic) and internal (verbal-musical) motivational forces, the two writers have projected a musical-dramatic vehicle that thoroughly engages without negating the necessity for scenic effects and stage action.

The opera never grows sentimental through the excess of music or obscure through verbal vagueness. Stravinsky's enormous skill at creating environment, complementing and vitalizing Auden's lovely and well-crafted verse and ennobling Auden and Kallman's dramatic situations, and above all his ability to capture character inscape is the primary source of greatness in *The Rake's Progress*.

Postlude: Going On

The joy of opera is in its inherent beauty and in discovering the meaning that beauty may mask then slowly reveal, rather than immediately elucidate. All narrative art lives from the creation and resolution of tension between dramatic entities, and it is here that opera sometimes compresses plot advancement and logical character development through the use of musical form, as well as the direct emotional appeal of music per se. Opera's power is in its characters and their stories, but its essence is in the musical web representing those character's dreams and strivings for completion. The constant, emotionally evocative presence of music in the flow of actions can easily degrade the action to the exaggerated sentiment of melodrama. Yet the greatest operas are never melodramatic. The greatest composers evolve formulae involving subtle tensions between elements that not only serve to refine the musical-dramatic form, but offer novelty of expression. Novelty may get the best of Stravinsky in *The Rake's Progress*, because I think the librettists and composer employ too many complex, sometimes precious aesthetic games to appeal to a wide audience. But even so, I love the opera quite irrationally.

All operatic masterpieces share one universal quality—great music. For this reason, it is easy to forget that opera began as an imitation of literature and remains literature of a special kind. To ignore opera's essential historical and causal relationship to literature is easy, but a poor practice. Literature not only furnishes most operas with their plot, characters, and imagery. It also gives most of us the firmest means by which to appreciate the sub-arcs of music, poetry and the visual arts that support the great arc of dramatic action. Music form is the source of much of this arc in the most successful operas. Sometimes music makes its own striking commentary on the human condition. In such cases the greatest pleasures occur when music rises out of the musical-dramatic context to make a profound statement about a character or idea.

Imagery is of vital importance in opera, for all the disciplines in opera—literature, drama, music and the visual arts—combine in ecstatic union to create what Puccini called "the luminous image." This idealizing of a loved one existed long before Puccini's particular conceptualization of the worshipful love of operatic characters for their mate, parent or spiritual twin. Literary imagery will often reflect the qualities of a dream, so naturally many arias are built on lyric poems concerned with vision, personal quest, dramatic fear and the search for fulfillment. Nature imagery is common: flowers abound, gardens are common; and each couple seeks to fulfill Adam and Eve's quest for a new Eden. Ultimately, imagery and character combine to form a general theme—the dream of love fulfilled. As in *The Rake's Progress*, the dream may become a nightmare, but the dream-as-literature claims to be eternal, undying.

Opera is not only ambitious, reformist, even revolutionary in its choice of subject matter, but it is decidedly moral in effect. The first creators of opera took their cue from the high-minded Greeks, with their sense of elemental and cosmic balance, and established an unspoken tradition of taking the moral high road. Perhaps they sensed that esoteric musical and poetic forms demanded moral verisimilitude. At all accounts, bad deeds, including illicit love and lust, are almost always punished—by death in tragic opera, by marriage in comic opera.

Opera is character-driven, fueled by dream and fantasy. These dreams and visions are expressed primarily in arias. When Tom awakens and exclaims to Nick, "Oh, Nick, I had the strangest dream," we find nothing strange about it. We may regret that it is Nick to whom Tom expresses any aspect of his inner world, but we come to see that nothing could be more natural, for Nick has controlled Tom so completely at this point that he has infected his dreams. Mimi dreams and fantasizes throughout her short life. Carmen's future is clouded with superstitious imaginings. Violetta's suppressed fantasies emerge only as she bares her soul to us in her great Act 1 aria. Micaela and Anne have strength of purpose, but suffer painful separation from their lovers.

The aria is a fundamental building block of character in opera. The aria's most striking characteristics emerge from the lyric images of poetry set to music and the soaring melody onto which the sung poetry mounts. These elements offer the composer opportunity to allow his character to open to the audience like a blossom and reveal the heights and depths of their inner world. Out of and above this world may emerge unexpected musical beauties of great symbolic and emotional power.

Given a million contradictory subtleties, musical form allows us to make certain generalizations about the role of music in opera. Arias are usually revelatory of character, as are Shakespeare's great soliloquies. Duets, trios and quartets often advance the plot, though they may—as is often the way with arias, choral ensembles—freeze the immediate action utterly and telescope time. Within the folds and creases of musical form, stage time ceases and we may explore the intricacies of character thought and dream. Listening to opera is the greatest imaginative act. The listener is capable of magnificent acts of consciousness when listening to a recorded opera (or, for that matter, experiencing any work of art). After that, there is viewing a live or filmed/taped performance, at which time opera fulfills its destiny in the plot in our own lives.

Be well. I hope opera has enriched your life.

SELECTED BIBLIOGRAPHY

The English National Opera Guides for *La Bohème*, *Carmen*, *La Traviata* and *Oedipus/The Rake's Progress*. New York: Riverrun Press, Inc.

Aristotle, *The Poetics*, Translation by T. Buckley, Buffalo, 1992.

Auden, W. H., *Secondary Worlds*, New York, 1968.

Bachelard, Gaston, *The Poetics of Space*, Boston, 1969.

Bekker, Paul, *The Orchestra*, New York, 1963.

Budden, Julian, *The Operas of Verdi*, 3 Vols. London, 1963-71.

Brown, Calvin S., *Music and Literature*, Hanover, 1948.

Cone, E. T., *Musical Form and Musical Performance*, New York, 1968.

Conrad, Peter, *A Song of Love and Death – The Meaning of Opera*, New York, 1987.

Romantic Opera and Literary Form, Berkley, Calif., 1978.

Cooke, Deryk, *The Language of Music*, London, 1959.

Copland, Aaron, *What to Listen for in Music*, New York, 1939.

Music and the Imagination, Cambridge, 1952.

Davie, C. T., *Musical Structure and Design*, New York, 1966.

Donington, Robert, *Opera and Its Symbols*, New Haven, 1990.

Goldovsky, Boris, *Bringing Opera to Life*, Englewood Cliffs, 1968.

Hamm, Charles, *Opera*, Boston, 1966.

Kerman, Joseph, *Opera as Drama*, New York, 1956.

Knapp, J. M., *The Magic of Opera*, New York, 1972.

Kupferberg, Herbert, *Opera*, New York, 1975.

Langer, Susanne K., *Feeling and Form*, New York, 1953.

Longyear, Rey M., *Nineteenth-Century Romanticism in Music*, Englewood Cliffs, 1973.

Long, H. L., *The Experience of Opera*, New York, 1971.

Meyer, L. B., *Emotion and Meaning in Music*, Chicago, 1956.

Payne, Darwin, *The Scenographic Imagination*, Carbondale, 1982.

Pinson, DovBer, *Inner Rhythms*, Northvale, 2000.

Robinson, Paul, *Opera and Ideas*, New York, 1985.

Schmidgall, Gary, *Literature as Opera*, New York, 1977.

Seashore, C. E., *Psychology of Music*, New York, 1967.

Tovey, D. F., *The Forms of Music*, New York, 1956.

Winn, J. A., *Unsuspected Eloquence*, New Haven, 1981.